ROOSEVELT
AND THE
RUSSO–JAPANESE WAR

Books by Tyler Dennett

AMERICANS IN EASTERN ASIA
ROOSEVELT AND THE RUSSO-JAPANESE WAR

ROOSEVELT
AND THE
RUSSO-JAPANESE WAR

*A critical study of American policy in Eastern
Asia in 1902-5, based primarily upon the
private papers of Theodore Roosevelt*

BY
TYLER DENNETT

GLOUCESTER, MASS.
PETER SMITH
1959

ACKNOWLEDGMENTS

THIS book is a continuation of a study begun some years ago the first results of which were published in "Americans in Eastern Asia" (N. Y., 1922). The former book comprised an investigation of the development of American policy in China, Japan, and Korea down to 1900. This volume, with some limitations, carries the study down through the Roosevelt administration and concludes with the change in American policy which was revealed in the Knox neutralization plan for the Manchurian railways in 1909. This book, however, has a narrowed scope, for it aims to present in detail only the facts with reference to Roosevelt and the Russo-Japanese War and his policies toward Japan, Korea, and China.

"Roosevelt and the Russo-Japanese War" is based upon the private papers of Colonel Roosevelt to which the writer has had the freest access. Thanks beyond measure, therefore, are due to the Roosevelt family for permission to search these hitherto unused sources. The papers in question are deposited in the Library of Congress, and it is a pleasure to acknowledge the good offices and generous attention of Dr. Charles Moore and Mr. John C. Fitzpatrick of the Manuscripts Division.

The substance of these chapters was given as lectures before the history students of the graduate school of Johns Hopkins University in the spring of 1924. The

ACKNOWLEDGMENTS

writer is under a debt of lasting obligation to Professors John H. Latané and W. W. Willoughby for much sympathetic and helpful interest in the preparation of this material and its presentation. Some of the chapters formed the basis of a lecture given before the Institute of Politics at Williamstown in August, 1924, and were subsequently elaborated in an article in *Current History* (October, 1924). Other portions of the material appeared in *World's Work* (February, 1925). Thanks are due to Hermann Hagedorn for reading the manuscript and for much friendly interest, and to Arthur W. Page for helpful suggestions as to the rearrangement of some parts of the text.

In undertaking this study the writer was so fortunate as to be able to lay heavy tribute upon his friends who are specialists in various phases of the European history which is so closely related to the events in the Far East of 1904–05. Professor Bernadotte E. Schmitt suggested important continental sources of information which the writer might otherwise have overlooked. Professor A. L. P. Dennis has been of constant assistance and, after having read critically some portions of the manuscript, added to his generous service by securing from the British Foreign Office certain information which is acknowledged on page 214. Finally, the writer will always treasure the memory that his dear friend, the late Baron Serge A. Korff, in the last weeks of his crowded life, with an abundant generosity unwarranted by his strength, insisted upon reading the manuscript critically and made important corrections and suggestions.

And yet, notwithstanding the help which has been acknowledged as well as the assistance of other unnamed

ACKNOWLEDGMENTS

friends, it must be added that for the conclusions which have been suggested in this highly controversial theme the writer alone must assume the responsibility.

TYLER DENNETT.

WASHINGTON, D. C.,
September 29, 1924.

vii

CONTENTS

ix

CONTENTS

CONTENTS

ROOSEVELT
AND THE
RUSSO–JAPANESE WAR

ROOSEVELT
AND THE RUSSO–JAPANESE WAR

CHAPTER I

Introductory

AS LONG as England succeeds in keeping up the balance of power in Europe," remarked Colonel Roosevelt to Baron Eckardstein in the *Outlook* office one day in 1911,[1] "not only on principle, but in reality, well and good; should she, however, for some reason or other fail in doing so, the United States would be obliged to step in at least temporarily, in order to reëstablish the balance of power in Europe, never mind against which country or group of countries our efforts may have to be directed. In fact, we ourselves are becoming, owing to our strength and geographical situation, more and more the balance of power of the whole globe."

This passage, preserved from a fleeting conversation, supplies us with a complete key to the interpretation of President Roosevelt's intervention in the affairs of Europe and in the Russo-Japanese War in 1904–05. The thought was not new to him in 1911; he had acted on it more than once. Twice during the Russo-Japanese War he intimated to restless Europe that when a Power seized the opportunity to profit by the existing disorder it would

---

[1]Von Hermann Freiherrn v. Eckardstein, "Die Isolierung Deutschlands" (Leipzig, 1921), p. 175.

have to reckon with the most positive opposition of the United States.

He wrote to his friend Cecil Spring-Rice, July 24, 1905:

As soon as this war broke out, I notified Germany and France in the most polite and discreet fashion that in event of a combination against Japan to try to do what Russia, Germany, and France did to her in 1894 [*sic*], I should promptly side with Japan and proceed to whatever length was necessary on her behalf. I of course knew that your government would act in the same way, and I thought it best that I should have no consultation with your people before announcing my own purpose.

In truth, the United States held the scales in Europe as well as in Asia in 1905, and could tip them either way. When the Moroccan crisis came in the spring and early summer of 1905 President Roosevelt was almost immediately drawn into the situation. The German Emperor made repeated appeals. Roosevelt was concerned lest Germany should actually start marching over the French border where the British fleet would be of no assistance. He feared that a war in Europe would imperil the peace negotiations between Russia and Japan, precipitating in all probability a world-wide conflict. On the evening of June 25th he took occasion to intimate to Baron Sternberg that "no one would understand or pardon wars entered into for frivolous reasons." He further stated to the Kaiser's ambassador that in case of war the support which would be brought to the aid of France would be "very formidable."[1] William II could not fail to understand such language in the light of previous communications, and that he did actually fear

---

[1] Joseph Bucklin Bishop, "Theodore Roosevelt and His Time," (2 vols., N. Y., 1920), Vol. I, p. 480. (Hereafter cited as Bishop.)

the intervention of the United States in European affairs
appears from his letters to the Tsar seven or eight months
earlier.

What was unique in President Roosevelt's view of the
world in 1905 was not only that he realized the importance
of Europe in American affairs but that he approached
Europe through the Pacific and Asia.   On June 17, 1905,
he wrote to President Benjamin Ide Wheeler:

I believe that our future history will be more determined by
our position on the Pacific facing China, than by our position
on the Atlantic facing Europe.

The assertion was reminiscent of Senator William H.
Seward's famous declaration that the shores of the
Pacific Ocean, its islands, and the vast regions beyond
would become the chief theatre of events in the world's
great hereafter.   Seward spoke in 1852 while Commodore
Perry was gathering his black ships for the opening of
Japan.   Roosevelt wrote on a day when, after two weeks
of the most exacting efforts, it was not yet clear that he
would succeed in bringing the belligerents into direct
negotiations for the conclusion of the Russo-Japanese War.
Only a little more than a half century had intervened.
The Japan which Perry opened had now defeated the most
populous state of Europe on a battlefield within the
dominions of the Chinese Empire, and the combatants
were about to come to America to make peace by the
mediation of the President of the United States.   So far
was Seward's prophecy realized and Roosevelt's vision
already justified.

We shall, in the following pages, seek to take the reader
to that lonely peak from which President Roosevelt so

thoughtfully scanned the Pacific, its shores and regions beyond, where he so earnestly sought to pierce the mysteries of the world's great hereafter, and where he reached his conclusion that human welfare would best be served by the preservation in Asia of a balance of power in which Russia and Japan would be left face to face to moderate each other's action.

President Roosevelt scanned the Pacific from the point of view of the chief executive of a state which had a chain of possessions, broken, to be sure, and yet a chain, which reached across that ocean and at two points, north and south, almost touched its farthest boundaries. First of all, he thought of the security of those possessions and of the obligations which had devolved upon the United States since 1898. This was an aspect which few of his critics in September, 1905, and later, appear to have considered. But he was at the same time not unmindful of the world's welfare. Happily he was presented with no choice between what he conceived to be national and world-wide well-being. He was not tempted to sacrifice the interests of either Asia or Europe to the political or commercial advantage of the United States. From the Peace of Portsmouth his country derived no material advantage of any sort. Indeed, we shall be led to observe the singular absence from Roosevelt's policy of any great concern for the commercial interests of the United States. In his mind commerce and diplomacy were plainly not closely associated, a fact which separated his statesman-ship from the statesmanship of Europe as far as the West is from the East. American commercial interests were wholly unrepresented at Portsmouth save as a few New York bankers came to interview M. Witte about a Russian loan, which Wall Street at length refused to make. This is the more astonishing when we come to see how poorly American commercial interests were served in the settlement. There were no "honest brokers" of the Bismarckian type at Portsmouth. Critics belonging to the nationalistic school may find here an opportunity to criticize, and yet it will ever be a glory in American history that the Peace of Portsmouth stands almost alone as one in which the peacemaker demanded no compensation. To Europe, to Russia, to Japan, Roosevelt was a mystery. He wrote to Senator Henry Cabot Lodge on June 16th:

Russia is so corrupt, so treacherous and shifty, and so incompetent, that I am utterly unable to say whether or not it will make peace or break off the negotiations at any moment. Japan is, of course, entirely selfish, though with a veneer of courtesy and with infinitely more knowledge of what it wants and capacity to get it. I should not be surprised if the peace negotiations broke off at any moment. Russia, of course, does not believe in the genuineness of my motives and words, and I sometimes doubt whether Japan does.

President Roosevelt's westward vision in 1905 was still a long look into the future. It is the more remarkable that he had it when we discover that on the very day when he was invited to come forward as peacemaker in Asia he was also presented with what appeared to him an opportunity to avert war in Europe. The Moroccan crisis and the Russo-Japanese conflict overlapped each other in time, but this was no mere coincidence. These two events were integral parts of world politics which already enfolded the malodorous embryo of what became ten years later the world's pestilence.

Even now, nearly twenty years after the events, with all our experiences of the World War, one never quite recovers from the first astonishment that in the private papers of a citizen of the United States who happened for a few years to occupy the highest office there is so nearly complete a record of the political conditions of Europe as well as eastern Asia in 1905. Only a dozen years before the Portsmouth Conference Count Aoki, Japanese Minister for Foreign Affairs, had remarked in the Diet, "If you look at the map of the world you will see that America has her back turned to us."[1]

In 1905 the United States no longer had its back turned toward Asia. The possession of Hawaii and the Philippines, the growth of population and commerce on the Pacific Coast, the increase of American trade in the Far East, the building of the Panama Canal, all these factors were entering into the change. Most significant was it that in looking westward the American Government was compelled to face Europe again, for Asia was but the back door of European politics. To any who have been accustomed to assume that the Far Eastern conflict was merely a contest for Korea the following pages may come as a surprise. Korea was one of the pawns, though not so important a one as Manchuria, but Morocco, far away on the other side of the world, on another continent, was another, and perhaps we shall conclude that the desire of the American Government to protect her possessions in Hawaii and the Philippines was also a factor in the settlement. The truth is that the United States, since 1898, had been so woven into the warp of world politics that American policies were no longer those of the gener-

[1]Quoted in Tyler Dennett's "Americans in Eastern Asia" (N. Y., 1922), p. 497.

ation following the Civil War. Time and space had been absorbed by the ingenuity of man; oceans were paths of communications, not barriers; deserts had been crossed, waste spaces were desired for human habitation; in 1905 for a few brief months the world had in truth become one, and the United States was the balance of power. We have not yet grasped the meaning of this momentous change.

* * * * * *

While these pages have been written to prove no conclusion and to point no moral, the writer has not overlooked the fact that the episodes here related to one another in what is believed to be their proper sequence must have their meaning for all thoughtful citizens.

For example, we shall have occasion to draw attention to the appalling deficiency of the American diplomatic service at the beginning of the present century, a deficiency for which a provincially minded Congress and a vicious spoils system were responsible. When President Roosevelt came to deal with questions of world politics he did not have at his command a diplomatic organization which could supply him with accurate information or advice. Important diplomatic posts were occupied by men of scant qualifications whose claims to such positions consisted of something other than diplomatic experience or skill. The consular service was still a stench which the President had not yet had time to abate. Instead of being able to draw upon a corps of experienced and trusted public servants to aid him, it became necessary for the President to gather, almost on the spur of the moment, a group of personal assistants, some of whom happened to be in public office, but all of whom were selected solely with regard to their peculiar fitness to render the necessary help. At least three of his most important aides, Spring-Rice, Jusserand, and Sternberg, owed their allegiance to other governments, by which we do not mean that they were any less true to their beloved friend the President. No man in whom he trusted at this time played him false, but taken all together, fine and loyal as they were, these friends were no adequate substitute for a competent American diplomatic service. President Roosevelt was often left to grope blindly in the dark, and that he did not make great mistakes was due solely to providence and a canny political instinct which often guided him when his information was defective.

The control of American foreign relations will frequently suggest itself as a subject for reflection. It does not fall within our purpose to discuss theories of government. We cannot refrain from pointing out, however, that it was under administrations characterized by the most literalistic interpretation of the constitutional provisions for the control of foreign relations, that American policy in the Far East during the preceding fifty years can be subjected to most criticism.

The perils of secret diplomacy are often the subject of popular discussion. Perils no doubt there are, but open diplomacy, carried on at the expense of the confidential exchanges which characterize the relation of intimate friends, also has its perils. It will be of interest to inquire, as one turns these pages, how open diplomacy joined to a direct popular control of foreign policy, would have been likely to secure a better peace between Russia and Japan.

INTRODUCTORY

DIVISION OF THE SUBJECT AND METHOD OF TREATMENT

The Russo-Japanese War was compounded of several different though not unrelated conflicts. We should be wholly unable to give a satisfactory explanation of the facts if we were to confine ourselves exclusively to the Far East. Throughout the first three quarters of the 19th Century the Far East was passive. The Orient did not rise to action until it rose in self-defence to meet the West. The origins of the Russo-Japanese War lie more in Europe than in Asia. Originally the conflict was between Russia and England. More immediately it was between Germany and all the European states which stood in the path of her ambitions. The war itself may fairly be viewed as a symptom of a world-wide disorder, the consequences of which we know now only too well. Japan, to be sure, was not without her national ambitions and they are not to be explained away or charged wholly to Europe. But they were only a small part of the causes of the war with Russia.

In taking this larger view of the Russo-Japanese War we are led to study first its European background. This involves a survey of European politics of the preceding decade. For the sake of unity we have carried this survey down to the summer of 1905 before entering upon a review of Japan in Korea or of Russia in Manchuria. There is therefore an unavoidable break in the narrative at the end of Chapter IV. Not until we know the European background are we likely to appraise the immediate causes of the war[1] without assigning to them a disproportionate importance.

[1]Chaps. V, VI.

The method of treatment is determined by the desire to place the reader as nearly as possible in the exact position to which President Roosevelt moved from month to month. We wish to set forth the facts as they came to him in their chronological sequence so that one may ask himself at each stage of the proceedings whether he could have devised a better policy. So far as the reasonable limits of space permit we shall present letters and documents in their entirety, or where excerpts are used for brevity or to avoid repetition of thought, we shall take care not to omit any evidence which Roosevelt thought important, or which seems important to the writer. In the case of a very few persons, where they are still in public life, the names are omitted for obvious reasons, but the dates of the letters are given and those who come again to search the Roosevelt Papers will have no difficulty in identifying the correspondence in question.

The information upon which President Roosevelt acted was derived from three sources. There were, of course, regular diplomatic channels, including the foreign diplomatic representatives in Washington as well as the American representatives abroad. These reports were usually transmitted to the President through the Department of State, and copies of many of the notes and despatches are preserved among the Roosevelt Papers. The President cultivated the acquaintance or friendship of a wide circle of journalists and press correspondents, some of whom were at times of very great service to him. Last and most important, he drew his information from the circle of his personal friends. No one person or group of persons, however, held his attention to the exclusion of

INTRODUCTORY

others. His mind was as open as the windows of heaven to any information which could be brought.

The substance of the narrative is as follows:

After a proclamation of neutrality and a circular calling for a declaration from the belligerent Powers to respect the neutrality of China and the open door, President Roosevelt took no further steps, aside from the warning to Germany and France already mentioned, until near the beginning of 1905. Meanwhile, he had been enthusiastically elected for a term which in truth would be his own administration. One of the first tasks which he set for himself early in 1905 was the study of the Far Eastern situation. He was immediately led into the mazes of European politics which were so far responsible for the war, and which became the most important factor in the peace. So far as possible we shall draw our materials for this survey from the Roosevelt Papers, thus utilizing a rich store of hitherto unknown material which throws light not merely on Europe of 1905 but also on Europe of 1914.

The immediate causes of the war in Korea and Manchuria lead naturally to a statement of the actual war aims of the belligerents. At this point we shall have before us the choice which was presented to Roosevelt.

The narrative of peacemaking has four phases: the various projects emanating from Europe before the close of the battle of Mukden in March, 1905; the overture of Delcassé to Japan on April 5th, doubtless with the approval of Russia, followed immediately by the intimation from Japan to Roosevelt that his good offices were desired; the negotiations of Roosevelt leading up to the agreement between Russia and Japan for direct. peace negotiations in the United States; and the Portsmouth Conference, which was at length brought to a successful conclusion by the direct intervention of Roosevelt, who became the mediator of the peace. We follow the account of the Peace Conference with two chapters on Roosevelt and his critics in which we seek to show, largely by quotations from both sides of the controversy, the nature of the criticisms and the President's specific answers, many of which have never before been published. In a concluding summary chapter we shall sketch the outlines of Roosevelt as the diplomatist and, so far as this fragmentary study permits, attempt to define the nature of President Roosevelt's contribution to the Far Eastern policy of the United States. It is proper, however, to observe at the beginning that we are dealing with a very small fragment of President Roosevelt's foreign policy, and do not even include enough of his Far Eastern policy to admit of broad generalizations. The years of President Roosevelt's administration were very crowded ones in American diplomatic history and no phase of his foreign policy was without its intimate relation to every other phase.

The Roosevelt Papers themselves warrant the attention of not merely the few who are interested in historical sources, but also of all thoughtful American citizens. We therefore append to this chapter a description of these papers and take the opportunity of discussing, in relation to them, some of the literature—biographies, memoirs, apologies, and authoritative articles—covering the diplomatic history of the world from 1900 to 1905, to which the Roosevelt Papers themselves yield such important supplements. While this review is designed primarily for the specialist it will not be without interest to the general

INTRODUCTORY

reader, for there he will have an opportunity to judge how little of the secret diplomacy of twenty years ago has remained a secret. Within the last six or seven years there has been published so much from authentic sources, so much that is corroborated from the Roosevelt Papers, that one seems warranted in the conclusion that no facts yet to be revealed will materially alter the general conclusions to which historians have recently come.

THE ROOSEVELT PAPERS AND OTHER SOURCES

The publication of official documents, memoirs, and other records, so marked a characteristic of the years since the World War, has already extended back to include many phases of European diplomatic history in 1905. The inner history of both the Russo-Japanese War and the Moroccan crisis has been largely revealed.

From the Russian orange book, the memoirs of Kuropatkin, Rosen, Witte, and the unpretentious diary of Korostovetz, supplemented by the documentary material in Dr. E. J. Dillon's "Eclipse of Russia," we are already in possession of most of the important facts relating to Russia's part in the war and in the negotiations at Portsmouth.[1] The disclosures of the secret letters and telegrams of the Kaiser to the Tsar supply many gaps in our previous knowledge of Germany's relation to Russia.

Professor Otto Franke's "Die Grossmächte in Ostasien," recently published in Germany, while quite deficient as a statement of Germany's relation to the immediate events of the Russo-Japanese War and the Peace of Portsmouth, supplies most important facts, based on the archives of the

---

[1]For Bibliographical List see pp. 340-49. Sources in the following footnotes are sometimes designated merely by the author's name. The bibliographical list supplies full information as to title as well as place and date of publication.

German Foreign Office, relative to the intervention of the
coalition of Germany, France, and Russia at the close of
the Sino-Japanese War. Baron Eckardstein's third volume, "Die Isolierung Deutschlands," sheds much light
upon the outbreak of the war in 1904 and the earlier
projects for intervention in 1904.[1] There are at present no
French or English sources or studies which make equally
large contributions.

On the Japanese side we have the memoirs of Count
Hayashi, the official publications of the Foreign Office
giving some of the correspondence with Russia which
preceded the outbreak of the war, and the protocols of the
Portsmouth Conference. Hayashi, while not specifically
covering the war, yields much information relative to
Japanese motives and gives one an account of the negotiation of the first Anglo-Japanese Alliance which çan be
corrected only by the publication of similar memoirs or
documents covering the British side. The diplomatic
correspondence published by the Japanese Government
during the war was evidently designed to justify the
commencement of hostilities by Japan; it is clearly in-
complete, as we learn from both Mevil and Eckardstein,
and must therefore be used with caution. This correspondence was first published in Japanese. There are two
translations, the official one made, perhaps, at the Japanese Legation in Washington, and a translation by
Professor Asakawa which claims to be more accurate.
The latter will be found distributed through the trans-
lator's volume, "The Russo-Japanese Conflict." Baron
Kaneko has recently published in Japanese some of his

---

[1] In the preparation of this work it has not been possible to obtain a copy of the second series of
"Die Grosse Politik der Europäischen Kabinette," recently published in Germany, which is
understood to shed much light on the Far Eastern situation down to 1899.

recollections of 1904–05. The *Japan Weekly Chronicle,* (Kobe) May 1 and 8, 1924, carried an abstract and translation. From this fragmentary English text it would appear that Baron Kaneko's recollections are to be used with discrimination. In many important details they do not agree with the documents upon which this study is based.

Much authentic information is to be found in American sources. The successive volumes of "Foreign Relations" covering the causes of the war are very full, less in volume than the corresponding British blue books, but rather more exact and detailed at critical points. Thayer's biography of John Hay helps us on our way. The correspondence and diary of Ambassador George von L. Meyer, edited by Howe, is a very important source of information which the writer has compared with the Roosevelt Papers. There is a chapter in Melville E. Stone's "Fifty Years a Journalist" which gives some documents relating to the close of the Portsmouth Conference. While the information contained in that chapter admits of somewhat different interpretation than was given to it, the chapter throws a most interesting light upon the relations of the press to the conference and when compared with Korostovetz's diary invites attention to the way in which Mr. Stone, working in close coöperation with President Roosevelt and Baron Kaneko, was able to promote the conclusion of the treaty by the handling of news at a critical moment. Korostovetz supplies the information, which from the account of Mr. Stone would appear credible, that the Associated Press representatives at Portsmouth had instructions, in case of a break in the negotiations, to place the blame on Russia.

Most important of all, of course, are the four chapters

in Joseph Bucklin Bishop's "Theodore Roosevelt and His Time" on the war, the treaty, and the Algeciras Conference. In these chapters most of the major facts are either stated or alluded to. The difference between the following pages and the chapters by Bishop, aside from the fact that the present study is more extended and detailed than was called for in a popular review of a very crowded life, is that Bishop was chiefly interested in the portrayal of Roosevelt, while this book is a critical examination of a chapter in diplomatic history in which President Roosevelt happened to play a major rôle. It is believed that the result of treating this episode in its historical rather than in its biographical relation, together with the publication of supplementary correspondence, throws the entire incident into truer perspective. It tends to place some of the parties concerned in a rather more favourable light. When many details of the events which were properly omitted from Bishop's narrative are placed before us, the basis of most of the criticism that Roosevelt's intervention was hasty almost wholly disappears. President Roosevelt was well aware that he was the object of much criticism, especially immediately following the conclusion of the conference. In private letters he met every charge specifically and, as it seems to the present writer, so adequately as to place upon his critics an impossible burden of proof.

There is another source of information, extremely difficult to use and yet of the utmost importance in any attempt to understand the diplomatic atmosphere in which President Roosevelt did his work. · In the contemporary journals of the United States, England, France, Korea, China, and Japan there appeared a vast number of articles about the war. They fall sharply into three groups: declarations or expositions by official representatives of the belligerent governments; "inspired articles" prepared by writers who may properly be looked upon as intimately related to official representatives of some government concerned and which reflect a more or less official policy; and articles by independent writers who often, according to the internal evidence of the articles themselves, derived their information from sources which can be identified as authentic and official. When one is in possession of a key to the use of these articles, a key such as the Roosevelt Papers supply, it would be possible to write practically the entire diplomatic history of the war from the articles without citing documents in the Roosevelt Papers. However, without such a key it would be impossible to winnow the wheat from the chaff. The following pages are based exclusively on the Roosevelt Papers and such other material as is acknowledged in the footnotes or by documents included in the text. The journalistic material we have made use of, not for information, but to supply atmosphere, and we have gathered some of it in the form of excerpts printed at the end of certain chapters under the caption "Contemporary Comment." Some further analysis of this information may be of value to those who are interested in the study of war propaganda as it was employed nearly twenty years ago.

Count Cassini and Minister Takahira, while very accessible to journalists, made few contributions directly to the magazines. In London neither the Russian Ambassador nor the Japanese Minister contributed anything directly. Russia undertook very little direct propaganda in the

British or American press, although the articles and monthly comment by Dr. E. J. Dillon in the *Contemporary Review*, and subsequently the statements, interviews, and articles by him at Portsmouth, constitute a body of information which may be regarded as having been drawn from the most authentic Russian sources. The Russian subvention of the French press has recently been exposed. Similar subventions by Japan would appear to have been confined to newspapers in Korea. On the other hand, the Japanese Government carried on an aggressive press campaign from the outset of the war. Baron Kaneko in the United States and Baron Suyemetsu in London presented somewhat evasive introductions to the public, but all doubt as to their functions disappears when one brings together the literature on the war, arranges it in chronological order, and scrutinizes the statements and explanations given out by these two gentlemen as addresses, signed articles, or in the form of interviews. For example, the Japanese version of the causes of the war is very fully given, with documents, in various scattered articles by Baron Kaneko in the American magazines, and in three consecutive numbers of the *Nineteenth Century and After* (August, September, and October, 1904), by Baron Suyemetsu. However, a relatively small part of the official Japanese promotion of their case appeared over the names of Kaneko and Suyemetsu.

Alfred Stead rendered yeoman service for the Japanese cause. Early in the war he published in England and the United States a collection of official statements regarding Japan under the title "Japan by the Japanese." This is an extremely important book. The chapter on Japanese diplomacy, prepared by Professor Nagao Ariga, contains the most authentic information, so far as the writer knows, of the diplomatic background of Japanese relations with Korea and China. Incidentally, unlike other portions of the book, it makes admissions which require qualification to the claim that Japan had reluctantly undertaken her wars in 1894 and 1904. Mr. Stead followed up the book by a long series of articles in the *Fortnightly Review* during the war. His indebtedness to Baron Suyemetsu is occasionally mentioned, but the internal evidence of these articles leads one to believe that the indebtedness was very much greater than that acknowledged. These articles, although of the nature of special pleading, had much force, and when Mr. Stead at length declared that Japan was much dissatisfied with the character of British neutrality, and intimated that when the Anglo-Japanese Alliance had come to its natural end it might be followed by a Russo-Japanese Alliance in which Russia would support Japanese ambitions in the Malay Peninsula and Archipelago, the threat could hardly have passed unnoticed. Mr. Stead's efforts in England were supplemented by numerous articles by other contributors to both British and American periodicals, among the most prominent being Captain Brinkley and Count Okuma. Mr. Kennan in Japan, according to President Roosevelt's opinion, appears to have been taken into camp by the Japanese, and in his articles in the *Outlook* one may read a considerable amount of promotion of the Japanese cause which was quite apart from his reports of facts. Mr. Foord, the editor of the *Journal of the American Asiatic Association*, like Mr. Kennan, was so devoted to the advocacy of Japan that he drew the charge from some who did not support her of being a "discredited adjunct, so to

speak, of the Japanese consulate." When Adachi Kinno-
suke published in the *North American Review*, May, 1905,
a statement of the probable Japanese peace terms we may
look upon the article as an exhibition of diplomatic kite-
flying similar to Mr. Stead's article of July, 1904, in the
Fortnightly Review, and the article by O. Eltzbacher in the
Nineteenth Century and After (July, 1905) on the indemnity due Japan.

As is almost uniformly the case under such circumstances the promotion was overdone and at length "Calchas," an extremely well-informed writer who feared that
the pro-Japanese sentiment in England might endanger
the hoped-for understanding with Russia after the war,
was led to remark in the *Fortnightly Review* (November,
1904):

As no man ever was so wise as Daniel Webster looked, no
nation ever could be quite so great as Japan is painted.

There was still a third class of contributions of import-
ance. The monthly letters of A. Maurice Low to the
National Review reveal an accuracy of information about
the policy of Secretary Hay and President Roosevelt and
an alertness in interpreting the news which are notable.
Professor Reinsch's article in the *North American Review*
(January, 1905), as well as his brief contribution to the
Outlook (September 16, 1905), is typical of an independent
American opinion which supported Japan because it
disliked Germany and despised Russia. The Kobe
Chronicle, unlike the Japan *Daily Mail*, reflected an
independent opinion favourable to Japan, yet not as a
slavish supporter of Japanese policy in Korea and China.
The *Korean Review*, edited by Mr. Homer B. Hulbert,

was plainly somewhat intimidated by the Japanese occupation of Seoul but eventually repudiated Japan and came out as the bold champion of the Emperor of Korea. There were, in addition to the articles mentioned, a large number of others, many of them signed with pseudonyms, which were based on authentic information. The *North American Review* in the United States, the *Contemporary, Fortnightly, Nineteenth Century,* and *National* Reviews in England, and the *Revue des Deux Mondes* in Paris, to mention only the most important, supply us with the atmosphere of the drama which we are about to narrate. This literary history of the war acquired something of a military quality, for it recorded the battles for the conquest of public opinion.

The Roosevelt Papers are deposited for safe keeping in the Manuscripts Division of the Library of Congress. These papers are now in the process of classification and for that reason each quotation from them is accompanied merely by a name or date, in most cases by both—a sufficient identification. As the papers came to the library there were four box letter files containing the bulk of the correspondence relating to the Portsmouth Conference beginning late in 1904 and ending in November, 1905. There was one box, similarly gathered, relating to the Moroccan crisis and the Algeciras Conference. Supplementing these are the letterpress copybooks containing copies of all the letters from President Roosevelt. These copies appear to have been preserved with very great care. Even when a letter was written out by hand it was usually first dictated and a copy preserved. Not all of the letters and documents relating to our subjects found their way into the five boxes, and the writer has, therefore, searched other files of correspondence where outgoing letters, or other references, revealed the fact that there is other material. The Roosevelt Papers are voluminous. Doubtless further searches in the correspondence of subsequent years would disclose other statements by President Roosevelt which are pertinent to the discussion. In fact, the writer knows of some such letters but has made no effort to locate them. The contemporary correspondence is the most authentic source and that has been found to be so complete that it raises no questions which it does not answer, and creates no mysteries. Indeed, so complete is the information that one seriously doubts whether a search of the archives of the Department of State would reveal any additional facts of importance.

During all of the period when President Roosevelt was intently studying the questions under review, it may fairly be asserted that he was his own Secretary of State. The relations between the President and Secretary Hay were, as is well known, extremely intimate, and there were no important differences of opinion. Long before 1905 Secretary Hay's grasp in the Department of State was relaxed and when he went abroad in the last vain quest for health in March, there was no abrupt transition. Already President Roosevelt had taken the important diplomatic relations into his own hand. From that time onward he was accustomed even to draft despatches and telegrams himself and send them to the Department of State for transmission. After the President's return from his speaking trip in New England at the end of June he transferred his residence to Oyster Bay, a fact which still further brought copies of diplomatic correspondence into his personal files.

INTRODUCTORY

Largely because of the inadequacy of the American diplomatic service already referred to, and the consequent utilization of unofficial channels of communication, there is a large mass of personal letters which have the quality of diplomatic documents. President Roosevelt did not exactly encourage his diplomatic agents abroad to communicate with him directly, but they often did so, and Ambassador Meyer, who carried the burden in Europe, wrote regularly to the President about once a week. There was a period of nearly two weeks, perhaps longer, in May and June, during which the Department of State was wholly ignorant of the fact that the President had been expressly asked by Japan to bring about the direct negotiations for peace. Indeed, there were days when Mrs. Roosevelt, as the correspondence shows, was absolutely the President's only confidant. One may go even further and state as a personal opinion, subject to correction when the Department of State archives for this period become accessible for study, that the Roosevelt Papers contain some important documents which were never a matter of record in the Department, and the existence of which was probably unknown except to a very few people long since unconnected with the administration of American diplomatic affairs.

President Roosevelt appears to have been fully conscious that even his most personal letters often acquired the nature of state papers. It was his habit at intervals in the midst of important negotiations to dictate long letters to personal friends in which he not merely reviewed the facts and explained them, but also included copies of the important documents and telegrams. There are such letters covering both the Portsmouth Conference and the

Algeciras Conference. Bishop has printed one of them as two chapters and utilized another very largely. At the same time it was the President's custom to send copies of important documents to various people, usually those in official position, in various parts of the world with a view to having their contents known in quarters where it seemed wise to convey the information. There must be more than a dozen such letters covering various phases of the Russo-Japanese negotiations.

The President's papers were carefully preserved. While here and there a letter may be missing owing to careless filing, there has been no destruction of records. President Roosevelt's diplomatic practice was secret, properly so, for the occasion required the cultivation of the most intimate personal confidences, but his habits were not secretive. On the contrary, they were frankness itself—a quality which some of the professional diplomats were unable to comprehend. One of the most astonishing aspects of the situation as revealed in the Papers is the fact that while so much information of the utmost importance was placed on paper and entrusted to a wide circle of people, some of whom were men whose profession it is to publish the news, nevertheless very little, even after the lapse of twenty years, has found its way into print. No man was ever better served than President Roosevelt by his friends. They did not violate his confidence.

The information hitherto published, parallel with that taken from the Roosevelt Papers, is referred to either in footnotes or in excerpts from contemporary comment at the end of the chapters. While the writer has sought and obtained interviews with many persons whose knowledge of the facts enabled them to throw light on their correct

INTRODUCTORY

interpretation, it is believed that nothing of importance has been stated in the following pages without an accompanying reference in the text, at the bottom of the page or at the end of the chapter, to a written or printed source from which it can be drawn.

CHAPTER II

Roosevelt and the Diplomats

IT IS of the utmost importance for us at the outset to remember that the Russo-Japanese War did not arise suddenly in 1904. The conflict had been maturing for nearly ten years. Japan disclosed her purpose in the Treaty of Shimonoseki (April 17, 1895) when she secured the so-called Liaotung Peninsula from China. A European coalition of Germany, France, and Russia demanded that Japan return this domain to China. Thus were revealed the beginnings of a contest for the domination of the Far East in which Europe was pitted against eastern Asia. Russia, lured on by the phantom of such a conquest of the Far East as England had accomplished in India through the British East India Company, yet not so much lured by economic prospects as instigated by Germany for political reasons, came forward as the protagonist of the West.

It now seems amazing that Europe should have been so ill-informed about the determination of Japan and about her preparations, and so absorbed in its own intrigues and conflicts that up to the very day of the outbreak of hostilities, February 8, 1904, the Foreign Offices in St. Petersburg, Berlin, and Paris were confidently asserting that there could be no war. Unquestionably the Russo-Japanese War took Europe by surprise.[1] President

---

[1]Baron Eckardstein's "Die Isolierung Deutschlands," pp. 187–93, 56–69, includes correspondence from Paris and Berlin clearly indicating the astonishment of the Foreign Offices. See also André

Roosevelt did most of his studying of the questions involved after the beginning of hostilities. It is of importance for our purpose therefore to begin where Roosevelt did and follow through with him, step by step, the various phases of the conflict and the development of his policy.

From the outset President Roosevelt's sympathies were with Japan. Almost four weeks before the attack on Port Arthur the Japanese Government had the assurance that in case of war the American Government would go even further than the observance of strict neutrality. The American policy would be benevolent toward Japan.[1] A declaration of neutrality was made soon after the Japanese declaration of war. Almost immediately President Roosevelt took a second step which marked him at once as the leader among the neutral Powers. Through Secretary Hay he addressed a note to the belligerents and to China February 20th, expressing an earnest desire that during the hostilities the "neutrality of China" as well as its "administrative entity" should be respected and that the area of hostilities should be so localized and limited that "undue excitement and disturbance of the Chinese people may be prevented and the least possible loss to the commerce and peaceful intercourse of the world may be

---

Mevil, "De La Paix de Francfort à la Conférence d'Algesiras" (Paris, 1909), pp. 87ff., and Witte's "Memoirs" (N.Y., 1921), Chap. V. It is possible that the outbreak of hostilities was less unexpected in Berlin than elsewhere, but the true situation at Tokio was known to only a very small group of people and the information was not conveyed even to the banks and financial interests in Germany.

[1]January 12, 1904. Eckardstein to Baron Alfred Rothschild ("Isolierung," p. 189): "The Japanese Minister told me this morning, that after the official declarations of Germany and the United States that they would observe strict neutrality and the latter even a very benevolent neutrality, the Japanese Government were pushing their war preparations as quickly as possible and that within two weeks very likely over 100 thousand troops would have been landed in Korea."

occasioned." Copies were sent to all the Powers interested in China with a request for their coöperation. It is significant that thus at the very beginning of the war the American Government showed its concern for China and at the same time made no mention of Korea.[1]

When we go back of this note, however, we find that the American Government was owing its leadership not so much to its own initiative as to the complications of European politics. The note appears to have been framed upon the initial suggestion of the German Emperor.[2] The significance of this action of the German Government can hardly be over-emphasized for the purposes of our study. Here we have the first illustration, and there are many more in the following eighteen months, of how the European Powers were preparing to make use of the war in the Far East to advance various nationalistic projects in Europe and elsewhere.

Throughout the war and the peace negotiations the greatest unknown factor was prospective European intervention. There were precedents for it. Russia had not forgotten the revision of the Treaty of San Stephano by the "honest brokers" at Berlin in 1878, and the German Emperor did not fail to keep this fear of intervention before the Tsar.[3] Japan could not forget that the war

---

[1]"Foreign Relations" (1904), p. 2.

[2]From the diary of Ambassador Meyer, then at Rome, it appears that in the correspondence with the Powers which preceded the issuance of the note of February 20th, the Russian Government was very reluctant to give its assent but was urged to do so by the Kaiser. Russia was, in fact, the last government to reply to it and excepted Manchuria, the field of military operations, from its assent. Russia was at that time fearful, and had been for more than a year, that Japan would form an alliance with China. M. A. DeWolfe Howe, "George von Lengerke Meyer" (N. Y., 1919), p. 86. Hereafter cited as Howe's "Meyer." Moore's "Digest," Vol. V, pp. 553-54.

[3]December 17, 1904. ". . . signs there are that some Powers are already [sic] working in that direction, especially Paris and London." Isaac Don Levine, "Letters from the Kaiser to the Czar" (N. Y., 1920), pp. 133-34. Hereafter cited as "Levine."

itself was a struggle on her part to reclaim what had been taken from her by the European coalition in 1895. None of the Powers could overlook the fact that it was the intervention in China in 1900 which had provided Russia with her opportunity to occupy Manchuria. There were reasons as well as precedents for intervention in January and February, 1904. The bankers desired the continuance of peace or the immediate termination of hostilities. War in the Far East, with Russia involved, was the last thing desired by France, who looked to Russia for protection against Germany. England could expect little benefit and much injury, and appears to have preferred peace to the many uncertainties of such a conflict. Nevertheless, England did not favour intervention to prevent the war.[1] Indeed, the spectre of intervention loomed up before Japan continually during the last stages of the negotiations with Russia and the first weeks of the war.

To the American Government this possibility of European intervention had two aspects. In the first place, Japan was undertaking a task, namely, the loosening of the Russian grip on Manchuria, which was distinctly a service for the United States, and just because European intervention would be aimed against Japan as in 1895, the American Government was naturally opposed to it. It was not to American interests that Russia be permitted to consolidate her position in the Far East. In the second place, European intervention probably would have involved compensations for all the Powers, and in fact would have provided the long-expected opportunity for the

[1] Delcassé even went so far as to intimate, late in January, that if Japan would not listen to England's advice to preserve the peace, the Powers would intervene together to make Japan listen to reason ("Isolierung," p. 192). Delcassé greatly exaggerated the degree of pressure which England would bring to bear upon Japan. See Spring-Rice to Roosevelt, below, p. 213.

division of the Chinese Empire.[1] England as well as the United States was wholly opposed to such a partition and her determination to stand by her ally caused France to abandon its plans for a joint intervention against Japan. President Roosevelt does not appear to have been well informed on this point and he was of the opinion that France or Germany, or both, were likely to take the side of Russia either just before or just after the outbreak of hostilities in Manchuria. This is the explanation, presumably, for his polite and discreet yet apparently unqualified notice to both France and Germany that he would go to the aid of Japan if they entered the war on the side of Russia.[2] President Roosevelt's astonishing notice to France and Germany served a very useful purpose. Not only did it encourage Japan when all Europe was arrayed against her, but the memory of it was a constant warning to Germany which was not forgotten. Later in the same year we find the Emperor busily arguing with the Tsar that there was a possibility of American intervention not only in the Far East but even in the affairs of Europe.[3] As late as the end of the year President Roosevelt wrote[4]:

If it were not for the attitude of England and the United States I think that Germany and France would probably have already interfered on Russia's side.

Almost surrounded by European intrigue, the President took up earnestly the study of the Russo-Japanese War shortly after his overwhelming victory in the November

[1]The early division of China was still one of the expectations of Europe as late as 1904. See, for example, "Isolierung," p. 198.

[2]See p. 2.

[3]Levine, pp. 123, 133.

[4]To Spring-Rice, December 27, 1904.

elections. He could now look forward to four years in which he would be President, as it were, in his own right. The Republican policy with reference to the Philippines was one of the policies which had been enthusiastically endorsed by the people, and the President had the satisfaction of knowing that he enjoyed to an extraordinary degree the confidence of the nation. He was now relatively freer than a year earlier to block out a foreign policy of his own. Before the first of the year he had "very definitely concluded" what he intended to do in the Far East "if circumstances permit."[1] He made an appraisal of the American diplomatic service and determined upon some changes with a view to his projected policy. This leads us to a consideration of the relatively small group of people in the United States and elsewhere who became the diplomatic agents and channels of communication for President Roosevelt.

In the making of peace the nations actively concerned were Russia, Japan, Germany, France, and Great Britain. There were two regular channels of communication, either through the diplomatic representative at Washington and the Department of State or through the American diplomatic representative abroad and the corresponding foreign office. To Roosevelt the choice in each case was important and he did not leave it to chance.

Count Cassini—the Cassini of China fame—represented Russia in Washington. He it was who was believed to have made the arrangements which prepared the way for the secret treaty between Russia and China in 1896. From Peking, Count Cassini had brought to Washington the reputation of his doubtful achievements in the

---

[1] See p. 45.

Chinese Empire. It is no secret, for it has already been disclosed both by Thayer and by Bishop, that the American Government entertained no high regard for Cassini. Secretary Hay disliked him and at one time appears to have been on the point of asking for his recall.[1] Cassini proved to be not only difficult to deal with but also untruthful, as appeared in the negotiations in regard to the evacuation of Manchuria in 1902. If it be the duty of a diplomatic officer to commend his government by his own gracious personal qualities, Russia was badly served. Yet in Cassini Russia was not misrepresented. All that her ambassador proved to be in the way of a shifty, arrogant, unscrupulous diplomat, his government was to an even greater degree. No man could have carried out the instructions of Count Lamsdorff in 1902–05 and retained the confidence of the American Government. Cassini merely played his rôle with fidelity, but his presence in Washington made it entirely necessary for President Roosevelt to find another means of communication with St. Petersburg.

President McKinley had sent George von Lengerke Meyer as American Ambassador to Rome in 1900, partially as a reward for his having obligingly withdrawn from a Congressional contest in Massachusetts. Mr. Meyer had proved to be an excellent diplomat. He had business experience, wealth, and charm; he was not unwilling to work; he was alert and a skilful negotiator. He had one qualification exceptional for an American ambassador, for he was not confined to the use of the English language.[2]

---

[1] William Roscoe Thayer, "Life and Letters of John Hay" (2 vols., Boston and N. Y., 1915), Vol. II, p. 373. (Hereafter cited as Thayer's "Hay.")

[2] Howe's "Meyer," p. 28.

ROOSEVELT AND THE DIPLOMATS

The death of President McKinley placed in the White House a personal friend of Meyer. Roosevelt and he had been at Harvard together and they had kept alive their undergraduate friendship. They had been associated in politics; President Roosevelt trusted the Ambassador very much. During the summer of 1904 Meyer came home to render most helpful service in the political campaign. He appears to have been promised a promotion to Paris after March 4th when the President would make his new diplomatic appointments. On account of the war and the possible peace negotiation, however, Roosevelt determined to send Meyer to St. Petersburg, which he considered the most important diplomatic post in Europe at the time. "Now at St. Petersburg I want some work done, and you are the man to do it."

The trouble with our ambassadors [he wrote to Meyer] in stations of real importance is that they totally fail to give us real help and real information, and seem to think that the life of an ambassador is a kind of glorified pink tea party;

and then he added a comment by no means flattering to other ambassadors but important as a clue to the diplomatic situation which we are studying:

It happens to be the only Embassy at which I do want work done just at present.[1]

Ambassador Meyer did not reach St. Petersburg until April, 1905, but already, both at Rome and in a brief visit to Berlin, he had rendered important service to the peace negotiations. Thus very early in January the channel of communication with Russia was assured.

[1]Howe's "Meyer," p. 109, Roosevelt to George von L. Meyer, December 26, 1904.

Roosevelt did not want activity in any other embassy on the Continent because the communications with Paris and Berlin could best be taken care of by his personal and intimate friends, M. Jusserand and Baron Speck von Sternberg, the regularly accredited ambassadors of the two countries, respectively. Jusserand and Sternberg were among Roosevelt's most intimate companions in Washington. With these gentlemen the President spent much of his leisure time. To them he spoke a language which they fully understood, and he could count on their transmitting his meaning with all its shades of emphasis, or he could count on them equally well to advise with him and keep silent. Practically all of the important diplomatic communications between Berlin and Paris, respectively, and Washington, were through these two men.

The Japanese Government likewise had selected Washington as its point of transmission for communications to Roosevelt. Mr. Takahira had the double advantage of being fully trusted by his own government and by the President. Under the most exacting burdens of representation and communication Minister Takahira never once stumbled or made a false step. In the midst of so much diplomatic informality he held himself rigidly to the diplomatic code and not once took the liberty of addressing a communication directly to the President. Always the notes were sent either through the Department of State, or, when Roosevelt went to Oyster Bay, through the President's Secretary. However, behind this exceptionally stiff formality the relations of the two men were friendly although not intimate.

We cannot dismiss the subject of Japanese representation without reference to another personage, Baron

ROOSEVELT AND THE DIPLOMATS

Kentaro Kaneko.[1]   Not long after the outbreak of the war Kaneko appeared in New York, to assist in the direction of the Japanese 'publicity." He had been in the Harvard Law School when Roosevelt was in college. He addressed a letter to the President and reminded him of the former acquaintance. A visit to the White House followed. Later he sent a review containing a recent article of his on Japan and the United States.[2]   This article reiterated the points of the argument which had been advanced some years before by Baron Shibusawa that American capital in alliance with Japanese skill and knowledge of the markets of eastern Asia would find great rewards. The article contained a brief yet significant note of warning, for a part of one sentence stated that American business men would fail if they disregarded "the importance of Japan in Chinese affairs." This Japanese claim on China was destined to play an important part in international relations in the course of the next fifteen years.[3]   The President expressed a desire to read some books on Japan. Takahira recommended a reading list and Kaneko supplemented it, adding a book or two written by himself. Roosevelt was much impressed with Bushido. He became interested in jiujitsu and the Japanese representatives supplied him with an instructor. Thus the acquaintance ripened and Kaneko was often at the White House. Between Takahira and Kaneko there was perfect team work and no apparent jealousy. It is difficult to assign to Kaneko his relative place in the subsequent drama. It was, perhaps, not quite so important as has been supposed. Kaneko's

[1]See "Kaneko in America," *Japan Weekly Chronicle*, Kobe, May 1 and 8, 1924.

[2]*International Quarterly*, Vol. VIII, December-March, 1903-04, pp. 399 ff., "Japan and the United States: A Proposed Economic Alliance."

[3]Kaneko to Roosevelt, April 20, 1904; Roosevelt to Kaneko, April 23, 1904.

little attentions were wholly unnecessary to keep the President sympathetic with the Japanese cause. In the end, however, Kaneko served a most useful purpose as a channel of the sort of communication to the Japanese Government which could hardly have been compassed within the bounds of diplomatic etiquette. For the moment we merely point to the contrast between Cassini calling at the Department of State and "shouting" at Secretary Hay and the Japanese representatives quietly supplying the President with reading lists and a teacher in jiujitsu. The nature of Kaneko's services may best be described by giving an extract from Roosevelt's farewell letter to him after the close of the Portsmouth Conference. He wrote (September 11, 1905):

Will you permit me at this time to say to you how much I have enjoyed our intercourse during the last year and a half, and how deeply I appreciate the services you have rendered throughout that period in keeping our two countries in close touch? You have rendered me invaluable assistance by the way in which you have enabled me to know, and also by the way in which you have enabled me to convey to your own government certain things which I thought it desirable to have known and which I hardly cared to forward through official channels.

Relations with Great Britain acceptable to President Roosevelt proved more difficult to establish. Sir Mortimer Durand, the British Ambassador at Washington, was an estimable gentleman who commanded respect but unfortunately he was not of a temperament to understand Roosevelt or win his intimacy. The President was never at ease in dealing with him and never felt quite sure that Durand was comprehending correctly his meaning. The relations were cordial enough but they were not useful. This was especially unfortunate because Ambassador Choate was about to leave London and the post at St. James's had been promised to Whitelaw Reid. The latter did not reach England until June and was never able to attain a position of great usefulness in the peace negotiations. Roosevelt, in the emergency, turned to his old friend Cecil Spring-Rice, who was then first secretary of the British Embassy at St. Petersburg.[1]

The relations between Spring-Rice and Roosevelt present one of the most important as well as the most interesting links in our narrative. The two men had been the closest of personal friends for more than twenty years. The President did all that he could with propriety to intimate to the British Government that he would like to see Spring-Rice appointed to Durand's place. Such an appointment would have been as fortunate for Anglo-American relations in 1905 as it was unfortunate ten years later. Yet even as it was the confidence which the two men had in each other came to assume an international importance during the closing months of the Russo-Japanese War, for it was this confidence which, more than any other one factor, kept the American and British governments from falling apart at the time of the Moroccan crisis and the earlier peace overtures to Russia and Japan. While President Roosevelt never quite distrusted the British Government he was not, on the other hand, any slavish admirer of British foreign policy. Fundamental in all that he did in 1905 was the assumption that British and American interests in the Far East, if not in Europe,

[1]Sir Cecil Spring-Rice had served as attaché at Brussels, Washington, Tokio, Berlin, and Constantinople. He was First Secretary in St. Petersburg, 1903-05. In 1912 he was appointed Ambassador in Washington and died February 14, 1918.

were identical and yet he was unable to win the confidence of Lord Lansdowne. The British Secretary for Foreign Affairs does not appear to have been quite willing to accept the leadership of this young and relatively inexperienced American. Furthermore, President Roosevelt occasionally betrayed a sympathy with the German Emperor which was incomprehensible to the English. The lack of confidence was deplorable and but for Cecil Spring-Rice, might have had serious consequences. Throughout these important months the President sent and received his most important communications to and from England, not through Sir Mortimer Durand, not through the American Embassy in London, but through the Secretary of the British Embassy at St. Petersburg. Most if not all of the subsequent misunderstandings would have been avoided if only the British Government had been adequately represented in Washington and the American Government had been adequately represented in London.

Roosevelt wrote to Spring-Rice, December 27, 1904, in answer to a letter of congratulation over the November election:

Largely because of what you set forth, I shall probably send George Meyer to St. Petersburg. He is a close friend of mine and I have told him that an Englishman (I did not mention your name) would speak to him and tell him that he had been in communication with me and, by my request, was to keep in full touch with him. You can show him this letter if you feel it is safe to take this letter with you to St. Petersburg. But it will not be necessary, for you can describe to him what I have said, and he will recognize the description and will know that I want you to go over all matters that come up with him.

ROOSEVELT AND THE DIPLOMATS

The establishment of this relationship in St. Petersburg, duly sheltered from the search of the Russian secret police who, according to a private letter from Meyer to Roosevelt, had already secured the code book of the American Department of State and were, of course, opening all letters addressed to the Embassy, gives to our narrative a romantic and dramatic interest. There may be other chapters in diplomatic history as amazing and unique, although the writer does not know of them, but surely there are none which might more justly invite the attention of the dramatist.

This was the stage and these the principal actors: Theodore Roosevelt, John Hay until his health forced his retirement in March, George Meyer and Cecil Spring-Rice at St. Petersburg, Sternberg and Jusserand in Washington, and a few others who still remain in public life. The conventions were observed to this extent: that in the correspondence Roosevelt was almost uniformly "Dear Mr. President," but the others were "Dear John," "Dear George," "Dear Springy," "Dear Speck," and, in the case of the Secretary of War, "Dear Will." Likewise, the late Senator from Massachusetts was "Dear Cabot." Surely never before in modern times was so much diplomatic correspondence carried on in such familiar fashion. The letters are in truth state papers and yet they are the missives of affection. Many a fleeting sentence of conversation such as is usually lost is here preserved to mark the path for the historian. There were moments of relaxation and sparkles of humour. Once President Roosevelt remarked to Secretary Hay that the more he saw of the Kaiser and the Tsar the more respect he had for American senators, to which Mr. Hay replied that he was unable to make such fine distinctions.

On the other hand, the letters breathe good faith and there is not a line which detracts from the reputation of its writer. Only gentlemen could have brought about the restoration of peace between Russia and Japan. The correspondence is dignified by evident feeling of grave responsibility, lofty purpose, and hard thinking.

CONTEMPORARY COMMENT

Baron Suyemetsu,[1] "How Russia Brought On the War," *Nineteenth Century and After*, September, 1904.

". . . it will be plain that the present war in the Far East is not in reality a conflict which has arisen merely out of a dispute between the two combatants. It is rather a general revolt of all the civilized peoples of the earth against the perfidy and insincerity of Russia who for many years past has sought to outwit the other Powers."

Sidney Low, "President Roosevelt's Opportunities," *Nineteenth Century and After*, December, 1904.

". . . much more surprising things might happen than that the foundations should be laid of a League of Peace, based on a genuine and effective Anglo-Saxon Alliance, before it is time for him [Roosevelt] to quit the Executive Mansion."

O. Eltzbacher, "The Balance of Power in Europe," *Nineteenth Century and After*, May, 1905.

"During the past few weeks various writers have eloquently recommended that the Anglo-Japanese Alliance should be renewed in the form of an unrestricted and long-termed offensive and defensive alliance, which, especially if the United States should join in, would prove an irresistible combination."

---

[1] Spelled Suyematsu.

ROOSEVELT AND THE DIPLOMATS

O. Eltzbacher, "The Collapse of Russia," *Nineteenth Century and After*, July, 1905.

"Germany and France could hardly intervene with success in favour of Russia unless the two Powers should be able to join either Great Britain or the United States, and such an event appears to be highly improbable."

CHAPTER III

England and the Continent

WE ARE about to enter with President Roosevelt the quicksands of world politics in 1905. It was a perilous journey. Companions had to be selected with care.

The diplomatic history of the period admits of few general statements and rarely justifies a sweeping conclusion. Every choice presented to President Roosevelt was qualified and contingent upon some speculative factor. The personal equation entered so largely into situations that one is often reminded of how quickly the relations of states resolve themselves into personal relations. Roosevelt placed great confidence in the British Government, and yet there were qualifications. He favoured Japan, yet with certain doubts as to the future. He distrusted the German Emperor, yet not without a certain degree of sympathy for him in his European difficulties. He wanted to stand by France, but he does not appear to have trusted Delcassé. He welcomed a defeat for Russia and yet he counted on Russia's strength. Lastly, he believed that his own nation was sound at the core and yet he was well aware of the inherent weaknesses of popular government and he though he detected a growing and ominous softness in the American people. Such distinctions as he made can only safely be given in his own words.

President Roosevelt's letter of December 27, 1904, to

ENGLAND AND THE CONTINENT

Cecil Spring-Rice, already quoted in part,[1] introduces us to his perplexities at the beginning of 1905. He wrote:

It is always possible that Japan and Russia may come to terms of agreement, as I supposed Count Ito truly wished them to do some few years ago.

He was quite justified in this supposition. Efforts never ceased during the war to bring Russia and Japan to an understanding. In Tokio there was the little group represented by Count Ito who would have preferred a Russian to a British alliance in 1902.[2] In St. Petersburg there were M. Witte and a formidable group of Russians, including many statesmen and most of the bankers, temporarily without influence with the Tsar, who deplored the war and notwithstanding the personal dangers involved never ceased to work for the initiation of peace negotiations. Nearly a fourth of French foreign investments were tied up in Russia.[3] Paris had by no means welcomed the war and the French financiers were eager to coöperate with their Russian correspondents to bring about peace. In the summer of 1904 the question of peace was being seriously considered both in Paris and in London. Not only was Witte seeking an interview with Count Hayashi, the Japanese Minister, but other unnamed Russians, vested with more authority than Witte, were in London and in communication with Hayashi through Baron Eckardstein.[4] Count Hayashi was at first non-committal, but after conferring with his govern-

---

[1]See, p. 38.
[2]See p. 56.
[3]André Tardieu, "France and the Alliances" (N. Y., 1908), p. 28.
[4]"Isolierung," pp. 75-80.

ment he received full powers to negotiate for a basis for peace. The assassination of Plehve, July 28th, interrupted negotiations, for Witte had to return to Russia, but communications continued for more than another month. Nothing came of them except the common agreement that whenever peace was to be made it must be by direct negotiations rather than by intervention or mediation. Again in February, 1905, Witte appears to have resumed the overtures to Count Hayashi only to be met by the blunt statement that the Japanese could not deal with a man who was without influence in his government.[1] These earlier overtures were known to the German, British, and presumably to the French governments. Doubtless Roosevelt was aware of them.

In his letter to Spring-Rice the President continues:

I have reason to believe that the Japanese were disappointed and unfavourably impressed by the English vehemence of speech and exceeding moderation of action in the Hull fishing fleet affair.[2] Personally I appreciate to the full the difficulty of committing oneself to a course of action in reliance upon the proposed action of a free people which is not accustomed at present to carrying out with iron will a long-continued course of foreign policy. It would be well-nigh impossible, even if it were not highly undesirable, for this country to engage with another country to carry out any policy save one which had become part of the inherited tradition of the country, like the Monroe Doctrine. Not merely could I, for instance, only make such an engagement for four years, but I would have to reckon with a

---

[1] Dr. E. J. Dillon, "The Eclipse of Russia" (London and Toronto, 1918), pp. 296–301.

[2] The Dogger Bank incident, in which vessels of the Russian fleet on its way to the Far East, in a panic, opened fire upon British fishing vessels in October, 1904. The possibility of hostilities between Great Britain and Russia was averted by French good offices, when both parties consented to submit the question to a Hague commission of inquiry. J. B. Scott, "The Hague Court Reports" (1916), p. 403; Graham H. Stuart, "French Foreign Policy" (N.Y., 1921), p. 134.

ENGLAND AND THE CONTINENT

possible overthrow in Congress, with the temper of the people, with many different conditions. In consequence, my policy must of necessity be somewhat opportunist; although as a matter of fact I have very definitely concluded what I intend to do if circumstances permit, so far as this Far Eastern question is concerned. I do not like to write my conclusions even to you, and unfortunately there is no one in your embassy here to whom I can speak with even reasonable fullness. I wish to Heaven you could come over, if only for a week or two, and I think it would be very important for your Government that you should come over.

Mr. Spring-Rice, in response to this invitation, paid a flying visit to Washington in February, 1905.[1] The Roosevelt Papers do not appear to reveal any memoranda whatever of the conversations which took place, and their nature must be left entirely to surmise. If one were to hazard a guess it would be that Spring-Rice was to carry back to the Foreign Office the message that in the following months President Roosevelt would take entirely independent action but that his views would be made known to the Foreign Office by way of direct letters to Spring-Rice and through the latter's conferences with Mr. Meyer. The whole arrangement, if such there was, rested upon the agreement of both the British and the American governments that their interests in the Far East were identical and that the policy which would serve one would equally serve the other. This assumption was, beyond a doubt, the corner stone of Roosevelt's policy.

[1] January 13, 1905, Roosevelt to Hay, upon learning that Spring-Rice was leaving London for the United States and wanted to stay with Henry Adams: "This is very interesting. Won't you ask Henry if he can put up this distinguished member of the kitchen ambassadorial circle—if there are members of the kitchen cabinet, why cannot there be kitchen ambassadors?" Baron Rosen knew of this visit and suspected its meaning. ("Forty Years of Diplomacy," [N. Y., 1922], Vol. I, p. 256); Lord Charnwood makes a veiled reference to it ("Theodore Roosevelt" [Boston, 1923], pp. 146-47.)

"For similar reasons," continued Roosevelt, who lived to realize that he had underestimated the British people—

I would hesitate in counting upon the support of your Government and your people. I am not quite sure of their tenacity of purpose, of their fixity of conviction, of their willingness to take necessary risks, and at need to endure heavy losses for a given end. Both your Government and ours must reckon with the possible clamor of the great business interests, who regard anything that will tend to "unsettle values," as they call it, with unaffected horror, as being worse than any possible future national loss, or even disgrace; and we have to reckon with a fundamentally sound, but often temporarily unstable or mistaken, public opinion. Moreover, in large parts of both of our countries there is undoubtedly too much softness. The amiable peace-at-any-price people who in our country have been prancing about as anti-imperialists for the last few years [are] not invariably but generally, men weak in body or mind, men who could not be soldiers because they lack physical hardihood or courage; and though in their extreme form these people are not very numerous, there are undoubtedly large sections of the population whose men, if drafted into the ranks, would need long training before they would become effective fighters against formidable foes, and who, stay-at-homes, moreover, simply because they are unused to it, would become utterly appalled by slaughter in the field. In the Spanish War, for instance, and in the Boer War, our generals and yours, our public leaders and yours, had to grapple with a public sentiment which screamed with anguish over the loss of a couple of thousand men in the field; a sentiment of preposterous and unreasoning mawkishness, as is instanced by the fact that the actual mortality in the two wars, taken in the aggregate, did not equal the aggregate mortality, during the same number of years, of the women who died in childbirth; nor, as regards my own country, of the men who were killed in private quarrel.   This softness and its attendant hysteria must be reckoned with.

Russia for a number of years has treated the United States as badly as she has treated England, and almost as badly as she has treated Japan.   Her diplomatists lied to us with brazen and contemptuous effrontery, and showed with cynical indifference their intention to organize China against our interests.   Russia could of course under no circumstances make any attack upon the United States, not even upon the outlying possessions of the United States, in the Philippines.   I should have liked to be friendly with her; but she simply would not permit it, and those responsible for managing her foreign policy betrayed a brutality and ignorance, an arrogance and short-sightedness, which are not often combined.

The Japanese, as a government, treated us well, and what they contended for was what all civilized Powers in the East were contending for.   But I wish I were certain that the Japanese down at bottom did not lump Russians, English, Americans, Germans, all of us, simply as white devils inferior to themselves not only in what they regard as the essentials of civilization, but in courage and forethought, to be treated politely only so long as would enable the Japanese to take advantage of our various national jealousies, and beat us in turn.

The President then alluded to reports which had come to him from newspaper correspondents and others who had recently returned from the Far East.   Some of these men had had very unpleasant experiences.   He mentioned the reports of two men particularly.   These two men grew to dislike the Japanese, although they greatly admired them as soldiers.

They were both originally pro-Japanese, and . . . at least struggled to remain such.   They feel that the Japanese have a most admirable army.   They do not believe at all that the Japanese are invincible, however, they become discouraged and unsteady, just like other men. They feel that the Russians have just as much courage, both in defence and attack, but that the Russian preparedness is nothing like as great, or the Russian plans anything like as clearly thought out, and they feel that on the whole the Japanese private soldier shoots a little better and has more initiative than the Russian, though not superior to him in either daring or dogged and obstinate endurance. They feel that the Russian officers were inferior to the Japanese; but that all these differences in the effectiveness of the two armies are tending to grow less and less instead of growing greater. Still they think the Japanese superior to the Russians.

They do not think that a Japanese regiment is superior to one of our good regular regiments, but of course they say that we could not gather even a small army which would be able to meet a Japanese army of similar size. They say that when the Japanese have not got their blood up and take Russian prisoners they treat them well; but that in the big and obstinate fights neither the Russians nor the Japanese take many prisoners, but bayonet all the wounded, and those asking quarter, in turn as the lines move forward and back. Moreover, they said that under the stress of victory the Japanese grew exceedingly insolent to the foreigners, and, curiously, particularly to the Americans; a latent feeling that I had not in the least expected becoming evident as to our having thwarted Japan's hopes not merely in the Philippines but in Hawaii. [One man reported] that toward the end of his stay the Japanese soldiers would sometimes threaten the various foreigners (the English and Americans just as much as the Germans or Frenchmen) if they met them alone, and that the tone of the Japanese officers was often insolent; in some cases to an almost unbearable extent. In short, the Japanese Army showed a disposition to lump all white men together and to regard them with a common hatred. I gather that the exceedingly obstinate resistance of Port Arthur and the very effective offensive return made by the

48

Russians at the close of the last great battle before Mukden have had a rather healthy effect in abating this insolence.

Of course, in a way the feeling is most natural. It is only ten years since the foreign nations ceased to treat Japan with official contempt in the matter of consular courts and the like, and I think, Springy, you and I will both admit that our travelling countrymen, not to speak of the inhabitants of Continental Europe, are not always ingratiating in their manners toward the races which they regard as their inferiors. If the circumstances were reversed and if English or Americans had been lorded over by one yellow race for a long term of years and then had won some striking victories over another yellow race, I doubt whether the victorious soldiers would have shown any great courtesy or consideration toward the men of the first yellow race. I yet have hopes that this is only a passing phase and that when Japan settles down she will feel a desire to enter more and more into the circle of the great civilized nations as one of their number. There are many individual Japanese for whom I have a sincere liking and there is much in their civilization from which we can with advantage learn.

But all this is aside from the main point which is that in international affairs, as things are in this very human world, each nation, while striving to act fairly by other nations, must rely for its own safety only upon its own forethought and industrial efficiency and fighting edge. Unless it has this fighting edge and this forethought it will go down. Whether Russia wins or Japan wins the victor will in the long run only yield either to England or to the United States substantially the respect which England or the United States is enabled to exact by power actual or potential. Moreover, looked at from the standpoint of a long course of years no nation can depend upon the mere friendship of any other, even though that friendship is genuine, unless it has itself such strength as to make its own friendship of value in return. When affairs come to the time of settlement in the Far East (even if previous to the peace no other nation

49

gets embroiled beyond the present pair of combatants) we shall have to look sharply lest our interests be sacrificed.

If it were not for the attitude of England and the United States I think that Germany and France would probably have already interfered on Russia's side. But of course this does not necessarily mean that all four Powers may not form a friendly agreement in the end, even an agreement as against us. But I hardly believe this. Japan has shown herself to be astute and far-sighted and she must know that if Russia made peace with her now, with the purpose of joint hostile action against some other Power, it would only be with the further purpose of eating her up a generation or so hence. So long as Japan takes an interest in Korea, in Manchuria, in China, it is Russia which is her natural enemy. Of course, if Japan were content to abandon all hope of influence upon the continent of Asia and to try to become a great maritime Power she might ally herself with Russia to menace the American, the Dutch, or perhaps the English possessions in the Pacific. But in any such alliance between Russia and Japan, do not forget what surely the Japanese would think of, viz.: whereas the sea Powers could do little damage to Russia, they could do enormous damage to Japan, and even though abandoned by Russia might well destroy the Japanese Navy and blockade the Japanese islands. In such an alliance the entire risk would be run by Japan and an altogether disproportionate share of the advantage would come to Russia. I hardly believe that Japan would fail to see this.[1]

But the summing up of the whole matter is that we must trust in the Lord and keep our powder dry and our eyes open. What turn the military and diplomatic affairs will take I have no idea, but so far as possible I intend, as your people should intend, to

---

[1]Japan and Russia actually did come to an understanding in the next ten years which was very similar to tne one Roosevelt outlined in 1904. See A. L. P. Dennis, "The Foreign Policies of Soviet Russia (N. Y., 1924), Chap. XI, for an authoritative review of the secret treaties and agreements between Russia and Japan in 1907, 1910, 1912, and 1916. S. A. Korff, "Russia in the Far East," *Am. Journ. of Inter. Law*, Vol. XVII, April, 1923.

be vigilant and reasonably ready to adopt whatever course is called for.

This letter which we have given at such length to introduce the subject brings us to a statement of the diplomatic situation which faced President Roosevelt. First we must consider the position of England.

Great Britain looked in two directions, toward Europe and toward her possessions. Her relations in Europe were primarily with France, Germany, and Russia; the relations in the colonies were with the same three Powers. It is difficult to say that one set of relations was more important than the other, and yet it may be observed that the concerns in Europe were more immediate to this extent, that for the sake of peaceful relations with France, Germany, and Russia, England was sometimes willing to sacrifice more remote interests in Africa, the Pacific, and the Far East. Indeed, we may go further than that when we view the effects of British policy, not from London but from the Far East, where it was applied. We suggest that a close study of European history, with the facts of the Far Eastern situation in mind, would probably reveal that it had been for half a century a regrettable principle of both Continental and British statecraft, confined to no single government, to pay debts, make concessions, and discharge obligations to neighbouring Powers in Europe by drawing demand notes on the foreign offices of the independent states of the Far East. This casual payment of debts with other people's property, for such it appears to be if one looks at it from the Far Eastern point of view, underlies most of the present sorrows of China and Korea and for many years was the great menace to Japan.

ROOSEVELT AND THE RUSSO-JAPANESE WAR

It was M. Delcassé who as far back as 1891 asserted that "it is in Europe that you will most surely defend your colonies.[1] He might also have said that it is in the Far East and Africa that one could least expensively build up a temporary security at home. In this practice the British Foreign Office was not unskilled, though never applying it so extensively as France and Germany.

By England, Russia was the Power most feared during the reign of Alexander III as well as after the accession of Nicholas II in 1896. Other Powers might be nearer, more intelligent, and in a way stronger, but Russia was the great menace because the Russian Government was so wholly irresponsible. Truth was not in it. At any moment a designing clique might gain ascendancy, or the Tsar might lift the control of foreign relations entirely out of the hands of his ministers and direct them for a time in utter disregard of good judgment or existing engagements. Whatever the ignorance and the weaknesses in Russia, the Tsar had at his command unlimited man power and much wealth. The menace to the British Empire along its whole frontier across Asia, as well as the menace to the peace of Europe, was very grave. It was the policy of England as much as possible to protect herself by means of friendly buffer states. Down to 1894 China, though not usually called such, had served that function. China lay next to Russia's eastern empire. So long as China could be kept friendly to England and would interpose an obstacle to the Russian advance, England secured a measure of safety. As Russia extended farther and farther her interest in the extreme East, England sought to extend her influence in China. There is reason

---

[1]Quoted in Stuart, "French Foreign Policy," p. 100.

to believe that this accounts for the sudden awakening of Chinese interest in Korea in 1882.[1] Back of the newly asserted Chinese claims on Korea was Great Britain opposing Russia. We may trace the Russo-Japanese War directly back to that contest in Korea in the 'eighties.

The Sino-Japanese War disclosed that the Chinese Empire was weak beyond the suspicions of any one. Japan was revealed as vigorous and promising. Suddenly, England, who up to that time had favoured China and treated Japan scornfully, turned to Japan as the Power most likely to offer effective resistance to Russia. The consequences were enormous. In thus transferring with little ceremony, in the midst of a war, her support from the Power which she had encouraged to aggress in Korea, England wounded Chinese feelings. While the transfer laid the foundations for the Anglo-Japanese Alliance of 1902 it also threw China into the waiting arms of Russia. The result was the more regrettable because it seems to have been so unnecessary. There was no good reason why England could not have retained the friendship of China and added to her resources the friendship of Japan— no reasons but the opium trade and British tactlessness.

The immediate consequence of the newly established Anglo-Japanese cordiality, and perhaps the result of it, was the secret defensive alliance between Russia and China in 1896. Li Hung-chang never forgave England for what he regarded as the desertion of 1894.[2] The next year England sought to come to a general understanding with Russia and the latter encouraged hopes of success.

---

[1] At this point we are merely summarizing an interpretation of Far Eastern diplomatic history which is treated at length in "Am. in East Asia," pp. 471 ff., and in an article in *Pol. Sci. Quart,* Vol. XXXVIII, March, 1923, pp. 82–103.

[2] See p. 122.

The price demanded by Russia was British acquiescence in the Russian lease of Port Arthur. The resulting disappointment to Great Britain may best be described by a paragraph from a letter of Cecil Spring-Rice to Roosevelt.[1] The writer cites the episode as an illustration of how impossible it had proved for England to trust Russia:

> She [Russia] held out hopes to England of a general understanding, part of which should be the acquiescence of England in Russia's having a port on the China Sea. England agreed provisionally, on the understanding that the port in question should be a commercial port. England withdrew her fleet from Port Arthur as an earnest of her friendly intentions. Russia occupied the port, proceeded to fortify it, and then said that she had no further desire to negotiate.[2]

Following this failure in 1898 England sought to come to an understanding in 1900 with Germany with a view to ranging the latter in opposition to the Russian advance in Manchuria. Russia had clearly showed her hand in the summer of 1900 both before and after the relief of the Peking legations. To meet this menace, which threatened the partition of China, England accepted from Germany an agreement (October 16, 1900), that in case another Power were to take advantage of the existing complications to obtain territorial advantages the two contracting parties reserved to themselves "the right to come to a preliminary understanding as to the eventual steps to be taken for the protection of their own interests." This was prefaced by a disclaimer of all territorial designs

---

[1] Undated, but about January 15, 1905.

[2] The published correspondence between London and St. Petersburg relative to the lease of Port Arthur is in "China No. 1" (1898) c8814. Note particularly numbers 123 and 133; compare Spring-Rice's statement with G. P. Gooch, "History of Modern Europe, 1878-1919" (N. Y., 1923), p. 226, and particularly p. 301.

by both England and Germany, and by an adherence to the doctrine of the Open Door. Germany gave her assent to the agreement because of its provision that the British sphere of influence would be limited to the Yangtze valley. In Germany it was known as the Yangtze Agreement.

The Anglo-German Agreement failed of its purpose and it immediately revealed the movement of German policy away from England. Germany was already morally committed to the side of Russia, and when it came to defining what territory was included in the agreement and what was meant by "the Chinese Empire" Bülow promptly asserted that it did not apply to Manchuria. Germany refused to join in a protest against Russian aggressions in the Far East in 1901.[1] Reventlow[2] takes the view that this interpretation of the Anglo-German Agreement was a turning point in Anglo-German relations. This may be true, but it would appear that there was little possibility of an agreement between Germany and England while the former was deliberately seeking, as she had been for several years, to involve Russia more and more in her mad adventure. However, this episode did have the effect of putting outside the bounds of possibility the inclusion of Germany in the Anglo-Japanese Alliance of 1902. Germany appears to have concluded that she could gain more by pushing Russia into the Far East than by joining with England and Japan to oppose her.

The incompatibility of British and German aims manifested itself in other ways than in the refusal of

---

[1] A. L. P. Dennis, "The Anglo-Japanese Alliance," University of California Publications, Bureau of International Relations, Vol. I, No. I, p. 16; Bernadotte E. Schmitt, "England and Germany" (Princeton, 1916), p. 151; K. Asakawa, "The Russo-Japanese Conflict" (Boston and N.Y., 1904), pp. 157 ff.

[2] "Deutschlands auswärtige Politik" (Berlin, 1916), pp. 167-73.

Germany to join England against Russia in the Far East. Germany was actively as well as passively opposed to England. In' the following chapter we shall elaborate this point and wish here merely to call attention to the fact that by the end of 1901 Great Britain was impelled to enter into an alliance with Japan for a much broader purpose than mere opposition to Russia in Manchuria and Korea. The Boer War had revealed Great Britain to be without a genuine friend among all the states of Europe. The German naval bills were alarming and there was the prospect that England would soon have to reckon not only with an indignant China, a hostile Russia, an unfriendly France, but also with an ambitious Germany whose navy was seeking practical equality with that of England. The biggest single factor in the approaching diplomatic revolution was the German Navy.

Japan wanted a free hand in Korea—wanted, in fact, to regain all that had been wrested from her by Russia, Germany, and France in 1895. There were two ways to work toward this object. One way, the peaceful way, was that proposed by Marquis Ito, an alliance with Russia. This solution promised only a measure of success, for it was unlikely that Russia could be persuaded to withdraw from more than Korea and would still be threatening Japanese interests in China through her control of Manchuria. The other choice, the belligerent one, the plan of Count Hayashi, called for an alliance with England and then a conflict with Russia. A Russo-Japanese alliance would have been a calamity to British interests not merely in China but in the Pacific and would have left Russia freer also for further advances in Afghanistan, Persia, and the Near East. Japan as well as Germany was rapidly becoming a seafaring nation and was building a large navy. Russia, supported on one side by Germany with a navy and on the other by Japan with a navy, would be more of a menace than ever. Russia was, of course, already in alliance with France. The isolation of England, now almost complete, would then have been crystallized by another treaty.

British statesmen went out to meet the growing danger with a triple plan. They would make the alliance with Japan, they would come to an agreement with France, and they would work as rapidly as possible for an agreement with Russia. When this plan was accomplished two triplicates of Powers would offset each other; the Triple Alliance of Germany, Austria, and Italy would be faced by England, France, and Russia, and the second group would have the advantage of the Anglo-Japanese Alliance in the Far East. This project occupied the attention of England during the next decade.

The Anglo-Japanese Alliance was greatly promoted by Russian policy in Manchuria in 1900–01.[1] It became as much a necessity for one Power as for the other. However, England could not be brought to the point of granting expressly to Japan a free hand in Korea, nor

[1] The only authentic published source of information on the motives in the negotiation of the first Anglo-Japanese Alliance is "The Secret Memoirs of Count Tadasu Hayashi," edited by A. M. Pooley (N. Y., 1915).

It is sometimes represented, as, for example, in A. M. Pooley, "Japan's Foreign Policies" (London, 1920), that the advances toward the Anglo-Japanese Alliance came exclusively from Japan. Pooley even represents England as having been tricked into the alliance. Likewise it is sometimes asserted that a prospective Anglo-Russian understanding did not enter the purpose of England until after the signing of the Treaty of Portsmouth. We do not accept either of these assertions. The Hayashi "Memoirs" are an *ex parte* account which must be accepted with reserve. As for the desire for an Anglo-Russian understanding we have the statements of Cecil Spring-Rice to Roosevelt, in January, 1905, and the writings of such men as Doctor Dillon and "Calchas" in the contemporary English journals, to show how strong was the sentiment for an understanding with Russia as early as 1904. Baron Eckardstein warned his government of the prospect in the summer of 1904, and the fear of it appears in the Kaiser's communication to Roosevelt.

could Japan be induced to extend the area of the alliance beyond China. The phrases were very carefully selected, and when the alliance was signed on January 30, 1902, if we interpret it in the light of the negotiations and its subsequent history, it amounted merely to this: In the approaching conflict with Russia, Japan had the promise that England would not permit a third Power to intervene on the side of her opponent. The publication of the terms, February 11th–12th, had two effects. Russia immediately changed for the moment her policy toward China and signed an evacuation agreement for Manchuria in which Chinese sovereignty over this area was clearly recognized.[1] The other effect proved to be of greater importance. On March 16th Russia and France, which composed the Dual Alliance in Europe, issued a joint statement which, to quote André Tardieu, "if it had any meaning, extended to the Far East the action of the Dual Alliance."[2] Delcassé stoutly asserted that such was not the intent of the statement. Yet the fact remains that it was issued in reply to the Anglo-Japanese Alliance, and that while professing to be fully satisfied with the declared purpose of the Alliance to assure the *status quo* in the Far East and to maintain the independence of China and Korea, nevertheless, it proclaimed that in case French or Russian interests were menaced either by a third Power or by troubles in China, "the two allied governments reserve to themselves the right eventually to provide means for their preservation."[3]

---

[1] See p. 131.

[2] "France and the Alliances," p. 19.

[3] There is an assertion from German sources that by a secret agreement Count Lamsdorff secured the promise of France specifically to come to the aid of Russia in the war with Japan in case a third Power entered on the side of Japan ("Isolierung," p. 198).

ENGLAND AND THE CONTINENT

Whatever may have been the express understanding in March, 1902, or whatever may have been added to the agreement subsequently, it had the effect of encouraging Russia in her wild programme in the Far East. At the very time when France, for her own safety as well as for the peace of the Far East, ought to have been restraining Russia and urging her to conserve her strength for the fulfilment of the purposes of the original Dual Alliance, France was taking the opposite course. She was helping Russia on toward her ruin, and, what was strangest of all, France was in this really helping Germany in a plot which had been contrived to injure France. When at the time of the Moroccan crisis in 1905 France found herself without the support of Russia, now so deeply involved in the war with Japan, France was reaping the harvest of her own sowing as well as of that of the German Emperor.

At the outbreak of the Russo-Japanese War the Anglo-French accord was still in part unrealized. The arbitration treaty had been signed the preceding October, and powerful commercial interests in both Paris and London were working to bring about the desired understanding on political matters. France had as many reasons as England for desiring it. The "pin-prick" policy of the past years had accomplished nothing. For the prosecution of French plans in north Africa, particularly in Morocco, an agreement with England had become necessary. Now Russia's entrance into a war in the East deprived France of a support upon which she had long depended. The Anglo-French Entente of April 8, 1904, was the result.

As in the Anglo-Japanese Alliance, so in the Entente, the terms had to be carefully limited. On the one hand France was allied to Russia, and, on the other, England was allied to Japan, and now Russia and Japan were at war. Therefore, while the Entente was concerned exclusively with colonial matters, and reached as far as the borders of Siam, it ignored China and Korea. The conflict of alliances was embarrassing. President Roosevelt was made aware of the delicacy of the situation. Spring-Rice told him that the alliance almost cost England the understanding with France.[1] The specific provision of the Entente which concerns our narrative was that in return for like recognition of British interests in Egypt, Great Britain recognized as paramount the French interests in Morocco. The broad significance of the Entente was that in coming to an accord on colonial matters England and France had become friends at home.

Between the Entente as such and the American Government there was no disagreement, for they moved in separate spheres. The relations of the United States to the two Powers, respectively, however, were not the same. President Roosevelt did not extend to the French Government that degree of confidence which he had in the British. France was the ally of Russia. France had sought to bring about intervention to prevent the war, prompted, not by a desire to see justice done in Asia or to Japan, but by a desire to preserve the strength of her ally and protect her own investors. Roosevelt had taken a position in this matter against France; he entertained no high regard for Delcassé. England was not only the ally of Japan but also the Power whose interests in China and in the Pacific were most similar to those of the United States. Roosevelt believed in the reality of the underlying Anglo-American friendship. On the other hand, he rather prided

---

[1] See p. 213.

himself on his independence of British influence and he was too good a politician to let it appear as though he were being directed from London. Again, he was aware of England's complicated relations with the Continent and this knowledge made him cautious. The net effect was that the transatlantic conflict in 1905 presented to President Roosevelt few perfectly clear issues upon which he felt that the American Government was warranted in expressing even an opinion.

CONTEMPORARY COMMENT

E. J. Dillon, "Our Friends, Our Allies, and Our Rivals," *Contemporary Review*, May, 1904.

"That one of the immediate effects of the 'clean slate' in our relations with France will be a similar agreement with Russia has already been emphatically affirmed throughout Europe."

René Pinon, "La Guerre Russo-Japonaise et l'Opinion Européenne," *Revue des Deux Mondes*, May 1, 1904.

"L'évolution de l'opinion publique dans les divers pays du monde civilisé en ces dernières semaines, a montré encore comment, sous l'influence des événements d'Extrême-Orient, se reforme peu à peu, dans la conscience des peuples, une notion qui, en Europe, commençait à s'affaiblir et à s'effacer, celle d'un ennemi extérieur menaçant de détruire leur civilization et leur vie même."

R. de Marmande, "French Public Opinion and the Russo-Japanese War," *Fortnightly Review*, August, 1904.

"The war was spoken of as a matter wholly outside the sphere of French interest." *La Vérité Française* stated: "God cannot do otherwise than give victory to the Russians, for they are only schismatists, whilst the Japanese are terrible pagans."

ROOSEVELT AND THE RUSSO–JAPANESE WAR

Baron Suyemetsu, "Japan and the Commencement of the War with Russia," *Nineteenth Century*, August, 1904.

"Only a little time ago an eminent French statesman told me that France understood Japan little; Russia still less. It was the sole cause of the present unfortunate war. "In that respect," he continued, "England was sharper, for she understood the Far East, and, consequently, the changing circumstances of the world, before any other Occidental nation."

"Calchas," "First Principles in the Far East," *Fortnightly Review*, February 1, 1904.

"The friendship of Japan could never compensate us for a renewal of enmity with France. . . . If you think Germany must prove, sooner or later, by far the most formidable enemy you have ever had, you must ask yourself by the light of that opinion to what extent you can wish Russia to be weakened."

CHAPTER IV

The Kaiser and Roosevelt

BEHIND Russia stood Germany. This fact was not so clear in 1904 as it is now.

The war grew in large measure out of Germany's purpose to weaken the Dual Alliance of France and Russia by incapacitating Russia through her involvements in the Far East. Closely related was the German contest for naval equality with England and the peculiar controversies with France.

Count Witte claimed the credit for having formed the coalition to force Japan to return the Liaotung Peninsula.[1] On the other hand, Count Hayashi and André Mevil have asserted that Germany was the leader of the coalition which was really the newly formed Dual Alliance with Germany added.[2] The obscurity which has hitherto surrounded this event has recently been largely cleared up by the researches of Professor Otto Franke in the records of the German Foreign Office.[3]

British and German foreign policy had this in common, that both Powers desired that Russia have a sufficiently free scope for her expansion in the Far East so that she

---

[1] Witte's "Memoirs," Chap. IV.

[2] Hayashi's "Memoirs," p. 82; André Mevil, "De la Paix de Francfort," pp. 73-74.

[3] Otto Franke, "Die Grossmächte in Ostasien von 1894 bis 1914." (Braunschweig and Hamburg, 1923.) The first hundred pages of this work are devoted to the relations of the Powers to the Sino-Japanese War, the Treaty of Shimonoseki, and the intervention of Russia, France, and Germany.

would not be too aggressive toward India, Afghanistan, Persia, the Near East, or, in the case of Germany, along the German border. As the Sino-Japanese War drew toward a close and the Japanese victory followed, another alarm spread among the European capitals that Japan might be able to effect an alliance with China, after the conclusion of peace, which would place the resources of the Middle Kingdom at the disposal of Japan and threaten the position and interests of the Powers in the Far East. The first project for intervention was discussed between St. Petersburg and London late in 1894. According to Franke, Germany was invited to join the discussion and her association in the proposed intervention was solicited. Later Lord Salisbury withdrew and Germany became the actual leader in the coalition. German motives were mixed. Von Brandt, formerly German Minister at Peking, urged that Germany adopt an aggressive policy in China. For a dozen years Germany had been looking about for a suitable naval base in the Far East. It was feared that if China were to come under the domination of Japan it would be impossible for Germany to secure the desired foothold. If Germany did not join the coalition it seemed probable to the Berlin statesmen that France and Russia would carry through the operation together and this would tend to strengthen the newly formed Dual Alliance, giving it, perhaps, an invigorating baptism of blood. The Emperor, however, did not overlook the argument that by thus helping Russia to secure a clear field for her operation in the Far East he would at the same time be increasing his own security along his northeastern border. While the German decision in 1895 was consistent with the Russian policy of Bismarck, it represented a very important advance, a fatal step, as it seems to Professor Franke.[1]

German policy matured very rapidly after 1895. While Witte claimed the credit for the coalition he does not fail to see that two years later the German Emperor had already begun to execute his scheme for the involvement of Russia with Japan. Witte wrote:[2]

It is certain that by the seizure of Kiao-Chow[3] Emperor William furnished the initial impetus to our policy. Perhaps he was not clear to what consequences our step would lead, but the German diplomats and the German Kaiser were clearly making every effort in those days to drag us into Far Eastern adventures. They sought to divert our forces into the Far East so as to insure the safety of their Eastern frontier.

This statement, published in 1921, is much less strong than one ascribed to Witte in 1905 by Doctor Dillon:[4]

"As soon as he (the Kaiser) decided to weaken Russia," [stated Witte to Dillon as the Russian peace delegation was approaching New York in August, 1905] "he pushed her into the Far Eastern swamp. Of this I am absolutely sure. . . . It was he who countered and thwarted my policy of peaceful penetration and no annexations. . . . Wilhelm II is the author of the war which we are on our way to America to terminate."

---

[1] *Op. cit.*, particularly pp. 38–43, 61–62, 74–75. See also, Otto Hammann, "Der neue Kurs, Erinnerungen" (Berlin, 1918), p. 113. During the peace negotiations at Shimonoseki Li Hung Chang was in communication with Berlin through Von Brandt and he did not sign the treaty with Japan until he had received a message from Von Brandt assuring him that the Powers would intervene ("Am. in East. Asia," p. 635, footnote).

[2] "Memoirs," p. 105.

[3] The spelling of Chinese and Japanese names presents great difficulty. In these pages we have sought to conform to the best recent standards of uniformity. However, we have not felt at liberty in direct quotations from other writers to change their spelling. For example, Kiaochow and Kiao-Chow; Korea and Corea; etc.

[4] "Eclipse of Russia," p. 347.

For many years it was supposed that Russia secured the preëmptive right to lease Kiaochow in the so-called Cassini Convention of 1896, and that the Kaiser persuaded the Tsar to relinquish this right to Germany. We now know that the text of the secret treaty which was actually signed contained no such stipulation.[1] According to Witte's statement to Doctor Dillon,[2] the Kaiser contemplated the lease of Kiaochow as early as 1896 and secured the definite acquiescence of the Tsar in a secret agreement which may have been unknown to the Russian Government. Witte inferred that the lease was made for the express purpose of compelling Russia to take Port Arthur and Talienwan. The German motive was not so simple as that.[3] One of the effects of the seizure of Kiaochow was to create a political situation in the Far East in which Russia felt it necessary to make sure of the Liaotung peninsula, but Germany accomplished much more than this. By this lease Germany secured a military and commercial foothold which would become more important if the partition of the empire were to take place. Meanwhile, it gave the German Emperor and Von Tirpitz another excuse for increasing the navy. But of greater actual importance was the leverage thus afforded for meddling both in the Far East and in Europe. Germany became one of the Powers directly interested in China.

It is clear from Bülow's interpretation of the Anglo-German Agreement in the spring of 1901 that Germany was already committed, either by promises to Russia or by the demands of her own policy, to support Russia in Manchu-

---

[1] J. V. A. MacMurray, "Treaties and Agreement With and Concerning China," Vol. I, pp. 79-82.
[2] "Eclipse of Russia," pp. 249-50.
[3] Otto Franke, op. *cit.*, pp. 117-30.

ria and to become in some degree, because of the position at Kiaochow, a protection for Russia against England.

As we shall see in another chapter, the Russian adventure in Manchuria met with the united opposition of many of the wiser Russian statesmen after 1900. The management of affairs was taken out of their hands and controlled directly by the Tsar. Men like Witte and even Kuropatkin knew that the Russian attitude toward Japan in the negotiations which began in the summer of 1903 was very likely to bring on war for which Russia was wholly unprepared. Witte, at least, made every possible effort to restrain the Tsar in his mad folly. Similar efforts appear to have been made in Paris. It is possible that even without the encouragement of the Kaiser the Tsar would have persisted in bringing on the war, but it is at least equally possible that if the Kaiser had thrown in his influence to prevent it the war would never have broken out. It is perfectly clear that the German Emperor, while professing to President Roosevelt so much zeal for the integrity of China, was deliberately encouraging the Tsar to destroy that integrity. In a letter (January 3, 1904) designed to reach the Tsar just at the most critical moment in the Russo-Japanese negotiations which a month later eventuated in the outbreak of hostilities, the Kaiser drew a contrast between his own sympathetic attitude toward Russia and the hostile tone of the British press, and explained:[1]

To us here on the Continent this hypocracy [*sic*] and hatred is utterly odious and incomprehensible! Everybody here understands perfectly that Russia, following the laws of expansion, must try to get at the Sea for an iceless outlet for its commerce

[1]Levine, pp. 99-100.

. . . it is evident to every unbiased mind that Korea must and will be Russian. When or how that is nobody's affair and concerns only you and your country. This is the opinion of our People here at home and therefore there is no excitement or "emballement" or war roumers [*sic*] or anything of that sort *here*. The sure end that Korea will once be yours is a foregone conclusion here like the occupation of Mandschuria [*sic*], hence nobody troubles themselves about it here!

More utterly treacherous encouragement for that particular moment it would have been difficult to devise.

What did Germany expect to gain by the war? A hypothetical answer to this question now rather than later may be of some assistance to the reader in weighing and interpreting the evidence which follows. The German Emperor, in common with all of Europe at the outset of the war in the Far East, did not anticipate such sweeping and repeated Japanese victories as came at Port Arthur, Mukden, and in the Sea of Japan. It was the common expectation that at length Russia would gather her forces and wear Japan down so that in the settlement the Japanese aims would still be unrealized. Russia would still remain a Power in the Far East. This was as Germany desired. Meanwhile, Russia would be weakened by the war and the drain on her resources. This also was what Germany wanted. The Kaiser contemplated the settlement of the war by a division of north China, including Manchuria, between Russia and Japan. Thus Russia would come out of the war even more deeply involved than when she entered it, with the prospect that hostilities would be resumed by Japan at some future date. Meanwhile the Kaiser hoped by the aid of President Roosevelt to secure a pledge from France and England that they would not take any Chinese territory. Thus the partition of China would in fact be accomplished but without Germany's two rivals having a share. Judging by subsequent developments it would appear to have been a part of the German plan, when Russia had secured a slice of the Chinese Empire, to come forward with a demand that Germany be compensated, not in Asia, but nearer home either in the Near East or in Africa. With Russia crippled, France could have opposed no effective resistance to such a German demand. The Anglo-French Entente had not yet been formed, and even when it was consummated the Kaiser was under the impression that England would not give to France other than diplomatic support. It would appear to have been a bolder plan than was ever dreamed of by the Tsar in his wildest moments, and far more cunning. We believe that there is enough evidence to make credible this statement of the German strategy.

The Kaiser's first move was an appeal to President Roosevelt shortly after the outbreak of hostilities to issue a circular calling upon the Powers interested in China to urge Russia and Japan to "respect the neutrality of China outside the sphere of military operations." At Secretary Hay's suggestion a note was sent, but the clause referring to the sphere of military operations was omitted and in its place was inserted a request to respect "in all practicable ways her [China's] administrative entity."[1] This change in the wording of the request converted it into a different proposition from what the Kaiser may have desired, but after conference between Germany and Russia

---

[1]Thayer's "Hay," Vol. II, p. 37; "For. Rel." (1904), pp. 2-3. Compare this circular with the one issued a year later, also at the request of the Kaiser, below, p. 81; Howe's "Meyer," p. 86.

the latter acquiesced (February 19th) with some reservations. Russia excepted Manchuria from the area of its operation, thus restoring the proposition to the form originally outlined by Germany. The neutral Powers agreed to it without reservations. Thus the Kaiser secured an international guarantee for Kiaochow, and also advanced one step with his scheme. France and England were again committed to the preservation of the integrity of China.

The signing of the Anglo-French Entente, April 8, 1904, presented to the Kaiser a new complication. In his letters to the Tsar later in the year we find him seeking to persuade his weak-minded friend that France had been false to Russia under the provisions of the Dual Alliance in not coming to Russia's assistance in the war. He intimated that France was now under British influence.[1] A year later Germany undertook the task of breaking the Entente, or testing it, by bringing on the Moroccan crisis. The Kaiser's policy was to sow discord wherever there appeared to be understanding between his rivals. We shall have occasion to point out how he sought to create a discord between the United States on the one hand, and France and England on the other. Germany would be unable to carry out her project if, at the close of the war, any two Powers remained sufficiently close together to oppose her jointly.

During the summer of 1904 there developed two matters of importance.

In July, Germany compelled Russia to negotiate a new commercial treaty which was exceptionally favourable to

[1]Levine, p. 113. "After many hints and allusions I have found out what I allways [sic] feared— that the Anglo-French agreement had the one main effect, viz.: to stop the French from helping you!"

Germany. Witte abhorred the treaty but he had no choice but to sign it.[1]

More significant was the attitude of Germany toward the peace negotiations which were inaugurated during that summer in London. Even as early as June 6, 1904, the German Emperor wrote to the Tsar that he would "certainly try to dissuade Uncle Bertie" as soon as he met him "from harassing" the Tsar "with any more such proposals."[2] In July, Baron Eckardstein became the intermediary for peace overtures from Witte to Count Hayashi, the Japanese Minister in London. Eckardstein was not unwilling to be utilized because he already foresaw that eventually England and France might join as mediators of the peace. He feared that this would not only strengthen the Entente but would also pave the way for an Anglo-Russian understanding which was the development most dreaded by Germany. Eckardstein made a full statement of his fears to Bülow, who instructed Eckardstein that while peace by Anglo-French intervention was of course not desirable, Germany was not at all eager for peace at that time and Eckardstein was not to encourage peace negotiations.[3]

On September 19th, the Kaiser urged the Tsar to send more men to Manchuria and stated:

There is no doubt to me that you will and must win in the long run, but it will cost both money and many men.[4]

Next the Kaiser took up the project of a secret Russo-German Alliance. The argument brought forward by the

---

[1]Levine, pp. 114–15; Witte's "Memoirs," p. 72.

[2]*Ibid.*, pp. 113–14.

[3]"Isolierung," pp. 81–4.

[4]Levine, p. 118.

Kaiser was that "as soon as it [the treaty] is accepted by us France is bound to join her ally." On November 30th, he forwarded the draft of the proposed treaty which had been made by Count von Bülow. The project was apparently unknown to any in Germany except Bülow and the Kaiser.[1]

The purpose of this treaty, as originally drafted, was "to localize as much as possible the Russo-Japanese War." Subsequently, the preamble was redrafted in Berlin and the purpose changed to "the maintenance of peace in Europe."[2] Article I provided:

In case one of the two Empires should be attacked by a European Power its ally will aid it with all its land and sea forces. The two Allies, in case of need, will also make common cause in order to remind France of the obligations she has assumed by the terms of the Franco-Russian treaty of alliance.

Further reflection led the Kaiser to fear that such an agreement might become known. The article

would lead the whole political world to infer that we had—instead of concluding a Defensive Alliance—formed a sort of chartered Company limited for Annexation purposes, possibly involving secret clauses for the private benefit of Germany. The general mistrust ensuing would gravely imperil our mutual Situation, because Amerika [sic] would immediately join England—which on no account must be allowed—acting under the suspicion that Russia and Germany were on the move for aggressive operations to further selfish ends. But it will just

[1]Levine; pp. 123-27. The manner in which this project was brought forward suggests that Baron Sternberg, the German Ambassador at Washington, may have been kept in ignorance of the project. Several months later we find him protesting to Roosevelt that no such treaty existed and acting as though he had never known of the negotiations. See below, p. 75.

[2]Levine, pp. 128-30 and 138-40, gives the texts of the two drafts.

be the main task of Russian and German diplomatists to stop America joining England.[1]

Therefore the phrase about reminding France was softened and a secret article was added by which Russia was to make common cause with Germany in case the latter received complaints arising out of delivery of coal to Russia in "pretended violation of the rights [duties] of neutrals." Other articles bound the two parties to common peace negotiations in case of war, fixed an indefinite duration for the treaty, subject to denouncement a year in advance by either party.[2] It is not essential to our purpose to dwell upon this extraordinary document. In the end the Tsar refused to sign it without first notifying France. The Japanese victory at Port Arthur came on January 1, 1905. The Kaiser visibly cooled even about the coaling agreement to which the treaty had been reduced.

As the Kaiser had feared, "walls have ears," and rumours of this treaty were soon circulating in the capitals of Europe.

Spring-Rice wrote to Roosevelt, about November 5, 1904:

Emperor William has got the ear of the Emperor here. He has his adjutant always bringing him messages and making all manner of suggestions. I don't think it follows Germany will seek for compensations after peace is concluded—in the Far East. Judging by analogy the compensations will be in the West and in Europe. . . . However, . . . it is plain

[1]Levine, pp. 132-33

[2]For a full discussion of the significance of this project see Sidney B. Fay, "The Kaiser's Secret Negotiations With the Tsar, 1904-1905," *American Historical Review*, Vol. XXIV, Oct., 1918, pp. 48-72.

that Germany naturally enough wants to see Russia have a free hand in Asia and hopes in exchange to have one in Europe; that if England could be engaged in a war with Russia which would require her fleet to be absent in the East, the German fleet, especially if France would come in, would have a good chance for a sudden descent on England. . . .[1]

The King of Italy had some information about the proposed secret treaty and was under the impression that it had actually been signed. On February 14th Ambassador Meyer reported a recent conversation with the King in which the latter stated without qualification:[2]

1 will even make a prophecy that your country sooner or later will have trouble with Russia over China. Russia, with everything tumbling down as to her internal affairs, cannot continue the war with Japan. She will hope to make up by taking from China the equivalent of what she loses to Japan. Russia's diplomacy is based on misrepresentations and lies and she cannot be trusted. In addition to her alliance with France, I feel sure that she has made some agreement with Germany even in writing. The fact that Russia is replacing her modern guns on the frontier with obsolete ones is additional proof.

Meyer was so impressed with this assertion that he took it upon himself to visit Berlin and seek a personal interview with the Kaiser with whom he was on friendly terms. The subject of the alliance with Russia was not introduced into the conversation and Meyer does not appear to have understood the significance of that feature of the King's assertion. In regard to the Far East the

---

[1] The project of the Kaiser for the treaty with Russia followed the Dogger Bank incident in which war between Russia and England was for the moment threatened. (See p. 44.) Spring-Rice also appears to have been writing with the Dogger Bank incident in mind.

[2] Howe's "Meyer," pp. 121-23.

Kaiser renewed in the most positive and emphatic manner his previous declarations. "Yes," he said, "most assuredly if there should be any partition *now* of China there is no knowing where it would end." This assertion was made March 5th, just before the Kaiser embarked for his cruise in the Mediterranean, and less than four weeks before he made his belligerent speech at Tangier.[1]

The story of the alliance did not easily down, and at length Roosevelt was led to record his own impressions that the report of Germany's secret encouragement of Russia both before and during the war was "all nonsense." In a letter to Spring-Rice, May 26, 1905, he wrote:

The other day Speck called upon me and said that they had learned from Japan that the Japanese quoted you as authority for the statement that there was a Russian-German alliance against Japan and against England; that the German Emperor had really put Russia up to the war against Japan and was hostile to both England and Japan.

I told him that I thought it was all nonsense, but evidently the Kaiser or some high official is concerned about it, and Speck has now written me to ask if I would find out from you from whom you got your information. I told him I doubted . . . you . . . any knowledge [?][2] In his letter to me he states that there is no kind of warrant for the report, and that Germany is not and never has been in such an alliance with Russia, and that the German Government believes that Russia is circulating this report in both Japan and the United States so as to cause a hostile feeling to Germany.

As I think I told you, the Kaiser, both through personal dispatches, through communications from the Foreign Office and

---

[1]Howe's "Meyer," p. 126.

[2]This sentence was added by pen to the typewritten copy and the ink has faded beyond the point where it can be surely deciphered.

the communications of his Ambassador, in repeating these statements has shown an astonishing willingness to put down in black and white what his feelings are. . . .

As you know, I cannot believe that the Kaiser has any deep-laid plot against England. That he may have dreamed at times of some such movement is possible. His actions and words in reference to Russia and France during the last few months are in my judgment incompatible with any serious purpose on his part to get these two countries actively or passively to support him in the war with England. His attempt to thwart France in Morocco, for instance, is proof that he did not meditate keeping France friendly and possibly an ally in the event that he went to war with England.

If Spring-Rice had disclosed the source of his information the German Foreign Office would have been able to trace the "leak" in the Foreign Office at St. Petersburg. So far as is known, this German inquiry through Roosevelt failed in this regard.

We are now in a position to appreciate how badly handicapped the President was because of the defective American diplomatic service. At the American embassies in Berlin, Paris, London, and St. Petersburg there do not appear to have been any suspicions, and even Ambassador Meyer, upon whom the President depended, had been thrown off the trail by the Kaiser's ingenious professions of zeal for the integrity of China.

While the German Emperor was still waiting for the Tsar to sign the secret treaty without showing it first to France, he turned his attention to the question of Anglo-French intervention which Baron Eckardstein had already called to the notice of Count von Bülow. President Roosevelt was to be enlisted as the tool for the next operation.

Incidentally the Kaiser would have an opportunity to strike at a possible Anglo-American understanding.

Baron Sternberg, German Ambassador at Washington, spent the Christmas holidays in Germany. On December 29, 1904, he had a long talk with the German Emperor in which the latter informed him that he had "all reasons to believe" that after the conclusion of peace between Russia and Japan the Open Door and the integrity of China "would be gravely menaced." The Kaiser stated that from Paris the German Foreign Office learned that Delcassé was then straining his whole ingenuity to create an entente between Russia and England by pointing out to England that her great chance of making up with Russia would come in the peace negotiations after the war.

Sternberg made the conversation the subject of a letter to Roosevelt, but on January 5th the Emperor requested his ambassador to cable the following more explicit statement and request:

He [the Emperor] is highly gratified to hear that you firmly adhere to the policy of the open door and uphold the actual integrity of China, which the Emperor believes at present to be gravely menaced. Close observation of events has firmly convinced him that a powerful coalition, headed by France, is under formation directed against the integrity of China and the open door. The aim of the coalition is to convince the belligerents that peace without compensation to the neutral powers is impossible. The formation of this coalition the Emperor firmly believes can be frustrated by the following move: you should ask all the powers having interest in the Far East, including the minor ones, whether they are prepared to give a pledge not to demand any compensation for themselves in any shape, of territory or other compensation in China or elsewhere

77

for any services rendered to the belligerents in the interests of peace or for any other reason. . . .

In the opinion of the Emperor, a grant of a certain portion of territory to both belligerents, eventually in the North of China, is inevitable. The open door within this territory might be maintained by treaty. Germany of course would be the first to pledge herself to this policy of disinterestedness.[1]

Sternberg added that conversations with leading men led him to believe personally that the danger of the demand for compensations was considerable.

The Kaiser continued to nourish this suspicion, and in an interview with U. S. Ambassador Charlemagne Tower on February 4th, he supplied more of the evidence upon which his suspicions were based. This conversation was reported in the following personal letter from Tower to Roosevelt:

EMBASSY OF THE UNITED STATES OF AMERICA
BERLIN

4 February, 1905.

MR. PRESIDENT:

I have just had a confidential interview with the German Emperor in regard to the present state of affairs in China and the war in the Far East, which I think it my duty to report to you directly; for I believe, from the manner in which he spoke of you throughout the course of it, that he intended me to bring it to your immediate attention.

The Emperor began the conversation by saying that your present attitude in relation to the integrity of China and Mr. Hay's recent note to the Powers have rendered an enormous service to the commercial interests of all nations. For, he declared, there is no doubt that a well-defined plan had already been formed in Europe to make encroachments upon China with

---

[1]Quoted in Thayer's "Hay," Vol. II, pp. 385–86.

a view to taking advantage of the negotiations that are likely to occur at the close of the war between Russia and Japan to seize by mutual agreement, and to occupy permanently, certain portions of the Chinese Empire.

I do not know how much of the Emperor's information upon this subject may have been communicated to you already, Mr. President, through his Embassy in Washington, though it is evident from the cipher telegram addressed to me by the Secretary of State that the existence of such a movement has come to your knowledge. But the Emperor said to me distinctly in the course of this conversation that he had been formally approached in regard to it through the medium of France, and that a definite proposition had been made to him which looked toward his coöperation with France and England for the purpose of establishing permanent control within Chinese territory. He told me that M. Doumer, the present President of the French Chamber of Deputies, had gone some time ago to see the German Ambassador in Paris, Prince Radolin, to whom he had unfolded this plan. M. Doumer gave Prince Radolin to understand that England was ready to join in the concerted action if France and Germany would agree, and he proposed that, if the Emperor were willing, England should be allowed to carry out her plan of territorial acquisition in China, France should move her frontier limits northward from Tongking, and Germany should have a free hand in the development of Shantung.[1] Prince Radolin, alarmed at this unexpected disclosure, reported it at once to the Emperor, whereupon he made an emphatic declaration that he would not only not take part in any such arrangement, which he considered to be fraught with disaster to the commercial interests of Germany as well as of the rest of the world, but that he should oppose it with all the strength of his authority and influence. "This is where

[1] The German Emperor is proved by the correspondence under review to have been so utterly untruthful that one does not know how much faith to place in this accusation. However, the fact that M. Doumer had been Governor General of French Indo-China and was a faithful agent of Delcassé makes it appear at least plausible (Stuart, "French Foreign Policy," p. 72).

79

America has done an incalculable good," he said. "She has defeated that plan, she has forced the Powers to come out into the open and define their intentions, and she has preserved the integrity of China!" He then reiterated what he had already said in the note of Count von Bülow which I reported to the Secretary of State by telegraph, last week, that Germany does not want to occupy any territory in China, that she is unequivocally in favor of the open door and that her policy is in this respect absolutely in accord with yours for the maintenance and extension throughout the East of the commerce and trade of the world. The Emperor said further that he had sent for the Chinese Minister in Berlin, to whom he explained the imminent dangers which threaten his country as the result of the present war, and he urged him in the most impressive manner to warn the Chinese Government against the slightest breach of neutrality, because, he told him, a complication of any kind arising now could result only in injury to China. "I told him," he said, "that the cost of any act of the kind, especially of any step which might induce an intervention, would be very high, and that the price of it will be taken out of your hide if you are not careful."

The Emperor said to me, however, that he considers the immediate danger to have been averted by your action and by the note of Mr. Secretary Hay to the Powers, at which he expressed repeatedly, throughout the interview, his highest gratification.

I have the honour to be,
Mr. President,
Your Obedient Servant,
CHARLEMAGNE TOWER.

To the President of
the United States.

The most significant part of the Sternberg telegram of January 5th, as Secretary Hay immediately saw, was not the vague charges against France and England but the specific proposition that northern China be divided between Russia and Japan.

In a letter to Senator Lodge, July 11, 1905, Roosevelt explained how this telegram from Berlin had been received in Washington. Roosevelt wrote:

He [Hay] had grown to hate the Kaiser so that I could not trust him in dealing with Germany. When, for instance, the Kaiser made the excellent proposition about the integrity of China, Hay wished to refuse and pointed out where the Kaiser's proposition as originally made contained what was inadvisable. I took hold of it myself, accepted the Kaiser's offer, but at the same time blandly changed it so as to wholly remove the objectionable feature (that is, I accepted it as applying to all of China outside of Manchuria, whereas he had proposed in effect that we should allow Russia to work her sweet will in all northern China) and Hay published it in this form.

"A most singular incident," Secretary Hay observed of the Kaiser's proposition.[1] But even with his suspicions aroused the Secretary of State does not appear ever to have comprehended the full significance of the episode.

The text of the note sent out was as follows:

It has come to our knowledge that apprehension exists on the part of some of the Powers that in the eventual negotiations between Russia and Japan claims may be made for the concession of Chinese territory to neutral Powers.

Recalling the traditional American policy with reference to China the American Government disclaimed any such

[1]Thayer's "Hay," Vol. II, p. 387.

intention for itself and invited the other Powers to make similar declarations.[1]

The note was dated January 13th. The Marquis of Lansdowne replied that the American Government might rely upon the full concurrence of England. The French reply was reported as favourable, but was not made public. Germany, already pledged to agree, was in an embarrassing position. Bülow gave his assent but skilfully qualified it by stating that it was the German policy "absolutely to stand by its former declarations," one of which was the Anglo-German Agreement of 1900. In view of the fact that this agreement had been interpreted in Germany as not including Manchuria as a part of the Chinese Empire, it would appear that even after agreeing to Roosevelt's proposition Germany was still free to support Russia in her purpose to appropriate Manchuria.[2]

President Roosevelt was disposed to credit the suspicion that France was seeking an opportunity to acquire additional territory in China. However, the way in which he replied to Ambassador Tower, February 16, 1905, clearly indicates how inadequately he grasped the Kaiser's purpose in thus troubling the waters. He wrote:

I am interested in the conversation you report with the Emperor. I cannot believe that England has any intention of taking part in the partition of China, but there certainly do

---

[1] "For. Rel." (1905), pp. 1–4.

[2] Thayer's "Hay," Vol. II, p. 388. There was a singular inconsistency between the note of January 13th, as sent out, and President Roosevelt's explanation in the letter of July 11th, quoted above. The note contained no qualification excepting Manchuria from its application. The note merely referred to the "Chinese Empire" and "Chinese territory." The American Government had never interpreted this to exclude Manchuria. The note was therefore more inclusive than the proposition which Roosevelt apparently had in mind. It is possible that we have here an indication of Roosevelt's relative indifference to the separation of Manchuria from China, an indifference to which we refer below, p. 320.

THE KAISER AND ROOSEVELT

seem to be suspicious indications as to the possible actions of France. I think the Emperor rendered a service by what he did.

Having failed in his intrigue for the alliance with Russia, but having easy success in his attempt to place the United States in opposition to France, the German Emperor turned his attention to Morocco. His efforts in Washington had been so far sufficiently successful to warrant another attempt to involve the United States against France and perhaps against England. With the support of the United States he hoped to test and perhaps break the Entente.[1]

Things were going badly with Russia. She had been defeated at Port Arthur and forced to retire northward. Toward the end of February she was locked in a deadly struggle to hold Mukden, which she was at length forced to surrender in a panic on March 10th. Russia could be of no assistance to France. This circumstance presented the German Emperor with a favourable moment to strike. If only he could secure the support of President Roosevelt against France, success would be reasonably assured. But if this support were not forthcoming there was still the possibility that American influence might be brought to bear either on France or else on England in such a way as to compel France to humiliate herself, or to reveal the Entente as a hollow sham. Thus the Kaiser appears to have schemed.

On March 6th, Baron Sternberg conveyed to the President the invitation of the Kaiser to join with Germany in informing the Sultan of Morocco that he ought to

---

[1] In what follows on the Moroccan incident we are following Bishop, "The Secret History of the Algeciras Convention," Vol. I, Chap. XXXVI, except as otherwise noted. This chapter is President Roosevelt's own statement of the facts, printed verbatim from one of his letters and fully supported by the Roosevelt Papers.

ROOSEVELT AND THE RUSSO–JAPANESE WAR

reform his government, and that if he would do so Germany and the United States would support him against France. President Roosevelt promptly replied that the American Government had no proper interest in the question. The letter was, however, cordial and friendly. The Kaiser embarked on his famous Mediterranean cruise, landed at Tangier on March 31st, and made his belligerent speech. Replying to the address of welcome made by the Sultan's uncle he proclaimed:

It is to the Sultan in his position of an independent sovereign that I am paying my visit to-day. I hope that under the sovereignty of the Sultan a free Morocco will remain open to the peaceful rivalry of all nations, without monopoly or annexation, on the basis of absolute equality.[1]

This was a direct slap in the face of the Entente, which had recognized Morocco as practically a French sphere of influence.

Germany felt assured, so Baron Sternberg explained to President Roosevelt, that England's aid to France in the situation thus created would not go beyond "diplomatic support." However, in the course of the next two weeks Germany became a little nervous about the British attitude. While the President was on his hunting trip in Colorado in April he received an urgent message from the Kaiser requesting him to find out how far Great Britain proposed to go in support of France. The German Emperor even went so far as to request Roosevelt to intimate to England that the American Government would be pleased to see England support not France but Germany.

---

[1]Text in Stuart, "French Foreign Policy," pp. 167-68.

THE KAISER AND ROOSEVELT

It now seems amazing that the Kaiser could have believed that he had President Roosevelt so under his influence that the latter would even listen to such a request. And yet, as we have seen, the Kaiser had reason to read into the previous correspondence at least a small degree of encouragement. It is clear that the President did not suspect the German motives. Yet it is fairly obvious that the Kaiser was laying a trap for Roosevelt just as a few months before he had laid a trap for the Tsar in the proposed Russo-German Alliance. Had Roosevelt yielded to the request from Berlin the consequences would have been endless. It would have ranged the American Government on the side of Germany against the Entente. It would have created an episode in Anglo-American relations as important as the Kruger telegram had been in Anglo-German affairs. Most important for our study is the fact that it would probably have placed France and England in opposition to any steps which the President might take to end the Russo-Japanese War. Compliance with the request of the Kaiser would have cost President Roosevelt his entire influence in both Europe and the Far East and would have made him ludicrous in history.

The absurdity was obvious to President Roosevelt. He was no more disposed to advise England in her Continental relations than he had been to join Germany against France in Morocco six weeks earlier. And yet the President, uninformed as to Germany's double-dealing with Russia and not crediting even the charges against Germany which had been made by his trusted friend Spring-Rice, was not entirely on his guard. This is clear from his instructions to Secretary of War Taft who, greatly to the joy of the cartoonists, had been left in

85

Washington to "sit on the lid." Roosevelt took the Kaiser as a joke; he would have been justified in taking him seriously. From Colorado he wrote (April 20th):[1]

The Kaiser's pipe-dream this week takes the form of Morocco. Speck has written me an urgent appeal to sound the British Government and find out whether they intend to back up France in gobbling Morocco. . . . I do not care to take sides between France and Germany in the matter.

At the same time, if I can find out what Germany wants I shall be glad to oblige her if possible, and I am sincerely anxious to bring about a better state of feeling between England and Germany. Each nation is working itself up to a condition of desperate hatred of the other; each from sheer fear of the other. The Kaiser is dead sure that England intends to attack him. The English Government and a large share of the English people are equally sure that Germany intends to attack England. Now, in my view this action of Germany in embroiling herself with France over Morocco is proof positive that she has not the slightest intention of attacking England. I am very clear in my belief that England utterly over-estimates, as well as mis-estimates, Germany's singleness of purpose, by attributing to the German Foreign Office the kind of power of continuity of aim which it had from '64 to '71. I do not wish to suggest anything whatever as to England's attitude in Morocco, but if we can find out that attitude with propriety and inform the Kaiser of it, I shall be glad to do so.

The President suggested that Secretary Taft see the British Ambassador and invite his statement on the Morocco affair.

Remember, however, that both parties are very suspicious. You remember the King's message to me through Harry White

---
[1]Bishop, Vol. I, p. 472.

and his earnest warning to me that I should remember that England was our real friend and that Germany was only a make-believe friend. In jùst the same way the Germans are always insisting that England is really on the point of entering into a general coalition which would practically be inimical to us—an act which, apart from moral considerations, I regard the British Government as altogether too flabby to venture upon.

The Germans were right to this extent, that the "policy of encirclement" had begun. England was bending her energies to isolate Germany, but this policy had been adopted in response to Germany's support of Russia and to the building of the new German Navy. King Edward, as it would appear from the foregoing pages, if nothing more was added, was likewise wholly right when he argued that the German Government was only a make-believe friend of the United States.

Our purpose at this point is not to review the Moroccan crisis beyond the point where it yields light upon the close of the Russo-Japanese War. The same mail which brought to the President the appeal from the Kaiser brought also a note from the Japanese Foreign Office stating that on April 5th Delcassé had informed the Japanese Minister in Paris that he was prepared to make peace between Japan and Russia. This concern of France for peace in the Far East was the most immediate result of the Kaiser's speech at Tangier. The Japanese note intimated that Japan would prefer Roosevelt to Delcassé as a peacemaker.[1]

The significance of the Moroccan incident for President Roosevelt was that, by ranging himself even in some degree on the side of the Kaiser, he lost, if indeed he had

[1]See p. 176.

ever held, the confidence of the British Foreign Office. President Roosevelt supported the German proposition for an international conference on Morocco. Lord Lansdowne regarded the proposal as "unfortunate, and as possibly planned to embarrass France."[1] At that very moment Roosevelt was looking to London for support in persuading the Japanese to moderate their peace terms. Lansdowne would not help Roosevelt. We shall return to this situation subsequently.[2] Suffice it now to observe that the Kaiser had again measurably succeeded, for he had placed President Roosevelt in the position where he appeared to be playing the rôle of a bull in the diplomatic china-shop.

Eventually the President came out right in the Moroccan affair. He supported the German demand for the international conference and then in the conference supported France against Germany and thus forced Germany into the very position of isolation which England had been planning for her. During the first six months of 1905, however, President Roosevelt was at times saved from the Kaiser's pitfalls not so much by his knowledge of the facts as by his political instincts.

The President was not unaware that he had brought himself under suspicion for his sympathy with the Kaiser, and on May 13, 1905, he put into the following letter to Spring-Rice his estimate of the Kaiser's character:

May 13, 1905.

DEAR CECIL:

Of course, in a way I suppose it is natural that my English friends generally, from the King down, should think I was under

---

[1] Telegram of June 5, 1905, Bishop, Vol. I, p. 475.

[2] See pp. 210-14.

the influence of the Kaiser, but you ought to know better, old man. There is much that I admire about the Kaiser and there is more that I admire about the German people. But the German people are too completely under his rule for me to be able to disassociate them from him, and he himself is altogether too jumpy, too volatile in his policies, too lacking in the power of continuous and sustained thought and action for me to feel that he is in any way such a man as for instance Taft or Root. You might as well talk of my being under the influence of [Russia?]. I very sincerely wish I could get England and Germany into friendly relations. While my business is to look primarily after the interests of my own country, I feel that I help this country instead of hurting it when I try to benefit other countries. I do not intend for a moment to be improperly meek about it. I have steadfastly preached a big navy, and I have with equal steadfastness seen that our navy is practised until I have reason to believe that ship for ship it is as efficient as any. I do not believe that as things are now in the world any nation can rely upon inoffensiveness for safety. Neither do I believe that it can rely upon alliance with any other nation for safety. My object is to keep America in trim so that fighting her shall be too expensive and dangerous a task to lightly be undertaken by anybody; and I shall try at the same time to make her act in a spirit of justice and good will toward others, as will prevent any one taking such a risk lightly, and will, if possible, help a little toward a general attitude of peacefulness and righteousness in the world at large. I have tried to behave in this way toward England primarily, and also toward France and Germany and toward Japan. As for Russia, I like the Russian people and earnestly hope for their future welfare, but I agree with all you say as to the Russian system of government. I loathe it.

Now in treating with the Kaiser I have simply applied in his special case my general rules. In one of your last letters you speak of the German Army as being a bulwark for civilization against disorder in view of the break-up in Russian affairs. I doubt if I really have as strong a feeling for Germany as this that you thus by implication express. I wish her well. I wish the Kaiser well. I should never dream of counting on his friendship for this country. He respects us because he thinks that for a sufficient object and on our own terms we would fight, and that we have a pretty good navy with which to fight. I shall hope that on these terms I can keep the respect not merely of Berlin, but of St. Petersburg and Tokio both. I know that except on these terms the respect of any one of the three cannot be kept. But by combining a real friendliness of attitude with ability to hold our own in the event of trouble coming, I shall hope to keep on good terms with all, and to lend some assistance to Japan in the present war in which I think she is right. The Kaiser has so far acted with me in the Far East. I do not for one moment believe that he has any long-settled and well-thought-out plans of attack upon England, such as Bismarck developed, first as regards Austria, and then as regards France. He is, and I think your people ought to be able to see it, altogether too jumpy and too erratic to think out and carry out any such policy. If England ever has trouble with Germany I think it will come from some unreasoning panic which will inspire each to attack the other for fear of being attacked itself. I get exasperated with the Kaiser because of his sudden vagaries, like this Morocco policy, or like his speech about the yellow peril the other day, a speech worthy of any fool Congressman; and I cannot of course follow or take too seriously a man whose policy is one of such violent and often wholly irrational zigzags. But I don't see why you should be afraid of him. You have told me that he would like to make a continental coalition against England. He may now and then have dreamed of such a coalition; and only last December your people were fully convinced he intended to make immediate war on them. But it is perfectly obvious that he had no such thought, or he would never have mortally insulted France by his attitude about

THE KAISER AND ROOSEVELT

Morocco. If the Kaiser ever causes trouble it will be from jumpiness and not because of long-thought-out and deliberate purpose. In other words he is much more apt to be exasperating and unpleasant than a dangerous neighbor. I have been reading De La Gorce's "Histoire du Second Empire," and I can imagine no greater contrast than that offered by Bismarck's policy from '63 to '71, with that of the Kaiser during the last eight years, the only ones in which I have watched him closely.

To turn to matters of more immediate importance, I am of course watching to see what the Russian and Japanese fleets will do in Eastern waters. France has obligingly given the Russians a base, but she may have to take it away from them. The Russian fleet is materially somewhat stronger than the Japanese. My own belief is that the Japanese superiority in morale and training will more than offset this. But I am not sure, and I wish that peace would come. Personally I wish that Japan had made peace on the conditions she originally thought of after Mukden was fought; as I pointed out to her government, a few months' extra war would eat up all the indemnity she could possibly expect Russia to pay. Just at the moment Russia is riding a high horse and will not talk peace. However, by the time you receive this letter all of what I have said may be an old story. I hope you like Meyer.

Give my love to Mrs. Springy.

Ever yours,
THEODORE ROOSEVELT.

Cecil Spring-Rice, Esq.,
St. Petersburg, Russia.

We have completed our sketch of the European background of the Russo-Japanese War, and have revealed the conditions of distrust, suspicion, and misinformation under which President Roosevelt began the task of bringing Russia and Japan together for peace negotiations. Obviously, the President was seeking to place himself in a position of neutrality and impartiality with reference to European politics. We are not to forget, however, that more than a year before he had politely warned Germany as well as France that if any Power went to the support of Russia he would go to the support of Japan. By this action he had ranged the American Government as an unsigned member of the Anglo-Japanese Alliance. Again, on June 25th, he intimated to Baron Sternberg, with reference to Germany's attitude in the Moroccan crisis, that if Germany were to start a war "for frivolous reasons" it would be unpardonable and likely to raise very formidable opposition.

Wherever the information at the President's disposal made the issue in Europe perfectly clear, he acted with promptness and his action in each case was directed against Germany, who alone threatened the peace. It is only fair to observe that the information upon which we have relied to show that the Kaiser's double dealing is drawn from literature of a very recent date. The information in the files of the Roosevelt Papers, while supporting our thesis, would not alone justify it. The charge, therefore, which we may bring is not so much against the President's defective judgment as against the American diplomatic service in Europe. Here was an appalling situation. It was not to be expected or desired that the private letters of the Kaiser to the Tsar would be reported to the President but, as we have seen, there was other information current in Europe as to the purposes of Germany which ought to have been brought to the attention of the American Government. So far as the files of the Roosevelt Papers reveal the facts, this information was **not** supplied except in small measure through British channels which Roosevelt regarded as almost fanatically prejudiced. For the lack of such impartial information the American Government was several times on the brink of very grave mistakes.

We shall have to look beyond Europe to the Far East, however, to find the clean-cut issue which placed the American Government definitely against Russia and Germany and on the side of Japan. We shall find this issue in Manchuria. But before reviewing the Manchurian question which enveloped the immediate causes of the war we must have before us the situation in Korea and President Roosevelt's policy toward Korea and Japan.

CONTEMPORARY COMMENT

"Calchas," "The New German Intrigue: A Note of Warning," *Fortnightly Review*, September, 1904.

> "The aim of German diplomacy at the present moment is to use the war as a means of ruining the effect of the Anglo-French agreement. . . . The present object of Berlin, therefore, must be, and is, this—to secure for Russia sufficient success in the Far East to keep her permanently entangled on that side of the world."

O. Eltzbacher, "The Indemnity Due Japan," *Nineteenth Century*, July, 1905.

> "When the secret history of the Russo-Japanese War comes to be written, it will become clear that Great Britain did her best to avert the war, and it will appear that the authors of the Russo-Japanese War not only hoped that

Russia would bleed to death in Asia, but that they did their best to draw France and Great Britain also into the struggle, in the hope that they would tear one another to pieces, and that they did everything in their power in order to attain that end."

Sir Charles W. Dilke, "The War in the Far East," *North American Review*, April, 1904.

"If Germany were to declare war on Japan, Great Britain would be forced by her treaty engagement to declare war on Russia and Germany; and France, it is understood, to declare war upon Great Britain and Japan."

André Chéradame, "Les Causes de la Guerre," *Le Correspondent*, May 23, 1904.

An appraisal of the responsibilities, respectively of the United States and England for having supported Japan, and of Germany for having urged Russia into the Far East consistently since 1880. ". . . l'Allemagne a discrètement, mais résolument poussé Russes et Japonais au conflit."

A. Maurice Low, "American Affairs," *National Review*, April, 1904.

"When the knowledge of Mr. Hay's note became public, it was announced in Berlin that the initiative was taken by Germany, who suggested it to the American Government, but if the United States refused to assume the responsibility, Germany would lead. . . . It is true that the original proposition was made by Germany, but it was in such form and coupled with such impossible conditions that it would have been instantly rejected by both of the belligerents as well as by the neutral Powers. I am not at liberty to say more than that at this time. . . ."

94

THE KAISER AND ROOSEVELT

A. Maurice Low, "American Affairs," *National Review*, March, 1905.

"Here in Washington it is understood that Mr. Hay by his move [the second circular to the Powers with reference to China] has frustrated one plot and given warning that another plot contemplated would be attended with disastrous consequences."

CHAPTER V

Korea, Japan, and the United States

FOR fifteen years 1882–98, one could study in Korea the maladies of Europe.

Russia disclosed her hand at Seoul in 1885 when she demanded the privilege of sending a large number of military instructors for the Korean Army, and appears to have contemplated the establishment of a protectorate in the peninsula.[1] This intrigue stirred England to action through China, and the interference of China at Seoul down to 1894 appears to have been promoted by the British representatives in Peking and by Sir Robert Hart.[2]

This new assertion of Chinese claims to suzerainty excited Japan and brought on the Sino-Japanese War, 1894–95. Shortly after the close of this war Russia transferred her attentions to Manchuria. With the Rosen-Nissi agreement between Russia and Japan, April 25, 1898, this conflict between Russia and England in Korea, which after the Treaty of Shimonoseki became in outward appearance a contest between Russia and Japan, came practically to an end. After 1898 Russia was in continuous retreat before Japan, and the signing of the Anglo-Japanese Alliance in 1902 measurably accelerated the retirement. Probably the Russian strategy was

---

[1]Dennett, "Early Am. Policy in Korea," *Pol. Sci. Quart.*, Vol. XXXVIII, March, 1923.

[2]See "Am. in East. Asia," Chaps. XXIII–XXVII, for an exhaustive examination of the facts and a discussion of sources and authorities upon which this and the following generalizations are based.

first to make sure of Manchuria and north China and then to appropriate Korea at some more convenient time. The ultimate disposal of Korea doubtless remained to be decided between Russia and Japan, but by the end of 1903 Japan was at least temporarily secure.

To Japanese ascendancy in the peninsula the American Government had no objections. Japanese control was to be preferred to Korean misgovernment, Chinese interference, or Russian bureaucracy.

The Japanese interests in Korea were very important. Whether or not we credit the claim that Japan had to have an outlet for her surplus population, and Roosevelt accepted this argument, a glance at the economic situation reveals clearly that Japan was dependent upon Korea as the nearest foreign market, and as a source of raw materials. A disorderly government in Korea would always expose trade and friendly relations to disturbance, while a hostile power in possession of this strategic area would be a menace.

Japan wanted Korea. In most of the war literature either prepared by Japanese or based upon Japanese sources during the war a contrary impression was given. It was customary to state that Japan desired to see Korea completely secured in its territorial integrity and complete sovereignty.[1] A more careful scrutiny of Japanese commercial and political history for the preceding forty years, a scrutiny which would have been difficult in 1904, would have cast a doubt over this assertion. Korea stood

---

[1]An excellent illustration is to be found in K. Asakawa, "The Russo-Japanese Conflict." This book is the most carefully written and detailed examination in English of the causes of the war. The author aimed to be coldly scientific. Yet he organized all his material to exemplify this assertion that Japan did not want Korea. Even before the publication of the book the first steps in the absorption of Korea had been taken. Note particularly pp. 368 ff.

between Japan and China, or between Japan and Russia. She could not serve two masters. Even the strongest nation under such circumstances would have had great difficulty in remaining neutral. Korea was unbelievably weak. There had been no time since the days of the Japanese Restoration (1868) when Japan had been content to allow Korea to incline in any other direction than toward the East. In the measures by which Japan had sought to bring about this dependent relationship conciliation had no part.

Every time when the subject was brought forward, in 1872, 1877, 1882, 1884, and in 1894, some clear-sighted leaders had pointed out the political inexpediency of taking Korea. On the other hand, we know of no voices raised to counteract the notion that annexation would be desirable if expedient. A good proof of Japanese purposes is the régime in Korea immediately after the signing of the Treaty of Shimonoseki. The Japanese conducted themselves as though they already possessed the land and were determined to remain. If the European coalition had not intervened and thus intimidated Japan it seems probable that the annexation would have taken place within a period not longer than elapsed between the Portsmouth treaty and the final act of appropriation. This is a speculative point, however, which we do not press. There is ample proof as to the nature of the intentions in the following ten years.

As a result of the unaccountably stupid and brutal acts of the Japanese, the King of Korea took refuge in the Russian legation at Seoul, February 11, 1896.[1] Under the

---

[1] About this time, with the approval of Russia the King of Korea assumed the title of "Emperor." The fact accounts for the use of both titles in the following pages.

tactful and gentle manipulations of Waeber, the Russian representative, Russian influence immediately became paramount. But in the course of the following twenty-seven months Japan and Russia negotiated and signed three agreements relative to Korean affairs. It is perfectly evident from the texts of these conventions that Russia was without conspicuously aggressive designs. The more recent testimony of Russian statesmen supports this conclusion.[1] In Russia there were divided councils and the War Department appears to have planned aggression in 1896 by means of Russian military instructors supplied to the Korean army, but this scheme was definitely abandoned in 1898. Henceforth Russia concentrated her attention on Manchuria and other portions of north China.

A brief summary of the three Russo-Japanese agreements will suffice.[2] By the first of them Japan secured the right to station guards along the Fusan-Seoul telegraph line. Japan was permitted to keep two hundred soldiers at Fusan, the same number at Gensan, and four hundred at Seoul. By the second agreement Russia and Japan agreed to unite in efforts to remedy the financial embarrassments of Korea, to consult each other about foreign loans, and to advise the reduction of the Korean army. The administration of the Fusan-Seoul telegraph line was retained by Japan while Russia reserved the right to establish a line from Seoul to the northern frontier. In the third agreement there was a definite recognition by

---

[1]General Kuropatkin, "The Russian Army and the Japanese War" (2 vols., N. Y., 1909), Vol. I, pp. 160-66; Baron Rosen, "Forty Years of Diplomacy," Vol. I, pp. 133 ff.; Witte's "Memoirs," p. 106; Dillon, "Eclipse of Russia," pp. 284-85.

[2]Waeber-Komura (May 14, 1896), Lobanoff-Yamagata (June 9, 1896), Rosen-Nissi (April 25, 1898) agreements. "Korea Treaties and Agreements," published by the Carnegie Endowment for International Peace (Washington, 1921), pp. 22-24.

both parties of the entire independence of the state, and both Russia and Japan agreed to abstain from interference in Korean affairs. Neither country was to send in advisers without the consent of the other. And yet, "in view of the wide development taken by the commercial and industrial enterprise of Japan in Korea, as well as the large number of Japanese subjects residing in that country, the Russian Government engaged not to "hinder the development of the commercial and industrial relations between Japan and Korea." Surely these documents contain no evidence of Russian aggression. What more could Japan ask for, if in truth she was content with Korean independence? And why the large naval and military bills by which Japan had already absorbed the indemnity received from China and partly borrowed by China from Russia?

Let us follow through the evidence contained in the later official documents.

A little more than five years after signing the Rosen-Nissi agreement in which Japan had given up the privilege of political interference in the peninsula her Minister for Foreign Affairs officially stated:

Japan possesses paramount political as well as commercial and industrial interests and influence in Korea, which, having regard to her own security, she cannot consent to surrender to or share with any Power.[1]

This sweeping statement referred not to intentions but to accomplishments. It was in the present tense. It was

---

[1]Correspondence regarding the negotiations between Japan and Russia. Presented to the Imperial Diet, March, 1904; translation probably printed in Washington (see Asakawa, pp. 296–97, footnote). This excerpt is taken from the initial instructions from Komura to Kurino, the Russian Minister in St. Petersburg, July 28, 1903.

an achievement of the preceding five years. Japan did not even recognize that Russia's interest in Manchuria balanced that of Japan in Korea. Baron Komura asked that Russia recognize "Japan's preponderating interests in Korea" in return for which Japan would recognize only "Russia's special interests in railway enterprises in Manchuria." Japan demanded the exclusive right to give advice and assistance in Korean affairs both civil and military.

Omitting the tedious steps in the negotiations, we come to the counter-proposals of Russia on December 11, 1903. Russia would allow a railway to be built from Seoul up to the Manchurian border where it could be connected with the Manchurian lines belonging to Russia. The entire administration and control of communications in Korea would be surrendered to Japan. The right to give advice in civil administration was granted. "Japan's preponderating interests in Korea" were recognized. The right for Japan to send troops into the peninsula to suppress disorders was acknowledged. On the other hand, Russia desired a pledge that Japan would allow free navigation of the straits of Korea by which Russia could maintain naval communication between Port Arthur and Vladivostok, and asked a further pledge that no part of the peninsula would be used for "strategical purposes." Russia also wished to have created a neutral zone along the northern border between Russian and Korean territory. Baron Komura immediately replied that Japan was not satisfied to limit her advice to purely civil administration, that she would not make the engagement about the use of Korea for strategical purposes, and that the neutral zone was objectionable. All these proposals and counter-drafts were prefaced, of course, by the usual formula of "mutual engagement to respect the independence and territorial integrity of the Korean Empire," a formula about which we are warranted in being somewhat cynical.[1]

At the outbreak of the war Japan was on record as having already established an influence in Korea which was expressly forbidden by the Rosen-Nissi agreement, and Russia was willing to recognize the *fait accompli* provided Japan would not use the new advantages to imperil Russian occupation of Manchuria. As matters stood at the end of 1903 there was certainly nothing to justify Japan in embarking upon a costly war for additional advantages in Korea.

The cause of the war lay not in Korea but in Manchuria.[2]

Students of the control of public opinion by the manipulation of the news will find an interesting field of exploration in the study of the news emanating from

---

[1] In the final exchange of proposals Russia made still further concessions, under the pressure, perhaps, of France, and it has been asserted that at length Russia was willing to meet all of the Japanese demands regarding Korea with the exception of the neutral zone where Japan was unwilling to pledge not to erect fortifications (André Mevil, *op. cit.*, p. 110).

[2] A review of events in Korea, with special reference to commercial and political affairs, leads to the same conclusion and is omitted from the text. Japan almost monopolized the steam tonnage in Korean ports, and the trade between the two countries about doubled in five years. The Japanese population in Korea advanced from 17,000 in 1902 to 30 or 40 thousand in 1904. Japan controlled the railways, the investment of the Fusan-Seoul line being guaranteed by the Japanese Government. The effort to dismiss McLeavy Brown, the superintendent of Maritime Customs, had failed because of the united opposition of Japan and England. Instead of the Russian Government having established a naval base at Masampo the fact was that Japanese had bought the foreshore to the area which the Russians had desired for a settlement, forcing the Russians to move to another location adjoining that of the Japanese settlement. Even on the Yalu, of which we shall speak later, the Russian timber concessionaires found Japanese lumbermen already at work. The sources for this information are accessible: *Monthly Summary of Commerce and Finance*, January, 1904, see especially pp. 2459, 2460, 2475, 2477-79; *Annual Return of Foreign Trade of the Empire of Japan*, Dept. of Finance, Tokio, 1902-03, tables 498-99; Asakawa's Introductory chapter; "Secret Memoirs of Count Hayashi," p.171; Advance Sheets of American Consular Reports, various dates, 1901-04; H. J. Whigham, "Manchuria and Korea" (N. Y., 1904), pp. 176-217; Angus Hamilton, "Korea" (N. Y., 1904), Appendices II-IV.

KOREA, JAPAN, AND THE UNITED STATES

Yokohama and Tokio in the years immediately preceding the war. The current misrepresentation of Japanese purposes in Korea was in the end very costly to Japanese prestige. Good faith with the public as well as with Korea would have yielded a larger net benefit to Japan.

AMERICAN INTEREST IN KOREA

It is barely possible that there was for a few moments nearly sixty years ago a fleeting political interest in Korea among a few Americans. At the close of the American Civil War there are some reasons to imagine that William H. Seward had in mind a grandiose plan for American expansion in the Pacific which included not merely the acquisition of Alaska and the Hawaiian Islands but even a share, of some sort, with the French in Korea.[1] This was in 1868. Whatever the interest, it was very limited, very secret, and never reappeared. It is true that some Americans developed an ambition to open Korea to the world, as the American expedition and hostilities in the Tatong River in 1871 bear witness and of course it is well known that Korea's first treaty with a Western Power was with the United States in 1882.[2] But there was less interest in the Far East among Americans in 1882 than there had been in 1868, and, so far as the American Government is concerned, the treaty of 1882 may truly be claimed as an act of absent-mindedness, the consequences of which for many years few thought to explore.

---

[1] Dennett, *Am. Hist. Rev.*, Vol. XXVIII, pp. 45-62; also "Am. in East. Asia," Chap. XXII. The significance of Seward's efforts to secure the Hawaiian Islands has not yet been fully worked out, but the evidence, upon which the present writer is now at work, is rather extensive.

[2] C. O. Paullin, "The Opening of Korea," *Pol. Sci. Quart.*, Vol. XXV, pp. 470-99; "Am. in East. Asia," Chap. XXIV; "For. Rel." (1871), pp. 111 ff.

ROOSEVELT AND THE RUSSO–JAPANESE WAR

The effect of the treaty of 1882 was to set Korea adrift on an ocean of intrigue. By recognizing the state as independent of China, the United States actually reinforced the contention of Japan, namely, that Korea was wholly outside the sphere of China's interest. It also stimulated the cupidity of certain Russians who probably had some slight support from St. Petersburg, and the resulting conflict of interest between China, Russia, and Japan in Korea aroused the American Government enough to create alarm.[1] This alarm over the possibilities of being drawn into either a Far Eastern or a European tangle was sufficient to extinguish wholly any lingering political interest in Korea. This was in 1887. The American Government was even unwilling to recognize that it had incurred any moral obligation by having given Korea the initial push which hurled the unhappy country into the arena of international politics.[2]

The American commercial interests were relatively strong, however, and rapidly growing in the opening years of the 20th Century. They were small, compared with Japan's, but larger than those of Russia or of any other Western Power. The philanthropic interest of Americans was very great, and increasing. There were in Korea in 1903 about two hundred and fifty Americans, half of whom were connected with the missions. The fact that practically all the Protestant missionary work was American and that it was extraordinarily successful

---

[1]Dennett, *Pol. Sci. Quart.*, Vol. XXXVIII, pp. 94–95, 100.

[2]In December, 1882, the Japanese, being alarmed at the prospect of trouble in Korea, instructed their Minister in Peking to propose to the American Minister a plan for the neutralization of the peninsula, by an international guarantee. He stated that Japan would support such a proposition and that Great Britain was favourable. John Russell Young approved of it, but the Department of State was wholly uninterested (Dennett, "American Choices in the Far East in 1882," *Am. Hist. Rev.*, Vol. XXX, p. 96).

served to nourish in the United States a growing sympathy with the Koreans.

The American commercial interests in Korea were those of capitalists, engineers, and promoters rather than those of manufacturers. The Koreans afforded very meagre markets in which to sell, but they were eager borrowers. Some American goods were being sold, but largely through Japanese agencies, and American manufacturers were not directly interested in the trade even to the small extent that they were in Manchuria. On the other hand, all the large financial undertakings had been started by Americans. The Seoul-Chemulpo railway, the first line to be built in the peninsula, was an American undertaking which, because of financial troubles, had been turned over to joint American and Japanese control. The street railways and electric lights of Seoul and the gold mines were entirely under American management until about 1900, when British, French, and German mining companies entered the field in a small way. In all these American mining and electrical enterprises the Emperor of Korea was directly interested as partner, owner, shareholder, or lessor.[1] Some American money had been loaned to the Emperor and some to the Government. The competition between American and Japanese capitalists from 1899 to 1904 was very keen, but in the main the feeling was friendly. To the Americans the Emperor extended a very great degree of confidence. Generally speaking, it would appear that American commercial interests had a bright future. It was plainly not likely to be beneficial to this interest for Russia to extend its bureaucratic influence over the peninsula.

---

[1] "Commercial Korea in 1904," *Monthly Sum. of Com. and Finance*, January, 1904, pp. 2449-82.

The American missionary opinion was more or less divided on the political question. No one favoured the extension of Russian control. Some inclined to feel that even non-Christian Japan might extend its political influence in Korea with benefit to the miserably mis-governed inhabitants. Most of the missionaries, however, were uncompromising champions of Korean *de facto* as well as *de jure* independence.

The first article of the American treaty with Korea contained the following stipulation:

If other Powers deal unjustly or oppressively with either government, the other will exert their good offices, on being informed of the case, to bring about an amicable arrangement, thus showing their friendly feelings.

This article had been drafted by Li Hung-chang at Tientsin in 1882 and in all the subsequent changes in the phrasing of the treaty the article had been retained. It was copied substantially from the second American treaty with China (1858). Li Hung-chang appears to have thought by the insertion of this article to have bound the United States to help China retain the suzerainty of the peninsula.[1] Later the King of Korea seized upon the article as creating an alliance between the United States and Korea and for more than fifteen years refused to learn that there was a very broad distinction between the exercise of good offices and the bond of an alliance.[2] The exercise of American good offices was interpreted uniformly in

[1] Dennett, "American 'Good Offices' in Asia," *Am. Jour. of Inter. Law*, Vol. XVI, Jan., 1922, p. 4.

[2] The writer has examined the history of this interpretation in detail. See "Early American Policy in Korea, 1883-87," *Pol. Sci. Quart.*, March, 1923, pp. 82-103. Also "Am. in East. Asia," pp. 504-06, Chap. XXVI.

China as well as in Korea to mean that upon appeal from the injured party the American Government would approach the offending government and express a desire to bring the two governments into agreement. In case the offer of these good offices was refused, as it almost uniformly was, the American Government held that it could go no further. In short, the exercise of good offices did not require intervention.[1]

There is no case on record where the American Government did not extend its good offices when officially requested by Korea. During his checkered and uncertain career the King or Emperor of Korea frequently applied to the American Government not merely for good offices but also for protection, though never with the idea that the protection of the American Government would in any way be paid for by any surrender of his royal prerogatives which were without limit and were the fountain head of Korea's sorrow. In every instance these invitations to intervene were declined, and several years before 1904 the King had come to realize that the American Government would in no case extend a protectorate over his unhappy land. The old notion about the alliance, resting upon a misinterpretation of the good-offices clause, was reviewed at the close of the war in 1905, and the misapprehension still widely exists that the United States in declining to intervene in Korea was violating the spirit if not the letter of a treaty.[2] The question is wholly apart from Roosevelt's policy, for the decision of the American Government in 1905 not to intervene was merely in

[1]Wharton's "Digest," 2d ed. (1887), Vol. I, p. 442.
[2]Homer B. Hulbert, "The Passing of Korea" (N.Y., Chicago, etc., 1906), Chap. V; Arthur J. Brown, "The Mastery of the Far East" (N.Y., 1919), p. 199; F. A. McKenzie, "Korea's Fight for Freedom" (N.Y., Chicago, etc., 1920), p. 22; and many other books on Korea.

line with the precedents of more than forty years. There is, however, no ground whatever for impugning the good faith of the United States.

ROOSEVELT AND KOREA

In defining the relations of the United States and Korea one must not overlook the acquisition of the Philippines in 1898. For more than thirty years before the Spanish-American War there had been among some Americans, especially naval authorities, a feeling that the United States ought to possess at least a naval base in the Far East. At times Korean ports had been discussed in that connection, but the acquisition of the Philippines definitely transferred all American political interests from the Asiatic mainland. This was especially marked during Roosevelt's administration because all the questions of Philippine government and defence were subjects of earnest debate, feverish activity, and much controversy. There never had been a time when the American Government had possessed so little interest in Korea as in 1904-05.

Another aspect of the situation, usually lost sight of, demands notice. Those were the days of the anti-imperialists at home, and those were also the days when, as appears from Roosevelt's letter already quoted,[1] Japan was particularly sensitive about American advances in the Pacific. Some Japanese had wanted not only the Philippines but even Hawaii. Having blocked Japanese expansion in the Pacific, seeking the exclusion of the Japanese from the Pacific coast, was the United States also to oppose Japanese expansion in Asia? In fact, there

[1]See p. 48.

had been for some years a feeling in diplomatic circles, recognized alike by Great Britain, the United States, and Japan, that there must be diplomatic give-and-take, that if the United States might stride across an ocean and seize an archipelago, just as Great Britain, the Netherlands, and France had already done, Japan had at least equal rights to similar liberties.[1]

Very early in the war Japan was compelled to throw off its mask in Korea. On February 26, 1904, Minister Takahira called at the Department of State and left a telegram giving the text of a protocol which had been concluded at Seoul between the Japanese and the Korean governments the day before. The agreement, which was never protested by the Korean Government, established a practical Japanese protectorate, and was reminiscent of the reforms which Japan had sought to establish in 1894–95.[2] Korea engaged to adopt the advice of Japan in regard to administrative matters, and in return Japan agreed to "insure the safety and repose of the Imperial House," and further to "guarantee the independence and territorial integrity of the Korean Empire." It was stipulated that the "governments of the two countries shall not in the future, without mutual consent, conclude with a third Power such an arrangement as may be contrary to the principles of the present protocol." It was a document worthy of Russia at her worst in Manchuria, but Korea accepted and acquiesced.

The following August the Japanese Government concluded a supplementary agreement by which Korea engaged to accept a Japanese financial adviser and

---

[1] "Am. in East. Asia," pp. 613–14.

[2] "For. Rel." (1904), pp. 437 ff. Compare "For. Rel." (1894), App. I, pp. 35–36.

yielded to Japan the right to direct her foreign relations.[1] Again Korea acquiesced. Korea ceased to be an independent state.

President Roosevelt reached an early conclusion with reference to Korea and then gave the subject little further thought. The Koreans, in their recent history, and in most of the diplomatic representatives in Washington during the period since the President had been a resident of the city, could not have commended themselves to his respect or admiration. One day at the end of January, 1905, in a brief note to Secretary Hay entirely about another matter, he added a postscript in his own handwriting into which we are probably justified in reading his entire personal feelings in the matter. He wrote:

We cannot possibly interfere for the Koreans against Japan. They could not strike one blow in their own defence.[2]

President Roosevelt never opened the subject again in his letters. On February 9th, Baron Kaneko submitted to him a *précis*, which he stated had been drawn up by "several gentlemen" of the Yale faculty "who are thoroughly conversant with conditions in the East." The first paragraph of this summary stated:

Japan has fairly earned the right to paramount influence in Korea, by reason of her sacrifices, to prevent the Russianization of Korea.[3]

This statement reflected the rather hazy notions then prevailing as to what was actually happening in the peninsula, but it would appear to have represented current

---

[1] "For. Rel." (1904), pp. 438–39, August, 1922.

[2] Roosevelt to Hay, January 28, 1905.

[3] Kaneko to Roosevelt, Feb. 9, 1905.

American opinion. There is no way of knowing whether Roosevelt was better informed as to which was the aggressive nation in Seoul, but in any event it appears to have been evident to the President that Korea, long a derelict state, a menace to navigation, must now be towed into port and secured.

In the letter of explanation which followed the announcement of the renewal of the Anglo-Japanese Alliance in August, 1905, Lord Lansdowne wrote:

The new treaty no doubt differs at this point conspicuously from that of 1902. It has, however, become evident that Corea, owing to its close proximity to the Japanese Empire and its inability to stand alone, must fall under the control and tutelage of Japan. . . . England has every reason to believe that similar views are held by other Powers with regard to the relations which should subsist between Japan and Corea.[1]

This was unquestionably the opinion of Roosevelt, and he had reached it at least six months earlier. Indeed, the history of the preceding twenty-three years would admit of no other conclusion. Korea might possibly have been saved in 1882 by an international protectorate, although the experiences in Samoa do not warrant great confidence, but in 1905 Korea could not be saved. Korea in her day had many false friends, but none of them so false as her monarch and his corrupt court.

The Lansdowne note of 1905 intimated that there had been a general agreement among the Powers as to the future of Korea. To one who has followed carefully the course of American policy for the preceding twenty years and has traced, step by step, the events from the be-

---

[1]Dennis, "The Anglo-Japanese Alliance," p. 24.

ginning of the war, it will come as no surprise that President Roosevelt had been among those whose views on Korea were a matter of record. On July 29, 1905, Count Katsura, Japanese Premier and Minister for Foreign Affairs, had what is known in diplomatic parlance as a "conversation" with a personal representative of President Roosevelt, not a member of the Department of State. An agreed memorandum of this conversation was drawn up and is to be found among the Roosevelt Papers of that date. The views expressed on behalf of President Roosevelt were confirmed in a telegram of July 31, 1905. The memorandum is of peculiar interest because (1) it was a full statement of a policy to which President Roosevelt had freely committed himself at least six months earlier; (2) it shows how the acquisition of the Philippines had brought the American Government into the realm of world politics; and (3) it records a very definite and official commitment of the Japanese Government as to its policy toward the Philippines. The memorandum reads as follows:[1]

. . . First, in speaking of some pro-Russians in America who would have the public believe that the victory of Japan would be a certain prelude to her aggression in the direction of the Philippine Islands, —— [the American] observed that Japan's only interest in the Philippines would be, in his opinion, to have these islands governed by a strong and friendly nation like the United States, and not to have them placed either under the misrule of the natives, yet unfit for self-government, or in

---

[1]Some allowance for the not very smooth phrasing of this memorandum might be made because of the telegraphic character of this report, but it would appear that it was drawn up by someone not wholly familiar with English idiom, presumably Count Katsura.

the hands of some unfriendly European Power. Count Katsura confirmed in the strongest terms the correctness of his views on the point and positively stated that Japan does not harbour any aggressive designs whatever on the Philippines; adding that all the insinuations of the yellow peril type are nothing more or less than malicious and clumsy slanders calculated to do mischief to Japan.

Second, Count Katsura observed that the maintenance of general peace in the extreme East forms the fundamental principle of Japan's international policy. Such being the case, he was very anxious to exchange views with —— [the American] as to the most effective means for insuring this principle. In his own opinion the best, in fact the only, means for accomplishing the above object would be to form good understanding between the three governments of Japan, the United States, and Great Britain which have common interests in upholding the principle of eminence [sic]. The Count well understands the traditional policy of the United States in this respect and perceives fully the impossibility of their entering into a formal alliance of such nature with foreign nations, but in view of our common interests he could [not] see why some good understanding or an alliance in practice if not in name, should not be made between these three nations, in so far as respects the affairs in the Far East. With such understanding firmly formed, general peace in these regions would be easily maintained to the great benefit of all Powers concerned.

—— [The American] said that it was difficult, indeed impossible, for the President of the United States of America to enter even to any understanding amounting in effect to a confidential informal agreement, without the consent of the Senate, but that he felt sure that without any agreement at all the people of the United States was [sic] so fully in accord with the people of Japan and Great Britain in the maintenance of peace in the Far East that whatever occasion arose appropriate action of the Government of the United States, in conjunction with Japan and

Great Britain, for such a purpose could be counted on by them quite as confidently as if the United States were under treaty obligations to take [it].

Third, in regard to the Korean question, Count Katsura observed that Korea being the direct cause of our war with Russia, it is a matter of absolute importance to Japan that a complete solution of the peninsula question should be made as the logical consequence of the war. If left to herself after the war Korea will certainly draw back to her habit of entering into any agreements or treaties with other Powers, thus resuscitating the same international complications as existed before the war. In view of the foregoing circumstances Japan feels absolutely constrained to take some definite step with a view to precluding the possibility of Korea falling back into her former condition and of placing us again under the necessity of entering upon another foreign war.

—— [The American] fully admitted the justness of the Count's observations and remarked to the effect that, in his personal opinion, the establishment by Japanese troops of a suzerainty over Korea to the extent of requiring that Korea enter into no foreign treaties without the consent of Japan was the logical result of the present war and would directly contribute to permanent peace in the East. His judgment was that the President would concur in his views in this regard, although he had no authority to give assurance of this; indeed, —— [the American] added that he felt much delicacy in advancing the views he did for he had no mandate for the purpose from the President. . . . He could not, however, in view of Count Katsura's courteous desire to discuss the question, decline to express his opinions. . . . [1]

Such a diplomatic *coup* was too much for the Japanese Government to keep entirely secret. On October 4, 1905,

---

[1] For a reproduction of a photostat of this document, see article by the writer in *Current History*, October, 1924.

the *Kokumin* published an allusion to the conversation which reveals how much they had misunderstood its purpose and character:

In fact, it is a Japanese Anglo-American alliance. We may be sure that when once England became our ally America also became a party to the agreement. Owing to peculiar national conditions America cannot make any open alliance, but we should bear in mind that America is our ally though bound by no formal treaty: we firmly believe that America, under the leadership of the world statesman, President Roosevelt, will deal with her Oriental problems in coöperation with Japan and Great Britain.

In judging this remarkable document it is of the utmost importance to keep in mind that it was not a sacrifice of Korea for the sake of the Philippines. On the contrary, in return for a statement of American policy toward Korea which had been fixed for more than six months, and which was consistent with the policy of more than twenty years, the American Government had secured from Japan a most official and explicit disclaimer of any aggressive designs on the Philippines.

As for the proposal to enter an alliance with England and Japan, President Roosevelt professed to be personally convinced of the desirability of such a measure. The proposal, which was not new to him, seemed, nevertheless, preposterous. To George Kennan, who had suggested it more than three months before, he had written:[1]

As to what you say about the alliance, the trouble is, my dear Mr. Kennan, that you are talking academically. Have you followed some of my experiences in endeavouring to get treaties

---

[1] Roosevelt to Kennan, May 6, 1905.

through the Senate? I might just as well strive for the moon as for such a policy as you indicate. Mind you, I personally entirely agree with you. But if you have followed the difficulty I have had even in getting such obvious things done as those connected with Panama and Santo Domingo you would get some faint idea of the absolute impossibility of carrying out any such policy as you indicate in your letter.

CONTEMPORARY COMMENT

Homer B. Hulbert, *Korean Review*, Seoul, 1904, 1905.

The editorial comment travels the gamut from credulity toward Japan to reproach and indignation at Japanese brutality and bad faith. "We believe that Japan fully intends to preserve the independence of the country but at the present crisis it is manifestly impossible to let the Koreans do as they please; nor would it be for their own best interests."—March, 1904. "We are waiting to see what Japan is going to do to establish the independence and autonomy of Korea in any such sense as America established that of Cuba. The die is cast and the future must be faced. Those who care for the Korean people must adjust themselves and work as best they may for the intellectual and moral uplifting of this Poland of the Far East."—September, 1905.

James S. Gale, "Korea in War Time," *Outlook*, June 25, 1904.

"Every day now the Government is busy with sorcerers, fortune tellers, medicine-men, wise women of the East, and others, trying to find out what it had better do about it."

K. Shigeoka, "What Japan Should Do For Korea." Translated in *Review of Reviews* (N. Y.), September, 1904, from the *Seiyo*.

"Japan placed herself in an extremely delicate position when she declared to the world that she stands for the independence and integrity of Korea. She was obliged to make such an illogical declaration in order to justify her cause in the eyes of the Powers."

Kogoro Takahira, "What Japan Is Fighting For," *World's Work*, April, 1904.
"We have no desire to interfere with the independence or territorial integrity of our neighbors."

Walter C. Hillier, "Korea: Its History and Prospects," *Fortnightly Review*, June, 1904.
"Korean independence is promised to the world but it stands to reason that it will be an independence strictly under the control of Japan, who has Egypt before her as a model."

Alfred Stead, "The Far Eastern Problem," *Fortnightly Review*, January, 1904.
". . . it would appear almost as sensible to the Japanese to negotiate with Russia for a right to the control over Korea as it would seem to the British Government to carry on long and serious diplomatic pourparlers with France as to the British right to control Ireland."

Count Okuma, "Japan's Policy in Korea." *Forum*, April–June, 1906.
"It is not a question of ambition, but a matter of necessity that Japan should become a great Power on the Asiatic Continent. Should she fail in that, there is but one thing left for her—national death. . . . It is forced upon us as a means of defense."

Edwin Winthrop Dayton, "What Russia Fights For," *World's Work*, April, 1904.
"There has never been a single act of aggression on the part of Russia against any scrap of territory to which Japan could make any claim whatever."

CHAPTER VI

Russia in Manchuria

WHATEVER may have been the confusion of issues in Europe and the misstatement of conditions in Korea, the conflict in Manchuria was perfectly simple: Russia had set out to become a Pacific Power, not in a modest way as when she held Alaska, but by the appropriation of as much of the Chinese Empire southward toward the Yangtze as she could get. This would have involved the extension of the blight of Russian autocracy over a large part of China and the closing, presumably, of the door of equal commercial opportunity at a point where American commercial prospects were bright. The complete partition of China probably would have followed. To such a project the American Government must inevitably be opposed. In this respect American interests were identical with those of Great Britain and Japan. By force of circumstances, therefore, the United States became for the moment as much a part of the Anglo-Japanese Alliance as though its signature had been attached.

Not only the fact of Russian aggression but also the methods by which it was being carried forward served to consolidate the Anglo-American and Japanese understanding. Russia had already been several times defeated even before the first shot was fired at Port Arthur. Her record would not stand a moment's examination. She was defeated in public opinion, and she was defeated in having lost the confidence of President Roosevelt. Even her domestic policy was such as to invite the indignation and contempt of all liberty-loving people.

Early in January, 1904, Mr. George Kennan forwarded to Roosevelt a digest of the important testimony in the trial of those alleged to be responsible for the Kishineff massacre. He wrote:[1]

> If he [Von Plehve] didn't plan—or at least encourage—that Kishineff massacre, for some dark purpose of his own, the circumstances of the case would seem to have been almost miraculously arranged to give that impression. . . . I only want you to know some of the facts which have convinced me that the present Russian Government is a government of cruelty, duplicity, and mediæval barbarity. We may have important dealings with Russia in the near future, and facts that throw light on the character and methods of "Adam-Zad" who "only walks like a man" may be useful.[2]

The Russian Government had entirely lost the confidence of President Roosevelt.

> No human beings, black, yellow, or white could be quite as untruthful, as insincere, as arrogant—in short, as untrustworthy in every way—as the Russians under the present system.[3]

This conclusion of Roosevelt's, which was repeated a great many times in different phrasing in his correspondence of the previous eight months, gives point to the review of

---

[1] Kennan to Roosevelt, January 8, 1904.

[2] In this connection it is amusing as well as instructive to note that Lamsdorff was reported to have told someone shortly before the American election of November 4, 1904, that Roosevelt's real name was Rosenfeld and that he was a Jew from south Germany. It was this incredible Russian ignorance of affairs outside the small circle of European politics which as much as anything contributed to Russia's disaster in the East. Spring-Rice to Roosevelt, undated, but about November 5, 1904.

[3] Roosevelt to W. W. Rockhill, August 29, 1905.

Russian activities in China and Manchuria. If the Russian Government had dealt honourably with the other Western Powers in the Far East, if its record had been as good as that of Japan, we believe that Roosevelt might have adopted a wholly different policy with reference to the war. As it was, the Russian record was so bad as to leave no choice whatever. Roosevelt did not incline toward the Japanese side because he was infatuated with Japan. On the contrary, as we shall see, his advocacy of Japan was uniformly qualified by his fears of how Japan might use its new power to the detriment of the world, but these fears weighed very little over against the plain fact that the Russian Government, which consisted of nothing more than a "preposterous little Czar" and his favourites, was an appalling menace.

The Russian record in China and Manchuria, even if one does not go back of 1895, supplies ample proof for the conclusion to which Roosevelt came. It was one long unrelieved chronicle of lying, brutality, and bribery rendered especially easy because Chinese officialdom likewise lived on bribery and protected itself by lying.

Arguing from the high ethical plane of the duty of protecting a weak and friendly state, Russia, in 1895, in company with Germany and France, had compelled Japan to return the so-called Liaotung peninsula to China. For the moment Russia represented the integrity of China as an important consideration, and later Lamsdorff even had the effrontery to claim that Russia was the originator of the policy to protect the integrity of China. The following year Russia made with China a secret treaty of defensive alliance in which Russia pledged to come to the aid of China in case she were attacked.

Two months later Count Witte negotiated through the Russo-Chinese Bank, and with the short-sighted support of France, whose bankers were interested, a railway contract by which China granted for the Trans-Siberian Railway a right-of-way across northern Manchuria. This would materially shorten the route of the famous railway line, not yet completed, to Vladivostok.

The railway agreement (Article VI) contained a most important concession which has been the subject of endless dispute in more recent years. The contract stated that *"la Société aura le droit absolu et exclusif de l'administration des ses terrains,"* that is of the *"terrains réelement nécessaires pour la construction, exploitation et protection de la ligne, ainsi que les terrains aux environs de la ligne, nécessaires pour se procurer des sables, pierres, chaux,"* etc. It was the contention of the Russian Government and subsequently of Japan which took over the Russian railway rights in southern Manchuria by the Treaty of Portsmouth, that the rights of administration thus conferred involved the political rights of municipal control. This interpretation would make the railway agreement practically equivalent to a cession of sovereign territorial rights. Following this interpretation Japan has now gone so far as to levy income taxes in Manchuria within the area of the railway concession in southern Manchuria. It has been the contention of the United States, on the other hand, that the railway contract conferred only the rights of business administration, and that the context clearly reserves to China all political jurisdiction over these lands.[1]

---

[1] "For. Rel." (1910), pp. 202 ff. Secretary Root's discussion of the subject April 9, 1908, p. 204; see also the *Note verbale* to the Russian Ambassador, November 9, 1909, pp. 218–20. It was the claim of Russia and Japan to sovereign rights over the areas of the railway concessions which immediately preceded the Knox neutralization plan of 1909.

ROOSEVELT AND THE RUSSO–JAPANESE WAR

In 1898 Russia still further forgot her concern for China and demanded the lease of Port Arthur and Talien-wan which only two or three years earlier the Coalition had required Japan to return to China. With the lease went the extension of railway rights similar to those already granted in northern Manchuria. Russia acquired the right to connect Port Arthur with the trans-Siberian and also to connect it with the Chinese railway. which ran northward from Tientsin to the Great Wall. Indeed, Russia stipulated that all the railways in Manchuria should be under Russian control. Mining rights and banking privileges were also provided for. This lease was secured by a Russian naval demonstration at Port Arthur, and by what the Chinese sometimes euphemistically call "presents" to Li Hung-chang and Chang Ing-huan to the extent of 500,000 and 250,000 rubles, respectively.[1]

Russian rights in the Far East, as they were understood at any time between 1896 and 1905, may be described as like three concentric circles: rights legally ratified and

[1]In these two paragraphs we have condensed with the omission of many details the terms of the following treaties and agreements: Lobanoff-Li Hung-chang, May, 1896; Russo-Chinese Bank agreement relative to railways and mines, September 8, 1896; Statutes of the Chinese Eastern Railway, promulgated by the Tsar, December 4, 1896; lease of Port Arthur and Talienwan, and railway agreement, March 27, 1898; agreement between Russia and China respecting boundaries, May 7, 1898. All these documents are collected in J. V. A. MacMurray's "Treaties and Agreements With and Concerning China" (2 Vols., N. Y., 1921), Vol. I, arranged by date. MacMurray also printed the documents necessary to dispose of the so-called Cassini Convention of 1896. The literature on this subject is immense. Most important is Count Witte's own statement in his "Memoirs," Chap. IV, "Dealings with Li Hungchang." E. J. Dillon, "The Eclipse of Russia," supplies additional facts, including telegrams containing Li Hung-chang's reports to Peking from Russia in 1896, pp. 260 ff. The most concise and lucid account of Russia's advance is in J. H. Gubbins, "The Making of Modern Japan" (N.Y., 1922), Chap. XXIII. H. B. Morse, "International Relations of the Chinese Empire" (N.Y., 1918), Vol. III, Chaps. II and V, supplies an excellent bibliography with special reference to British blue-books, contemporary journals, and also contains some interesting and otherwise unpublished correspondence of Sir Robert Hart. For a concise and suggestive treatment of the whole question see S. A. Korff, "Russia's Foreign Relations," and by the same author, "Russia in the Far East," in *Am. Journ. of Inter. Law*, Vol. XVII, April, 1923.

published; rights suspected to exist but not published; and prospective rights not yet acquired but known to be desired from demands already put forward in Peking and allowed to leak out into news channels. Altogether, Russia was fairly chargeable before 1904 with the intent to seize eventually all of eastern Asia as far south at least as the Yangtze. It was a mad project.

For the accomplishment of such vast designs the Boxer uprising was most opportune. "This will give us an excuse for seizing Manchuria," exclaimed General Kuropatkin, according to Count Witte.[1] "We will turn Manchuria into a second Bokhara."[2]

This design was immediately suspected. Russia came forward soon after the relief of the legations in Peking with the proposition that all of the Powers should immediately withdraw their troops. It was recalled that in 1860 Russia had asked for and received from China the gift of the maritime province between the Amur and the sea in return for Russia's supposed, but in fact entirely fictitious, good offices in securing the withdrawal of the British and French forces from Peking. It was suspected in the summer of 1900 that Russia had made a similar deal with Li Hung-chang, whose previous surrender to Russian rubles was already credited.[3] A withdrawal of the foreign troops very likely would have been followed by Chinese

---

[1]"Memoirs," pp. 107-08.

[2]Bokhara was a Russian protectorate with a resident Russian political agent whose function was broadly similar to that of a British Resident in a native state of India. Similarly, three years later, when Iswolsky, Russian representative in Tokio, recommended that Japan be allowed a free hand in Korea in return for Russian liberty in Manchuria, the Tsar had replied that Korea also must become to Russia what Bokhara already was (Dillon, pp. 284-85). Kuropatkin subsequently became alarmed at the prospect of war in the Far East and in 1903 joined Witte and others in opposition to Russia's belligerent policy. Kuropatkin, "The Russian Army and the Japanese War," Vol. I, Chap. VI, particularly p. 164.

[3]Sir Robert Hart to E. B. Drew, September 28, 1900. Printed in Morse, III, p. 306, footnote.

consent to a Russian protectorate over Manchuria and perhaps by even greater concessions.

During the relief of the legations and the settlement of the Boxer protocol it was the policy of Secretary Hay, supported by England and Japan, to keep all the Powers united and to prevent any separate negotiations with China. It was the Russian policy to act in coöperation with the other Powers as little as possible, to oppose a common settlement, and in any case to keep the Russian claims for damages in Manchuria segregated from the claims of the other Powers and not under the review of the foreign representatives in Peking.[1] Russia was so far successful as to keep any statement relative to the evacuation of Manchuria out of the protocol of 1901, but in other respects she failed. While the protocol was still under consideration Admiral Alexeieff entered into a secret agreement with the Tartar General at Mukden which was happily exposed by Dr. George Morrison, the famous Peking correspondent of the London *Times* early in January, 1901.[2] This agreement, had it been ratified, would have confirmed the Russian protectorate over Manchuria, placed the Chinese military forces under actual Russian control, and excluded all other foreigners from all of Manchuria except Newchwang. It would have granted the most sweeping and exclusive railway, mining,

[1] See American circular telegram, August 29, 1900, "For. Rel." (1901), App., p. 19, and many other communications in this document which is the Rockhill report on the Boxer protocol. Morse, III, pp. 241, 251, and Chap. X, p. 271. Witte's "Memoirs," pp. 111–13.

[2] "China No.2" (1904), cd. 1936. This blue book is a collection of correspondence relating to the Russian occupation of Manchuria and the steps leading up to the outbreak of hostilities between Russia and Japan. The various attempted secret agreements of Russia and China are given in great detail. This blue book, however, must be supplemented by earlier ones such as "China No. 1" (1898), c8814, and "China No. 1" (1899), c9131, and more especially by "For. Rel." (1901, 1902, 1903), to have a complete description of Russia's astonishing diplomacy with reference to her Manchurian policy.

and commercial rights, and would have bound China herself to relinquish all right to build railways in Mongolia and Chinese Turkestan. Indeed, all north China, including the province of Chihli and Peking itself, would have come under the domination of Russia. The dramatic exposure of this plot delayed its execution and caused a progressive modification of the Russian demands. Eventually it failed. The circumstances and causes of the failure may be noted after we review the experience of the American Government with Russia at Newchwang.

THE AMERICANS IN MANCHURIA

When U. S. Minister William B. Reed negotiated with China the treaty of 1858, at the time of the similar British, French, and Russian treaties, he was particularly pleased that Newchwang was included among the newly opened ports. He expected that the Americans more than any others, because of their dominance in the coastwise shipping, would profit by this new avenue of trade leading directly into one of the most fertile and prosperous sections of the Chinese Empire.[1] His hopes were at first realized, but the retirement of Americans from the maritime commerce of China, and indeed their relative retirement from the China trade itself, left Newchwang quite outside the range of direct American interest before 1885. For many years American interests were slight. Following the recovery from the panic of 1893, the trade with China had shown new vitality. This was particularly noticeable in North China, and in 1901 Newchwang stood third among the Chinese ports in the value of American imports.

---

[1] "Am. in East. Asia," pp. 320-21; S. Ex. Doc. No. 30, 36th Cong. 1st Sess. Reed to Cass, No. 29, July 29, 1858.

Exports amounted to almost nothing, but kerosene, cotton goods, and flour brought up the value of American imports to between seven and eight million haikwan taels,[1] the exact amount being difficult to determine because American cottons were usually shipped either from Japan or by British firms from Hongkong and Shanghai. Compare with this the British imports amounted to only 5,000,000 and the Japanese to about 2,160,000 taels.[2] While the Japanese exports from Manchuria were so large as to make the total Japanese and total American trade about equal, the rapid rise of the American imports justified the hope that at last American trade in China might return to the former relative position from which it had fallen after the American Civil War. Thus the Russian advance, with the threatened sealing in Manchuria of all prospective American markets except Newchwang, cut directly across a growing American commercial interest. Nowhere else in the world at that moment were American commercial interests so directly threatened.

In May, 1901, U. S. Consul Henry B. Miller was ordered by cable to proceed to Newchwang and reopen the consulate which had for years been in charge of a merchant

---

[1] Value of haikwan tael at that time about $.72 gold.

[2] The most illuminating way to follow American trade conditions in Manchuria in this period is through the Advance Sheets of Consular Reports published by the Bureau of Commerce from information supplied in the letters of consuls to the Department of State. These Advance Sheets have the advantage for the student that they are dated and reflect, in some degree, the business interests of the country which they were designed to serve. It will be observed in these pamphlets that the opportunities of the Manchurian market were being advertised frequently. Indeed, this fact in itself suggests that possibly the Department of State was even seeking to promote American trade relations with Manchuria as an offset to Russian designs. Note particularly Advance Sheets of Consular Reports, October 3, 1901, No. 1152; October 8, 1901, No. 1156; October 15, 1901, No. 1162; March 4, 1902, No. 1280; April 25, 1902, No. 1325; May 7, 1902, No. 1337; May 28, 1902, No. 1353. See also the *Oregonian* (Portland, Ore.) current files in which much of the current interest in Manchuria of the northern Pacific Coast was reflected.

vice-consul.[1] Miller found the Russian military and civil authorities in full control of the city. On August 6, 1900, Admiral Alexeieff had notified the consuls that the city had been occupied only temporarily. It was the opinion of all the consuls when Miller arrived more than a year later that there was no good reason why the port should not be handed back to the Chinese authorities. The Chinese Maritime Customs, nevertheless, were still under the "supervision" of the Russians, the funds were being deposited in the Russo-Chinese rather than in the Customs Bank, and the Russians were also collecting or receiving the native customs and even levying direct taxes. Miller was shocked to find that he must secure Russian permission even for the Americans to celebrate the Fourth of July. A few days later the Russian civil administrator took over the judicial functions of government, thus at one stroke practically abolishing the extraterritorial rights of the foreigners.

The winter of 1901–02 proved very difficult for everyone at Newchwang. The U. S. gunboat *Vicksburg* (Capt. E. C. Barry) and H. M. S. *Algerine* were stationed there, pulled up on the mud above the ice as a protection for foreign interests. The introduction of American and British sailors with too little to do and scant opportunities for amusement into a town where the Russian authorities were unwilling to recognize the jurisdiction of the consuls presented many embarrassments. Before the winter was half over the Russian Civil Administrator, after

---

[1] Miller, according to regulations, corresponded directly with the U. S. Minister at Peking on all political matters. Many of these reports cited below were published in "For. Rel." (1902, 1903), where they are included as enclosures of despatches from Minister Conger. The fact that so many of these letters were published in "For. Rel." is a still further indication of the disposition of the Department of State to present an extraordinarily full record of Russian pretensions in Manchuria.

reviewing a series of disorders, addressed Consul Miller as follows:

In conclusion I can assure you that the perfect order which existed here before the arrival of the American man-of-war will be maintained by me with energy and I will be very much obliged to you and the honourable officers of the U. S. S. *Vicksburg* for the smallest symptom of your mutual desire to put an end to the delinquencies of the sailors when they come on shore.

Indeed, the troubles at Newchwang had already been made the subject of diplomatic exchanges not merely between the American and Russian representatives at Peking but even between Washington and St. Petersburg. It was complained that the Americans were persistently obstructing the Russian Government. The facts were quite otherwise than as the Russians alleged.

The correct procedure at Newchwang, provided that extraterritorial rights existed, and the United States certainly had not consented to their abrogation, was that in case of complaint against any American, even a sailor from the *Vicksburg*, the Russian or Chinese authorities would supply the American consul with the information relating to the action, whereupon the consul would delegate his marshal to arrest the party and bring him to the American consular court where he would be tried by the consul according to American law and procedure. At Newchwang the Russian authorities had arrested American sailors, subjected them to brutal treatment, had arrested even an officer of the *Vicksburg* while in performance of his duty, had forcibly entered the sailors' club, and in other respects were interfering with American rights, but in no instance had the authority or jurisdiction of Consul Miller been recognized. It was the opinion of Miller that the Russian administration was seeking to make life in Newchwang intolerable for Americans. The Russian representative at Peking informed Minister Conger that the Russians regarded "the coming of the *Algerine* and the *Vicksburg* as a sort of combined naval demonstration against the Russians."[1] Later came complaints from American business houses and commercial bodies in America and Shanghai that Russia was permitting merchandise to enter Manchuria through Dalny, the new Russian commercial port at Talienwan, without the payment of any duties whatsoever. Such discrimination against Newchwang had the effect of diverting the foreign trade from Newchwang to Dalny. Early in this first winter the telegraph service between Peking and Newchwang was suspended, so that the little foreign colony in Manchuria was almost wholly isolated from the world, a condition favourable for the exercise of still further Russian pretensions.

In the spring of 1902 Consul Miller made a tour as far as Harbin. He reported that, regardless of the promises of their government, the Russians had little expectation of leaving the country or of settling merely in open ports. They would rely, he thought, upon the military protection of the Russian railway guards, whose jurisdiction along the railways was claimed by Russia even in case of evacuation. He also reported that "judging from the talk of Russian officials there is a gradual tendency on the part of Russia toward war with Japan, and they freely express their

---

[1] "For. Rel." (1902), pp. 145-59.

desire to fight Japan in Manchuria." Almost immediately after the publication of the Anglo-Japanese Alliance (February 11–12, 1902) Miller reported a new and conciliatory policy on the part of the Russians, and by summer better relations had been established. Nevertheless, a year later, March 5, 1903, Miller stated that in his judgment the Russian commerce was so thoroughly spread over all Manchuria, and so well protected by the railways and the railway guards, that any military evacuation would confer only illusory equality in commercial privileges. He believed that the only remedy would be to demand the complete opening of Manchuria to foreign trade. This was, in fact, the only solution, and thus we pass to another phase of the subject, namely the negotiations of the United States, Great Britain, and Japan, through the regular diplomatic channels to secure from Russia an execution of her often-repeated pledges to evacuate.

RUSSIAN BAD FAITH

The disclosure of the secret agreement between Admiral Alexeieff and the Tartar general at Mukden aroused the suspicions of the United States as well as of the other interested Powers. On February 1, 1902, Secretary Hay addressed to China, Russia, and the other Powers a strong telegram of protest against the contemplated agreement. He charged that the terms would restrict American rightful trade, tend to impair the sovereignty of China and also diminish her ability to meet her international obligations. Other Powers would doubtless seek compensating advantages, and the result would be to wreck the Open Door policy which Mr. Hay was now defining rather more broadly than in 1899. He submitted these protests to Russia with "confidence that due weight will be given to them and such measures be adopted as will relieve the just and natural anxiety of the United States." It was a sharp protest, but it probably would not have had any effect if the terms of the newly formed Anglo-Japanese alliance had not been published ten days later. Immediately upon receipt of this news Pring Ch'ing refused to sign the already much modified Russian agreement. On April 8, 1902, Russia consented to evacuate Manchuria within eighteen months. The evacuation agreement was prefaced by a clear recognition of Chinese sovereignty.[1] So close had been the dates of the American telegram and the publication of the alliance that Secretary Hay felt called upon to explain to Russia that there was merely a coincidence and that he had not known of the Anglo-Japanese negotiation. The effect had been, nevertheless, much the same as though there had been a triple alliance.[2]

Promises meant nothing to Russia even though they sometimes embarrassed Witte and even Lamsdorff. The Tsar had been nurtured in the comfortable belief that he was responsible to none but the Almighty whose vicegerent he was. The first section of the evacuation was accomplished according to schedule, but in the course of the year the faction at St. Petersburg which later appeared as the concessionaires in the Yalu timber company secured the ear of the Tsar and persuaded him that Russia might still retain Manchuria without incurring hostilities.

---

[1]For the American negotiations, "For. Rel." (1902), pp. 275-83; for the British, "China No. 2," (1904), cd. 1936.

[2]"For. Rel." (1902), pp. 929-30.

Commercial conditions were not greatly altered by the first step in Russian evacuation. The customs at New-chwang continued to be under Russian supervision, and the civil administration continued to exercise jurisdiction over the courts and to collect taxes. Even customs stations not under the Chinese Maritime Customs were established. Mr. Hay weakly instructed Mr. Conger that "the only point with which we can be concerned is that the duties levied at these places do not exceed the regular tariff duties levied at all other points in the Chinese Empire open to foreign trade."[1]

Matters, however, soon came again to an issue over two related points. Notwithstanding the recommendation of Consul Miller, and the prevailing opinion among foreigners in Peking, that only the complete opening of Manchuria would thwart the Russian designs to retain exclusive privileges, the American Government had decided to demand only the opening of three ports—Tatong, Mukden, and Harbin. China proved strangely reluctant to open these cities, and in time it leaked out that instead of carrying out the second stage of the evacuation which was due March 8, 1903, Russia had presented to China a new set of demands, among which was the requirement that no port other than Newchwang should ever be opened to foreign trade. Other conditions were: no foreigners but Russians to be employed; Newchwang customs to be deposited as before in the Russo-Chinese Bank; the sanitary regulations to be under Russian supervision; no change in the status of the civil administration after evacuation. Further investigation revealed that Mon-

---

[1]"For. Rel." (1903), p. 47, January 3.

golia and perhaps Chihli were within the purview of Russian immediate designs.

Then began a series of diplomatic exchanges between Russia and the Powers of a sort peculiarly adapted to enrage President Roosevelt. The memory of them was still fresh when the war began less than a year later. Lamsdorff, very positively assured United States Minister Robert S. McCormick in St. Petersburg, on April 29th, that there were no such demands, yet two days later the Russian representative at Peking reiterated them and the same day Count Cassini, in Washington (May 1st), confirmed them in an interview in the New York *Tribune* to this extent, that he reasserted that Russia did not wish other ports to be opened. Less than three weeks later M. de Plançon in Peking again confirmed them and meanwhile their existence was painfully evident in China. Lamsdorff complained that the newspapers were making intolerable trouble and drew attention to the fact that much of the current information was coming from Yokohama, a phase of the subject which it must be admitted was not without significance. Japan was remaining quiet, but she had a very active intelligence service not only in Peking but throughout Manchuria. Japan was fighting her battle in the newspapers. Public opinion was now running strongly against Russia. Russia persisted in denying that she was blocking the opening of the new ports, yet the fact remained that the troops in Manchuria were being increased and shifted rather than moved out. The Chinese reasserted that they did not dare to grant the American request. The Russian representative at Peking declared to Mr. Conger that without orders from St. Petersburg, orders which had been promised to the

American Government and never sent, he was not at liberty to tell China that Russia did not object to the opening of the ports.

The Russian bear was eventually smoked out, and on July 11th, in a formal statement,[1] the Russian ambassador at London replied to Lansdowne that Russia would not admit foreign settlements in Manchuria. By this he meant such foreign settlements as existed in the other treaty ports of China. As for Harbin, Russia did not regard that city as "unrestrictedly subject to the Chinese Government," because of the railway agreements. On July 29th the ambassador suggested to Lansdowne that it would be appropriate for Russia and Great Britain to come to a formal agreement, and the latter did not discourage him, readily admitting that Russia "had special interests in that part of China which adjoined her possessions." But Secretary Hay, unembarrassed by the requirements of European politics, continued to insist upon the opening of Tatong and Mukden, retiring, however, on the demand for Harbin. On August 13th, Hay's firmness was crowned with victory and Prince Ch'ing gave a letter agreeing to sign on October 8th, the day when the final evacuation was due, a commercial treaty in which Mukden and Tatong, later changed to Antung, were to be opened to foreign trade. A similar promise was made to Japan.[2]

AMERICAN POLICY IN MANCHURIA

Before taking up the negotiations between Russia and Japan which commenced about this time, we may examine

[1] "China No. 2" (1904), p. 79.

[2] "For. Rel." (1903), pp. 46–74.

rather closely the exact scope of American policy in the Far East at this stage of its development. In his notes of September 6, 1899, Mr. Hay had called for an Open Door in China for the exchange of commodities. Notwithstanding the preferential railway and mining rights already granted, his notes contained no direct protest against them. He merely requested that these privileges should not be used to discriminate, as for example in railway rates, against American trade. In 1902 Mr. Hay had advanced a point, and basing his contention on the principle of the Open Door, he combated the exclusive railway and mining, as well as commercial rights which Russia was demanding in Manchuria. We must not confuse this increased demand with a subsequent development of the policy by which it came to include, as it does now, the doctrine of the integrity of China. To whatever efforts Russia was making to appropriate Manchuria, Hay offered little direct opposition. He merely insisted that, whatever the changes, American rights must not be reduced. In one of those succinct paragraphs by which he was accustomed to sum up his policy for the use of President Roosevelt, he defined it rather more clearly than he appears to have done in the published correspondence. He wrote (May 1, 1902):

I return herewith Mr. Crane's letter. He evidently does not understand, nor, so far as I may judge from our brief conversation, does Secretary Hitchcock, the attitude of this Government. We are not in any attitude of hostility towards Russia in Manchuria. On the contrary, we recognize her exceptional position in northern China. What we have been working for two years to accomplish, if assurances are to count for anything, is that, no matter what happens eventually in northern China and

Manchuria, the United States shall not be placed in any worse position than while the country was under the unquestioned dominion of China.

Mr. Hay was not contending for the integrity of the Chinese Empire, and it is important also to observe that presumably Russia, had she been disposed to employ any sort of fair or honest methods, might have come to an understanding with the United States in regard to Manchuria which would have materially modified the line-up of the Powers in 1904–05. Russia after 1902 was madly bent on her own ruin.[1]

One may ask at this point why the American Government was content with such halfway measures, why it did not seize the moment to demand of Russia the fulfilment of her pledge to evacuate, and why it did not also demand the complete opening of Manchuria to trade. It now seems wholly probable that bold, energetic measures of this sort would have not merely prevented the war between Russia and Japan but would also have made impossible the further conflict between Japan and China which in the following decade was destined to mar so deeply the friendly relations of eastern Asia and involve the United States with Japan. To the critic of American policy in the East the American measures in 1902–03 seemed merely another one of those weak compromises such as had characterized American policy from the beginning. Writing in 1904 or 1905 Bertram Simpson,[2] after reviewing at some length, yet

---

[1] On January 9, 1904, at the last stage of the negotiations between Russia and Japan, Hay told Takahira that while the American Government had not surrendered its treaty rights in Manchuria, it was not then insisting upon "foreign settlements" such as existed in other parts of China and which Russia refused to permit China to grant in Manchuria (Thayer's "Hay," Vol. II, p. 371).

[2] Putnam Weale, "The Re-Shaping of the Far East" (2 Vols., N. Y., 1905), Vol. II, p. 328.

with little accuracy, the history of American policy in the Far East, remarked:

If that treaty [of 1903] had been more sweeping in its provisions; if it had made the question of the throwing open the whole of Manchuria its vital issue as a strong and resolute America could have done, and if America had headed a fresh triplicate of Powers—with England and Japan as her companions—and demanded of Russia the execution of the Evacuation Protocol of April 19, 1902, would the present war have been averted?

Simpson thought it would.[1]

We may pause a moment to put ourselves back in 1902 and recall the elements in the American domestic situation: a vice president hitherto famed more for impetuousness and zeal than for poise and good judgment had only recently been elevated to the White House after the assassination of the man who had been the people's choice for chief executive; a still large portion of the voters and taxpayers were deprecating the acquisition of the Philippines, and earnestly opposing the building of a large navy; the troubles over the acquirement of rights to the Panama Canal were at their height. It was now proposed to have an alliance with Japan and Great Britain or a joint threat of war against Russia over a strip of territory in eastern Asia which was only a name in a gazetteer to all but one in a thousand Americans. The combination of circumstances is regrettable, but the mere statement of

---

[1]This was the opinion of U. S. Minister Conger at Peking. On March 31, 1905, he wrote: "Had the Powers in 1901 and 1902—as it has always seemed to me they ought to have done—demanded of Russia the fulfilment of all her promises, made nominally to China, but actually to all the Powers, Manchuria would have been handed back to the Chinese then and probably the terrible war averted." Conger to Dept. of State, March 31, 1905; copy of despatch in Roosevelt Papers, filed by date.

them is a sufficient explanation. Secretary Hay put the case tersely May 22, 1903:[1]

The Manchurian matter is far more delicate and more troublesome. Russia, as you know, has given us the most positive assurances that the famous "convention of seven points" never existed. We have a verbatim copy of it as it was presented, with preamble and appendix, by Monsieur Plançon to the Chinese Government. . . . The Chinese as well as the Russians seem to know that the strength of our position is entirely moral and if the Russians are convinced that we will not fight—as I suppose we will not—and the Chinese are convinced that they have nothing but good to expect from us and nothing but a beating from Russia, the open hand will not be so convincing to the poor devils of Chinks as the raised club. Still, we must do the best we can with the means at our disposal.

THE YALU TIMBER COMPANY

As soon as Hay secured the promise (August 13, 1903) that two additional ports in Manchuria would be opened by treaty the following October, the American Government dropped out of the controversy which had already been taken up by Japan. Lansdowne still continued the conversations in London and St. Petersburg, but Russia was well assured that Great Britain, now on the point of forming the entente with France, was not likely to go to war with France's ally over the presence of Russian troops in Newchwang or on the Yalu.

The factions in the Russian court were sharply differentiated in 1902 and 1903. Witte, Rosen, Iswolsky, and many others had urged the withdrawal of Russia from Korea in 1898. That withdrawal had been accomplished,

---

[1]Thayer's "Hay," Vol. II, p. 369.

yet with an accompanying consolidation of Russian interests in Manchuria. Witte opposed the aggressive measures in 1901 and supported the Evacuation Protocol of 1902. The opposition was reinforced by General Kuropatkin. Eventually Lamsdorff, at least if we may trust his plain statement to Witte, saw the negotiations with Japan taken out of his hand and conducted directly by the Tsar.[1]

Two events in Russia revealed the trend of affairs—the formation of the Yalu timber company and the creation of the office of Viceroy of the Far East.

The Yalu timber company was designed, perhaps, to operate on the ancient model of the British East India Company. The very fact that at the beginning of the 20th Century there were those in Russia who supposed that there was in eastern Asia any such opportunity as the East India Company possessed a century and a half before reveals the abysmal ignorance of facts which characterized all the measures of the aggressive court faction. Prospect of great profits was held out and a select group of grand dukes, court favourites, and even the Tsar himself were led to make heavy investments of capital.[2] Captain Bezobrazoff was the leading spirit in the adventure, supported by Admiral Abaza and others and later by Admiral Alexeieff. A concession for timber, originally granted to a Vladivostok merchant by the King of Korea while he was a guest in the Russian Legation in Seoul in 1896, was secured and revived by the assent of the King, now Emperor by Russian support. Active work was

---

[1]Witte's "Memoirs," p. 126.

[2]Witte's "Memoirs," pp. 118-19. The Tsar invested at one time 2,000,000 rubles (Kuropatkin, Vol. II, App. 1, pp. 306-13).

started on the Yalu in a small way in April, 1903. The matter was quickly reported to Seoul and Tokio and no one could fail to note that the new operations coincided with the failure of the Russians to fulfil their promise to evacuate Newchwang on April 8th. This combination of bad faith at Newchwang and advance on the Korean side of the Yalu was added proof that Russia had no intentions of actual withdrawal from Manchuria. Further observations led to the discovery that Mukden, having once been evacuated, was almost immediately reoccupied, and that Russian troops, instead of being evacuated, were merely being shifted.[1]

As usual Lamsdorff professed to know nothing about the operations of the timber company and the delay in the evacuation of Newchwang he ascribed merely to the necessity of providing for the continuance of the sanitary regulations. Meanwhile Plehve, Minister of the Interior, is alleged to have joined forces with the Yalu concessionaires for the deliberate purpose of encouraging a war which he regarded as likely to avert the maturing revolutionary movement at home.[2]

In the summer of 1903 there was a general agreement in the reports from Manchuria that the Russians were seeking war with Japan. In St. Petersburg, on the contrary, the Tsar at least was still fatuously clinging to the belief that Japan would not fight and that a firm policy would result in the peaceful acquisition of the province.[3]

---

[1]Kuropatkin, *op. cit.*, reveals that even as early as 1902 the evacuation of Manchuria had been stopped by Alexeieff in the interest of the timber company, in violation of orders from St. Petersburg.

[2]Witte's "Memoirs," p. 250.

[3]*Ibid.*, Chap. V; Dillon, "Eclipse of Russia," pp. 283-84.

RUSSIA IN MANCHURIA

As if still further to provoke, or perhaps, as the Tsar supposed, to intimidate, Japan, Admiral Alexeieff was appointed "Viceroy of the Far Eastern Provinces" and released from the jurisdiction of the ministers at St. Petersburg, that is, from all control either civil or military. He took his orders directly from the Tsar and, in fact, supervised the replies to Japan. This appointment was accompanied by the organization of the "Committee of the Far East" in which the Tsar himself was the presiding officer. The Committee was wholly controlled by the Tsar, who had the power to nominate an unlimited number of members to the board.[1]

JAPAN AND MANCHURIA

Japan also wanted Manchuria. This fact had been disclosed in the Treaty of Shimonoseki when she retained the Liaotung peninsula. Even at the end of 1903 Russia had not acquired as much as Japan had been forced to relinquish in 1895. Where Russia had leases Japan had actual cession of territory by treaty. In April, 1895, and again in 1904 Japan was where England had been in the 16th Century. As an insular empire she was seeking to safeguard her markets and protect herself from an adjoining continent by the acquisition or retention of continental territory. At the outbreak of the war Japan did not officially include the annexation of Manchuria as one of her war aims. That fact is beside the point, for neither did Japan state in 1904 her purpose in Korea.

Japan took up the final negotiations with Russia on July 23, 1903, about two weeks before Secretary Hay had

[1] "China No. 2" (1904), pp. 85, 92.

secured from China the promise that two additional ports in Manchuria would be opened after October.[1] Kurino, the Japanese Minister in St. Petersburg, was directed to ask for a settlement of all existing troubles, the recent additional demands at Peking and the Yalu timber concession being cited as the immediate cause of the proposal. Baron Komura, the Japanese Minister for Foreign Affairs, asserted that Japan possessed paramount political, commercial, and industrial influence in Korea, and in an instruction of August 3rd, he expressed a willingness to recognize Russia's special railway interests in Manchuria. On the other hand, Japan proposed a reciprocal undertaking for both Powers not to impede each other's "industrial and commercial activities" in Manchuria, and asked for the right to extend the Korean railways *into* Manchuria to connect with the Russian lines which did not touch the Korean border. In other words, Japan desired in 1903 that Russia make with her with reference to Manchuria another Rosen-Nissi agreement such as had been the starting point in 1898 for the growth of the existing preponderating Japanese influence in Korea.[2]

Russia was wholly willing to join in a definition of Japan's rights in Korea but was equally unwilling to admit that Japan had any rights whatever in Manchuria (October 5th). Japan, in the course of the negotiations, retired considerably from the initial proposals. Russia at length, January 7, 1904, assented to recognize the rights

[1]Correspondence regarding the negotiations between Japan and Russia (1903–04). Citations to this document will be by date only, a sufficient identification, for there are only sixty-one pages of text. This correspondence is not complete, some of the later Russian communications having been omitted.

[2]For Rosen-Nissi agreement, see pp. 101–02.

acquired by Japan and the other Powers under the existing treaties with China, with the exception that Russia would admit no new foreign settlements in Manchuria. Japan would not yield this point and demanded the right of settlements as well as all other privileges such as the Powers enjoyed under the treaties with China. These of course included extraterritorial privileges and the 5 per cent. conventional tariff. In the end the Russian concessions to Japanese demands amounted to this: Russia would admit Japan's position in Korea provided Japan would agree not to fortify the northern border, but in Manchuria Russia would practically exclude Japanese in common with all foreigners, and Russia would not renew the pledge to respect the integrity of China. Japan broke off diplomatic negotiations February 5, 1904.[1]

It is not now apparent that there was any great difference between the territorial ambitions of Japan and those of Russia. There was, however, a vast difference between the two governments of that date, and between the European associates of the two Powers respectively. Behind Russia stood France, her ally, and Germany, her instigator. Behind Japan stood Great Britain, whose commercial interests in China and whose concerns for peace in the Pacific were similar to those of the United States.

The Russo-Japanese conflict was essentially a war, not for the integrity or independence of either Korea or China but for the *control* of both. It is not perfectly clear whether President Roosevelt realized this aspect of the situation. We incline, however, to believe that he did

---

[1]Text of Imperial Rescript declaring war on Russia, Appendix A, pp. 145-46.

realize it. The choice presented to him was not between the independence of these states and their dependence, but between their dependence on Russia and their dependence on Japan. President Roosevelt preferred Japan to Russia.

APPENDIX

*Japanese Imperial Rescript Comprising Declaration of War
Against Russia, February 10, 1904*

We, by the grace of Heaven, the Emperor of Japan, seated on
the same Throne occupied by the same dynasty from time
immemorial, do hereby make proclamation to all Our loyal and
brave subjects as follows:

We hereby declare war against Russia, and We command Our
army and navy to carry on hostilities against that empire with
all their strength, and We also command all Our competent
authorities, in pursuance of their duties and in accordance with
their powers, to attain the national aim with all the means within
the limits of the law of nations.

We have always deemed it essential to international relations,
and made it Our constant aim, to promote the pacific progress
of Our Empire in civilization, to strengthen Our ties with other
States, and to establish a state of things which would maintain
enduring peace in the extreme East and secure the future of Our
dominion without injury to the rights and interests of other
Powers. Our competent authorities have also performed their
duties in accordance to Our will, so that Our relations with the
Powers have been steadily growing in cordiality. It was thus
entirely against Our expectation that We have unhappily come
to open hostilities against Russia.

The integrity of Corea is a matter of constant concern to this
Empire, not only because of Our traditional relations with that
country, but because the separate existence of Corea is essential
to the safety of Our realm. Nevertheless, Russia, in disregard
of her solemn treaty pledges to China and her repeated as-

surances to other Powers, is still in occupation of Manchuria, has consolidated and strengthened her hold upon those provinces, and is bent upon their final annexation. And since the absorption of Manchuria by Russia would render it impossible to maintain the integrity of Corea, and would, in addition, compel the abandonment of all hope for peace in the extreme East, We determined in those circumstances to settle the question by negotiation, and to secure thereby permanent peace. With that object in view, Our competent authorities by Our order made proposals to Russia, and frequent conferences were held during the course of six months. Russia, however, never met such proposals in a spirit of conciliation, but by her wanton delays put off the settlement of the question, and by ostensibly advocating peace on the one hand, while she was on the other extending her naval and military preparations, sought to accomplish her own selfish designs.

We cannot in the least admit that Russia had from the first day serious or genuine desire for peace. She has rejected the proposals of Our Government; the safety of Corea is in danger; the vital interests of Our Empire are menaced. The guarantees for the future which We have failed to secure by peaceful negotiation We can now only seek by Our appeal to arms.

It is Our earnest wish that, by the loyalty and valour of Our faithful subjects, peace may soon be permanently restored, and the glory of Our Empire preserved.

Contemporary Comment

"Junius," "The Overlord of the Pacific and the Admiral of the Atlantic," *National Review*, April, 1905.

"America is therefore bound to do everything in her power to maintain the principles of the integrity of China and the Open Door. . . . America cannot herself preserve the integrity of China by force, and will not ally herself with the Power which possesses an army adequate to the task. What, then, is the solution of the difficulty in its present form? Obviously it is to be found in the mere existence of that island Empire whose vital interests are also closely interwoven with the integrity of China and the Open Door, whose land and sea forces are formidable, and who is allied with the greatest naval State on the globe."

Sidney Low, "President Roosevelt's Opportunities," *Nineteenth Century and After*, December, 1904.

". . . much more surprising things might happen than that the foundations should be laid for a League of Peace, based on a genuine and effective Anglo-Saxon Alliance, before it is time for him [Roosevelt] to quit the Executive Mansion."

"Calchas," "First Principles in the Far East," *Fortnightly Review*, February, 1904.

"M. Bazobrazoff is not a more sinister figure in the minds of imaginative, or rather unimaginative, Britons than was Cecil Rhodes in the mind of the German people."

C. A. W. Pownall, "Russia, Japan and Ourselves," *Nineteenth Century and After*, March, 1904.

"That the control of China, the copying on their own account of the European occupation of Peking, was for long an objective to the Japanese is proved by the existence of a detailed map covering the whole region of Korea, Manchuria, and the coast of the Gulf of Pechili, with the roads all marked, the contours of the hills given, and an amount of detail shown which must have occupied the clandestine surveys of the most inquisitive race on earth for many years until it came into use by the Japanese staff in the war of 1895. A copy of that map was given to the present writer at that time and is now in his possession.

ROOSEVELT AND THE RUSSO–JAPANESE WAR

It in itself furnishes evidence of the long-cherished design to invade China, and disproves the assertion, then made, that Japan was forced into the war on that occasion. On the contrary, it was a deliberate and carefully planned invasion. . . ."

Comte Cassini, "Russia in the Far East," *North American Review*, May, 1904.
"... Manchuria was a question to be settled between Russia and China in which Japan was no more legitimately concerned than any other Power. . . . It is not a thoughtless statement that were Japan to obtain supreme control in Manchuria, the dominant military spirit of the Japanese would lead them to organize the Chinese into a modern army of such proportions that England and America would stand aghast at the menace to their peace and well-being. This is a phase of what has been called the 'Yellow Peril' that it would be well for all the thoughtful and intelligent classes to consider carefully."

Kogoro Takahira, "Why Japan Resists Russia," *North American Review*, March, 1904.
"The fundamental purpose of Japan's action has been to safeguard vital interests which would be seriously menaced if Russia absorbed Manchuria, and followed that by the inevitable sequence of such action, the absorption of China."

Baron Kentaro Kaneko, "The Yellow Peril Is the Golden Opportunity for Japan," *North American Review*, November, 1904.
"By reconciling and inter-assimilating the two civilizations, Japan hopes to introduce Western culture and science into the continent of Asia, and thus to open up for the benefit of the world, with equal privilege for every nation, and peace assured to all, the teeming wealth of the Chinese Empire."

RUSSIA IN MANCHURIA

"Ivanovich," "The Russo-Japanese War and the Yellow Peril," *Contemporary Review*, August, 1904.

"With such a reservoir of force at her disposal, Russia could dictate terms to Europe."

Thomas H. Reid, "The Menace of the East," *Contemporary Review*, May, 1905.

"Germany, not Japan, is the menace of the East."

Alexander Ular, "Le Panmongolisme japonais," *La Revue*, February 15, 1904.

"Le Panmongolisme japonais mourrait, en ce cas, écrasé par le Panmongolisme russe."

"Anglo-American," "Some Revelations of the War," *North American Review*, April, 1904.

As a preface to an intimation of the necessity for an Anglo-American alliance. "No pen has flowed faster than Mr. Hay's since he first launched his Circular to the Powers in September, 1899; but the Chinese question, I must again insist, is not one of those cases in which the pen is mightier than the sword. Had Mr. Hay all the qualities of a Bismarck . . . he would still, in the last resort, be fundamentally helpless without a Moltke in the background."

CHAPTER VII

War Aims and American Interests

ONLY the barest outline of the military events of the war is essential to our purpose. On February 8, 1904, Japanese torpedo boats attacked the Russian fleet in the roadstead at Port Arthur. This was the opening of hostilities. Two days later came the Japanese declaration of war. The attack at Port Arthur continued, supported by land as well as sea forces. There were no less than six extensive battles around the fortress and on January 1, 1905, General Stossel surrendered to General Nogi, leaving the city in possession of Japan. The battle of Mukden began on February 23d, and ended in the complete rout of the Russian forces on March 10th. The major actions of the war closed in the great naval battle off Tsushima May 27–28th, in a complete victory for Japan. On June 10th and 12th, Japan and Russia, respectively, publicly accepted the good offices of President Roosevelt and agreed to direct negotiations for peace.[1]

Europe not only did not expect the war, but also was wholly unprepared for the unbroken succession of Russian reverses. Until the Russian disaster at Port Arthur, Europe expected daily to learn that the tide had turned against Japan. The Japanese victory at Mukden still left Europe unconvinced that Russia would be defeated.

---

[1]Frederick McCormick, "The Tragedy of Russia in Pacific Asia" (2 Vols., N. Y., 1907), Vol. II, pp. 403–19, supplies a useful chronology of the war.

WAR AIMS AND AMERICAN INTERESTS

It was generally believed that Russia's greater resources both in capital and in man power would in the end be sufficient to wear Japan down and secure a victory by attrition, if not by military success. The battle of the Sea of Japan, resulting in Russia's complete surrender of the sea, was more convincing, but even then it was the Moroccan crisis and the spread of the Russian revolutionary movement, more than the Russian defeats, that brought about the peace negotiations.

Russian war aims and British policy were graphically summarized for President Roosevelt in a letter from Spring-Rice early in January.[1] He wrote:

> No doubt exists (I quote the best Russian authority) that Russia never intended to evacuate Manchuria; but allowed her representatives in Europe to make declarations to that effect with a view to quieting for a time European opinion. Her experience with England . . . made her sure that Europe would acquiesce. Everyone would have acquiesced. Japan, however, having, unlike Europe, no other question except just the Korean and Manchurian questions, determined to resist; and has resisted.
>
> The reason she did resist was that from authentic sources Japan had learnt that it was the intention of Russia to strengthen her position in the Far East gradually, and, when it was firmly established, to repudiate her engagements. This was openly proposed by Russian officials who also were convinced that Japan, like England, was only "bluffing" in pretending to object and would like England accept the *fait accompli*. . . .
>
> With regard to the issue of the war. We have it from the highest authority here that if the war is quickly successful for Russia the demands made by Russia will be excessive—and amount to the practical annexation of all N. E. China and Korea and amount also to putting Peking in tutelage—with

---

[1] Undated, but before January 15, 1905.

the gradual absorption of the whole of the Chinese Government in Russian hands. By the extension of the railways in nominally Belgian hands, this power will be extended to the Yangtze and Tientsin.

Should the war, as is more probable, be long and difficult but end in the practical victory of Russia, the demands of Russia will be: (1) Manchuria in Russian hands, with all the country except Newchwang under Russian control—all enterprises, trade transport, and local government in Russian hands; (2) a fortified post on the Yalu; (3) another in E. Korea; (4) prohibition to Japan to have a fleet; (5) her exclusion from the Korean and Manchurian markets.

To Spring-Rice the prospect seemed alarming. The Tsar was to be "Admiral of the Pacific" while the Kaiser was to be "Admiral of the Atlantic." France, he thought, would continue to support Russia. England, where there was no prospect of compulsory military service, would then be faced by autocracy with unlimited reserves of military power. Russia could take peasants from their farms and put them on trains to fight anywhere in the world, even when police had to beat off the clinging arms of women and children. England could not make war that way. A Russian victory would open up the vast reserves of man power in the East. He cited instances in which Russia had drawn on the resources of the East to conquer the West. This, it seemed to him, was the real "yellow peril." In the face of such force the British Government had no choice. It could not fight such a combination. It must come to an agreement with Russia as soon as the war was over. He continued:

We are trying our best to come to some sort of understanding with Russia (when the war is over), so as to put an end to the continual régime of panic in India, Persia, etc. The reason we are doing so is that with the establishment of a strong German navy on our flanks we cannot afford to have a life-and-death struggle in Asia and the Far East. Germany is rapidly acquiring a very strong position in Russia. . . . In any case, if we were at war with Russia, Germany would either take Russia's side, or exact very hard terms from us for her neutrality. The German fleet has really revolutionized politics. . . ."

This letter must have reached the President just after the exposure by the Kaiser of the project of M. Doumer, President of the French Chamber of Deputies, to begin the partition of China.[1] Roosevelt credited this charge. Plainly the American Government, as he had already written to Spring-Rice (December 27, 1904), would have to look sharply lest its interests be sacrificed in the peace settlement in the Far East. With European affairs the United States was only indirectly concerned, although such a prospect as Spring-Rice had sketched could not be reassuring, but in the Pacific and Far East the American Government had extremely important interests.

ROOSEVELT AND THE CHINESE EMPIRE

The President did not have that somewhat sentimental though wholly honourable regard for the Korean and Chinese people with which we have been made familiar in the last few years. Neither Koreans nor Chinese were a fighting stock—a fact which did not commend them to one who could so readily drop affairs of state to practise jiujitsu or study pugilism. We have already noted Roosevelt's lack of regard for the Koreans who were allowing the

---

[1]See pp. 78ff.

Japanese such an easy victory. Toward the Chinese he had a somewhat similar feeling. His contribution to the American vocabulary of the verb "chinafy" implied no compliment to China. A series of misunderstandings with the Chinese Government during the year 1905 added to the prejudice against China which already existed.

For a quarter of a century the Chinese immigration question had troubled Sino-American relations.[1] In many details of the controversy the Chinese Government was wholly right, but Chinese tactics were equally wrong. The effect of raising the question in the form in which it was raised in each instance served only to increase anti-Chinese prejudice in the United States and imperil friendly feeling which China urgently needed to utilize in her losing struggle against Europe and Japan. The lines of Chinese exclusion were drawn steadily tighter and tighter in spite of China's continued protest, while the often unreasonable prejudice against the Chinese mounted higher and higher. The advocates of Chinese exclusion deemed it necessary to foster the most absurd notions about the barbarism and degeneracy of the Chinese people, and each new assertion, however baseless, left its increment of anti-Chinese feeling in the United States. President Roosevelt had grown to maturity in the period of this prejudice the intensity of which younger Americans of the present day can hardly realize. We suggest this as one of the psychological factors in the situation the actual importance of which cannot be easily valued.

China selected an inopportune moment, just before the war (January 25, 1904), to denounce the immigration

---

[1] "Am. in East. Asia," Chap. XXVIII.

treaty which was to expire in the following December.[1]
This brought the consideration of the Chinese immigration
question into the period when Roosevelt was forming his
policy in regard to Japan. In March, 1905, the Chinese
Minister, the victim apparently of very poor advice, addressed to the Department of State an almost insolent
note. China protested against certain alleged executive
orders relative to the Chinese in the United States which
were without the sanction of Congress.[2] It was a slap at
Roosevelt's known exaltation of the powers of the executive. It seems never to have occurred to the Chinese
Government and its adviser that in the settlement of the
differences between Russia and Japan, Chinese interests
would be gravely affected and that therefore it would be
well to conciliate rather than irritate President Roosevelt.
Furthermore, in a somewhat shifty manner, though not
entirely without reason, the Chinese Government selected
this time to cancel the Hankow-Canton railway concession
which had been given to Americans in 1898.[3]

To complicate matters still more the Chinese, stimulated
perhaps by the victories of the yellow race in Manchuria,

---

[1] "For. Rel." (1904), p. 117.

[2] "For. Rel." (1905), p. 166, March 31.

[3] Control of the company holding this concession had been acquired by King Leopold and
Belgian interests. The charter had stipulated that the control must not pass out of the hands of
Americans. In 1904 the banking house of J. P. Morgan re-acquired a controlling interest in the
corporation and proposed to resume operations in China. Either the fact that Americans had
regained control was not made clear to the Chinese Government or the pressure of British interests in China became too strong to resist. The concession was cancelled and Roosevelt was
much annoyed at this loss of American prestige in China. He blamed the Chinese Government.
Behind the cancellation of this concession appears the British Government which feared that the
Belgian interest would still control. Behind Belgium stood Russia. England was thus striking
again at Russia. The *Times* (London), September 5, 1904, and September 4, 1905, gives an
interesting account of the transaction from a British point of view. See also "For. Rel." (1905),
pp. 124–35. For an American statement of the controversy, see *Journal of the American Asiatic
Association*, Feb., 1905, p. 24.

started in May, 1905, a boycott of American goods in protest to the American immigration laws.[1]   The boycott exasperated Roosevelt.

Back of all was the fresh memory of the siege of the Peking Legations in 1900 and the brutal murder of many foreigners.   It is very easy to understand why President Roosevelt did not admit the Chinese to a place in his estimation equal with that assigned to the Japanese. Very few Americans did in 1905.

All this was very unfortunate for China.   The defeat of Russia might have provided a convenient opportunity to restore to China some of the rights in Manchuria which had been extorted in 1896–98.   If only the Chinese Government had shown itself able to administer those rights in 1905 it is possible that something would have been done.

JAPANESE WAR AIMS

Japanese war aims revealed a marked tendency to increase as one Japanese victory followed another.   An absolutely free hand in Korea and the payment of an indemnity by Russia were among the demands known to Baron Eckardstein in the summer of 1904.[2]   On the other hand, Japan was reported at that time, from what were believed to be authentic sources, to be willing to see Port Arthur returned to China, and to see the Manchurian railways placed under international control.   As late as December, 1904, the Japanese Minister at Madrid stated to his British colleague that Japan might be willing to concede Port Arthur to China if England would guarantee

---

[1] "For. Rel." (1905), pp. 204–34.
[2] "Isolierung," p. 80.

that the fortress would not again revert to Russia.[1]
The Japanese Minister stated that the island of Sakhalin
was to Japan more important than the fortress in Manchuria. President Roosevelt was always agreeable to the
transfer of Sakhalin to Japan.[2]

After the capture of Port Arthur the Japanese demands
increased. About the middle of January, Takahira had a
conversation with the President in which the latter stated
that in his opinion the Japanese had earned Port Arthur
and had a right to keep it.[3]

In the same conversation the President stated, in
response to the Japanese Minister's question, that he
believed that Manchuria should be restored to China
"under the guidance of the Powers." He stated that in
his opinion the British Government would approve of this
disposition, but he had no information on the subject from
Germany, Italy, or France. Just what Roosevelt meant
by a restoration under the guidance of the Powers one does
not know, for he did not elaborate the idea in his letters.
On March 31st, after the Japanese victory at Mukden,
Minister Conger at Peking suggested, on behalf of the
Chinese Government, that the Manchurian railway be
transferred to China under an international guarantee
both for its protection and for whatever payment might be
necessary either to Russia or to Japan. Such an arrangement, Conger believed, would interpose a most formidable
barrier, impassable in the future to Russia and Japan
alike. The plan appeared to those familiar with the

---

[1]Meyer to Roosevelt, February 21, 1905. Howe's "Meyer," pp. 124-25.

[2]See pp. 251, footnote 3; also pp. 261, 284.

[3]Meyer to Roosevelt, January 20, 1905. The accuracy of this statement which was made to
Ambassador Meyer in Rome was confirmed by Roosevelt.

conditions in north China to offer hopes of permanent peace. This scheme, as will be observed, foreshadowed the neutralization plan of Secretary of State Knox which was put forward in 1909 to prevent the very aggressions which Conger had feared. To the Knox plan in 1909 Roosevelt, no longer President, was wholly opposed.[1] One does not know the exact date when the President abandoned his suggestion that Manchuria be restored to China under international supervision and agreed to the Japanese demand, which was put forward after the victory at Mukden, for the transfer of Russian railway rights to herself.[2]

The only restrictions which President Roosevelt is known to have imposed upon Japan were that she must give a full pledge to respect the Open Door in Manchuria and to restore it to China. This pledge was asked for on April 20th, and given five days later.[3]

The President does not appear to have been greatly concerned with the details of the geographical settlement, nor does he seem to have given a great deal of thought to Manchuria and its future. He trusted to the broad promise of the Japanese to maintain an open door there even when the area was restored to China. One questions whether he meant more by this than that the commercial opportunities in Manchuria should be kept as open as they were in Korea up to the outbreak of the war. If he erred in his policy at this point, in the light of subsequent developments, it was on the side of trusting Japanese promises too implicitly. His policy, however, must be

---

[1] See pp. 320 ff.
[2] Loomis to Loeb, May 19, 1905.
[3] Chapter VIII, pp. 178, 179–80.

correlated with another phase of it, namely, Japan in her relation to Europe and the Pacific.

JAPAN IN THE PACIFIC

President Roosevelt took a long view of the situation in the Pacific. He was greatly concerned about the relation of Japan to the Philippines and Hawaii, and gave much thought to Japan's future relations with Europe. If we may judge by the number of times he returned to the subject in his letters, he was never really sure that all would be well. We give a number of excerpts of various dates.

The claim was put forward by Russia and by Russian advocates that the war was a colour conflict in which she was fighting the battle of the white race. Spring-Rice disposed of that plea in a letter already quoted.[1] Such appeals to prejudice stirred Roosevelt quite oppositely from what was intended. To a missionary, Dr. D. B. Schneder, of Reading, Pa., he wrote, June 19, 1905:

I have just your feeling about the Japanese Nation. As for their having a yellow skin, if we go back two thousand years we will find that to the Greek and Roman the most dreaded and yet in a sense the most despised barbarian was the white-skinned, blue-eyed and red- or yellow-haired barbarian of the North— the men from whom you and I in a large part derive our blood. It would not seem possible to the Greek and Roman of that day that the northern barbarian should ever become part of the civilized world—his equal in civilization.

On the other hand, the effect of a Japanese victory on the military situation in the Pacific and on the American possessions at Hawaii and in the Philippines was to

[1]See p. 152.

Roosevelt more disturbing. As early as January, 1905, there had been reported to him a smouldering resentment among the Japanese officers against the United States for having thwarted Japanese ambitions in these directions.[1] During the closing months of the war the President watched the Japanese closely and was very alert to meet any growing danger. Early in the year reports from Honolulu indicated that the Japanese, who far outnumbered the whites, were being aroused by the unbroken succession of Japanese victories and were showing an "insolent temper" which might create a most formidable problem. "After reading Carter's [George Robert Carter, Governor of Territory of Hawaii] letter," wrote Roosevelt February 9, 1905, to Mr. Taft, Secretary of War, "would it not be well for you to communicate with him and see if he needs a regiment or two of troops in the islands?"

The protection of the Philippines gave him even more concern and he weighed the question carefully. Always he came to the conclusion that the Japanese statesmen were too astute to adopt a policy of aggression in the Far East which would find them arrayed against the Western world. Some time in January or February he sent a message to George Kennan, then in Japan. This message, paraphrased by Richard Barry, who carried the message and confirmed as to substance when repeated back to Roosevelt, was as follows:[2]

I have, from the beginning, favoured Japan and have done all that I could do, consistent with international law, to advance

---

[1]See p. 48; also "Am. in East. Asia," pp. 637–38 and 623, for a review of the Japanese attitude toward the American acquisition of the Philippines and Hawaii.

[2]Kennan to Roosevelt, March 30, 1905; Roosevelt to Kennan, May 6, 1906.

her interests. I thoroughly admire and believe in the Japanese. They have always told me the truth, and the Russians have not. Moreover, they have the kind of fighting stock that I like; but there is one thing that I hope will be impressed upon them, and that is the necessity for a broad, intelligent self-restrained attitude at the close of this war. I am confident that Japan will prove to the end, as she has proven so far, victorious; but then she will have before her a very great problem, and it is the solution of this problem that I fear.

If Japan is careful, and is guided by the best minds in her empire, she can become one of the leaders of the family of great nations; but if she is narrow and insular, if she tries to gain from her victory more than she ought to have, she will array against her all of the great Powers, and you know very well that however determined she may be, she cannot successfully face an allied world. Now I don't believe that Japan is going to make any mistake . . . but there are so many adverse critics abroad in our country—and more especially on the continent of Europe —who prophesy that her extraordinary exploits will breed a spirit of self-conceit which will lead her to think that she can conquer the world, that, while I do not give any credence to them, yet, at the same time, I must recognize that they have some force. What I want to do is to assure Japan that she will have the entire support of the United States in whatever legitimate claim she may make.

In another letter Roosevelt carried this thought a little further and intimated that his policy would be to seek the friendship of Japan so that the latter would not be driven, through fear of America, into the arms of Russia. To Ambassador Meyer he wrote (February 6, 1905):

Japan ought to have a protectorate over Korea (which has shown its utter inability to stand by itself), and ought to succeed to Russia's right in and around Port Arthur while I should hope to see Manchuria restored to China. Of course it would be out of the question to forecast the details of peace now because no one can tell whether the military situation will continue unchanged, or what will be the result if Russia keeps on the war for another year. I do not believe that Japan has the slightest intention of making an alliance with Russia or that she will do so unless affairs change very much for the worse as regards herself and the war. If the Russians beat her, and she finds that America and England separately or together will give her no help, she may conclude that she has to make what terms she can with Russia. But this is not among the probabilities.

To Congressman J. A. T. Hull, chairman of the House Committee on Military Affairs, he wrote March 16, 1905, while deprecating any menacing language toward Japan:

It may be that the Japanese have designs on the Philippines. I hope not; I am inclined to believe not; for I like the Japanese, and wish them well, as they have much in their character to admire. But I believe we should put our naval and military preparations in such shape that we can hold the Philippines against *any* foe. If we do this, and act justly towards, and speak courteously of, our foreign neighbours, we shall have taken the only effective steps to make our position good.

In February, 1905, the *Chronicle* of San Francisco opened a campaign along the Pacific Coast for Japanese exclusion. In March the United States Immigration Commissioner at Dallas, Texas, refused naturalization papers to some Japanese on the ground that the Japanese were ineligible for citizenship. A few days later the California Legislature, incited and supported by the *Chronicle*, indulged in a most regrettable debate full of objectionable language and charges against the Japanese.

Both the Assembly and the Senate then passed a resolution calling on Congress to protect California against Japanese immigration.[1] President Roosevelt was unable to separate this agitation from a marked apathy on the Pacific Coast in support of an effective naval programme. To Senator Lodge, in an extremely confidential letter, he wrote, June 5, 1905:

Of course, not only Cassini but Jusserand are very gloomy over Japan's attitude toward outside nations in the future. That Japan will have her head turned to some extent I do not in the least doubt, and I see clear symptoms of it in many ways. We should certainly as a nation have ours turned if we had performed such feats as the Japanese have in the past sixteen months; and the same is true of any European nation. Moreover, I have no doubt that some Japanese, and perhaps a great many of them, will behave badly to foreigners. They cannot behave worse than the State of California, through its Legislature, is now behaving toward the Japanese. The feeling on the Pacific slope, taking it from several different standpoints, is as foolish as if conceived by the mind of a Hottentot.

These Pacific Coast people wish grossly to insult the Japanese and to keep out the Japanese immigrants on the ground that they are an immoral, degraded, and worthless race; and at the same time that they desire to do this for the Japanese and are already doing it for the Chinese, they expect to be given advantages in Oriental markets; and with besotted folly are indifferent to building up the navy while provoking this formidable new power—a power jealous, sensitive, and warlike, and which if irritated could at once take both the Philippines and Hawaii from us if she obtained the upper hand on the seas. Most certainly the Japanese soldiers and sailors have shown themselves

---

[1]See Raymond Leslie Buell, The Development of Anti-Japanese Agitation in the United States " *Pol. Sci. Quart.*, Vol. XXXVII, Dec., 1922, pp. 616 ff., for review of the California situation.

to be terrible foes.   There can be none more dangerous in all the world.

But our own navy, ship for ship, is I believe at least as efficient as theirs, although I am not certain that our torpedo-boats would be handled as well as theirs.   At present we are superior to them in number of ships, and this superiority will last for some time.   It will of course come to an end if [Senator] Hale has his way, but not otherwise.   I hope that we can persuade our people on the one hand to act in a spirit of generous justice and genuine courtesy toward Japan, and on the other hand to keep the navy respectable in numbers and more than respectable in the efficiency of its units.   If we act thus we need not fear the Japanese.   But if, as Brooks Adams says, we show ourselves "opulent, aggressive, and unarmed," the Japanese may some-time work us an injury.   In any event, we can hold our own, whether against Japan or Germany, whether on the Atlantic or the Pacific, only if we occupy the position of the just man armed —that is, if we do the exact reverse of what the demagogues on the one hand and the mugwumps on the other would like to have us do.

President Roosevelt's intervention in the Russo-Japanese War did not stand as an isolated policy and may not fairly be judged without reference to other phases of his policy in the Far East.   A foundation stone of Roosevelt's Far Eastern policy was a navy adequate to protect the Philippines and Hawaii, and adequate to command the respect of Japan.   Coördinate with a large navy in his mind stood a courteous handling of the Japanese immigration question.   In a somewhat academic way, for Roosevelt was not a business man and did not have a highly developed commercial sense, he also favoured an aggressive commercial policy in the Far East.   The building of the Panama Canal was also intimately associated with the Far East both in its political and its commercial aspects. All these phases of Far Eastern policy were independent of the Russo-Japanese War. The decision to intervene in this conflict must therefore be studied in its true relation to the policy as a whole.

Roosevelt was prepared to support Japan in 1905, but not blindly. There were definite limits to the support he would give. In another letter to Senator Lodge, June 16th, he remarked:

Japan now has Port Arthur and Korea and the dominance in Manchuria, and I should feel that the less she asks for in addition, the better it would be.

THE BALANCE OF POWER IN THE FAR EAST

Lastly, President Roosevelt held to the theory of the balance of power in the Far East. He argued that while Russia had about one chance in three of defeating Japan, the probabilities were for a Japanese victory. After the naval battle of the Sea of Japan he felt that the Russian cause was hopeless. He believed that in six, eight, or twelve months more Japan would be able to drive Russia out of all Siberia as far west as Lake Baikal. But he did not wish to see Russia driven completely out of eastern Asia. We shall return to this subject in Chapter XIII. He observed (June 16th):

Russia had far better make peace now, if she possibly can, and find her boundaries in east Asia left without material shrinkage from what they were ten years ago, than submit to being driven out of east Asia. While for the rest of us, while Russia's triumph would have been a blow to civilization, her destruction as an eastern Asiatic Power would also in my opinion be unfortunate. It is best that she should be left face to face with Japan so that each may have a moderative action on the other.

As for Japan, she has risen with simply marvellous rapidity, and she is as formidable from the industrial as from the military standpoint. She is a great civilized nation; though her civilization is in some important respects not like ours. There are some things she can teach us, and some things she can learn from us. She will be as formidable an industrial competitor as, for instance, Germany, and in a dozen years I think she will be the leading industrial nation of the Pacific. The way she has extended her trade and prepared for the establishment of new steamship lines to all kind of points in the Pacific has been astonishing, for it has gone right on even through the time of this war. Whether her tremendous growth in industrialism will in the course of time modify and perhaps soften the wonderful military spirit she has inherited from the days of the Samurai supremacy it is hard to say. Personally I think it will; but the effect will hardly be felt for a generation to come. Still, her growing industrial wealth will be to a certain extent a hostage for her keeping the peace. We should treat her courteously, generously, and justly, and we should keep our navy up and make it evident that we are not influenced by fear. I do not believe that she will look toward the Philippines until affairs are settled on the mainland of Asia in connection with China, even if she ever looks toward them, and on the mainland in China her policy is the policy to which we are already committed.

President Roosevelt was looking beyond the present generation to the next one. It is possible to charge him at this point with failure to foresee that Japan might change her policy in the Far East and adopt one to which the United States would in a very few years be wholly opposed. One may observe that he also failed to give sufficient attention to the fact that Russia and Japan were not, after all, so much natural enemies as natural friends who were very likely to make up their differences and even stand together against the other Powers. On the other hand, we must point out that a generation has not yet elapsed since President Roosevelt made his decision and that already the growing industrial wealth of Japan has become measurably a hostage for peace in the Far East and in the Pacific. We may also point out that in the course of the following decade two other parts of his Far Eastern policy, coördinate with his support of Japan in 1905, were not sustained at the level where he placed them. In spite of all that the Federal Government could do, the Japanese immigration question was not always handled courteously; and, after the famous voyage of the American Fleet around the world in 1907–08, Japan was not made to feel that a violation of the confidence which President Roosevelt had reposed in her in 1905, would be accompanied by prompt action other than verbal protest on the part of the American Government.

Contemporary Comment

Paul S. Reinsch, "Japan and Asiatic Leadership," *North American Review*, January, 1905.

"Japan is fighting our battle. . . . The very least that the Anglo-Saxon races can do for the representatives of their policy in the Orient is to counteract the diplomatic influence that would by roundabout means again deprive the Japanese of the fruits of their unexampled self-sacrifice."

Chester Holcombe, "Some Results of the Eastern War," *Atlantic Monthly*, July, 1905.

"It must constantly be kept in mind that this is not merely a war between Japan and Russia. It is rather a conclusive struggle between the Powers of the Far East and the ambition, lust, and greed of the great Powers of Europe, to determine, once for all, the right to existence and the status of the first named."

Arnold White, "Anglo-Russian Relations," *Fortnightly Review*, December, 1904.

"If an understanding with Russia is the logical consequence of our understanding with France and (short of the destruction of the German fleet on the Copenhagen precedent of September, 1807) the only means by which the isolation of Germany can be assured, the present Foreign Minister deserves well of the country."

Pierre Leroy-Beaulieu, "Le Japon et Ses Ressources," *Revue des Deux Mondes*, March 15, 1904.

"À vrai dire, s'il est une prévision qu'on puisse faire avec quelque certitude, c'est celle d'une intervention des neutres à la fin du conflit, pour empêcher le vainqueur de pousser trop loin la victoire. . . . De cette lutte déplorable, il est ainsi douteux qu'aucun des combattants puisse retirer de grands fruits, à moins qu'elle ne se termine par l'effroyable drame d'une conflagration universelle."

Professor Edwin Maxey, "Why We Favour Japan in the Present War," *Arena*, August, 1904.

"In this war Russia stands for reaction and Japan for progress. . . . The organization and control of the millions of Chinese by Russia is far more dangerous to the rest of the world than would be their control by the Japanese. . . ."

Alfred Stead, "A Question of Good Faith and National Expediency," *Fortnightly Review*, January, 1905.

". . . there are several flagrant examples of Great Britain's lack of good faith towards Japan (such as the delivery of coal to Russia, sale of war vessels to Russia and the North Sea Convention). . . . 'It is strongly felt' [quoting Baron Suyemetsu] 'that the nations of Europe are assisting Russia in a way never contemplated by us. I do not suggest that England is not fulfilling her duty as an ally, but even in this country much indirect assistance is being rendered to Russia by individuals.'

"Besides the immediate benefit to us from the alliance [Anglo-Japanese] it may lead us to that most desired goal of a new triple alliance, for Peace, when the United States, Japan, and Great Britain shall stand together as the guardians of international justice and morality."

Demetrius P. Boulger, "The Yellow Peril Bogey," *Nineteenth Century*, January, 1904.

"Japanese influence has asserted itself not merely in Korea, but also in Manchuria, and, more remarkable still, it has acquired an ascendancy over the councils of China . . . whereas the Peril under the direction of the Japanese would never be more than a phantom for any state except Russia, it might become in the hands of Russia a menace to the peace of the world, and the means of overthrowing the British Empire in Asia and of laying the whole fabric of British commercial prosperity level with the ground."

CHAPTER VIII

Peace Overtures

EFFORTS to restore peace between Russia and Japan almost never ceased from the outbreak of hostilities.[1] Four different methods of peacemaking were advocated: an international conference; mediation through England and France, the allies, respectively, of the belligerents; mediation by the United States; and direct negotiation between Russia and Japan. Over all hung the shadow of intervention by a concert of Powers.

Russia desired nothing which reminded her of 1878; Japan could not forget 1895. Both Powers feared intervention. The Kaiser, never zealous for peace until the Russian revolutionary movement raised before him a disquieting spectre, did not want peace by Anglo-French mediation, nor did he favour an international congress. The danger was that such a conference would demand compensations for its members as well as for the belligerents. An international congress might resolve itself into a committee on the partition of the Chinese Empire and it was a part of the German Emperor's plan to save China as a lure for Russia. The outward appearance of the German policy, however, was that of perfect neutrality. The American Government might justly be suspicious of any plan emanating from Europe, for Japan was without friends there. Any plan coming from Europe, whether for

[1]See pp. 26 ff.

PEACE OVERTURES

international conference, intervention, or mediation, was likely to be aimed at Japan with a view to robbing her again of the fruits of her victories. To Russia, to Japan, to the United States, and to Germany, though for a different reason, direct negotiation between the belligerents was the most satisfactory.

The war, as is well known, was never popular in Russia. It was not approved even by those, like Witte, who before 1904 had come to be known as representative Russian statesmen. In a sense Japan was fighting the Yalu timber concessionaires of whom the Tsar happened to be one. The timber company had as its defender the Committee of the Far East in which the Tsar was the presiding officer. The Tsar took the war under his immediate supervision and made it in a peculiar sense his own private enterprise. In a way the Japanese hostilities were directed only in a limited degree against the Russian Empire or people. There was always the possibility of reconciliation if at any time the conservative Russian statesmen returned to power. The continued peace talk during the war is therefore not surprising.[1]

Following the negotiations in London in the summer of 1904, M. Witte resumed the overtures to Hayashi in February, 1905. Japan was less willing, after the capture of Port Arthur, to give the matter serious consideration, but the Japanese Minister sent a reply that while Japan would require Russia to make the first proposal, nevertheless, the former would "welcome peace" and "cultivate friendship with her present enemy after the conclusion of peace."[2]

[1]See pp. 138-41; Dillon, "Eclipse of Russia," pp. 296 ff.
[2]Dillon, *op. cit.*, p. 301.

Thus in the midst of hostilities some Japanese and some Russians would appear to have been thinking about the cultivation of future "friendship," perhaps of the practical alliance which was consummated within the next decade. The important point is that these communications in February were carried by French messengers. The French and the American governments became, in a sense, rivals for the position of peacemaker.

Japan, always fearful of a repeated experience with European intervention, was of course especially suspicious of France, the ally of Russia. The German Government, unwilling to permit any growth of French prestige, determined if possible to break up the Anglo-French Entente, craftily planning according to an opportunist programme to take as much advantage as possible of the war in the Far East to advance German interests elsewhere, was likewise wholly opposed to French intervention in any form. Immediately after receiving the news of the fall of Port Arthur the Kaiser addressed to the Tsar, in an injured tone, a request for an outline of the Russian terms of peace. The Kaiser had learned that Russia had already given to France a memorandum of her terms of peace and he was greatly annoyed. "Now I prefer being informed by yourself directly, instead [sic] in a round about way through other agencies," he wrote.[1] However, the Kaiser took no chances on the failure of his letter to draw the desired information. Three days earlier he had instructed Sternberg to notify President Roosevelt of the fact that France was in possession of the Russian terms, and he coupled this information with the suspected plot in Paris to bring about intervention and the par-

---

[1] Levine, p. 146.

tition of China.[1]   Again on February 12th, Baron
Sternberg informed Roosevelt, upon advices from Berlin, that the British Ambassador in St. Petersburg had
pointed out to Lamsdorff the advantages of an early
conclusion of peace.   The German Government wished
to keep in touch with the Japanese attitude and intimated that it would like to know the Japanese peace
terms.

President Roosevelt had "definitely concluded" as early
as December 27, 1904, what he intended to do "if circumstances permit."[2]   Just what he had in mind at that time,
or whether the intention was in any way modified by the
visit of Mr. Spring-Rice to Washington the following
February, one does not know.   Mr. Hay recorded in his
diary on January 1, 1905, that the President "is quite
firm in the view that we cannot permit Japan to be robbed
a second time of the fruits of her victory."   This observation was doubtless prompted by the news of the fall of
Port Arthur.[3]   Almost immediately after this he expressed
to Cassini the opinion that Russia ought to make peace.
He was informed that Delcassé had expressed a similar
opinion.   We have already noted how Roosevelt and Hay
took steps, at the suggestion of the German Emperor, to
obstruct the alleged plan of M. Doumer to settle the war
with an international conference and compensations to the
Powers.[4]   It must have been reasonably clear both to the
Japanese Government and to President Roosevelt before
the battle of Mukden that in case the good offices of any

[1]See p. 79.
[2]See p. 45.
[3]Thayer's "Hay," Vol. II, p. 361.
[4]See p. 81

Power were utilized in making peace the choice would lie between France and the United States.

All doubt on this subject was removed in April while Roosevelt was hunting in Colorado. We shall dwell at length upon the following episode because of its significance. Russia plainly made an overture for peace through France. France, with the Moroccan incident in full view, greatly desired that Russia make peace. Japan also was willing to enter negotiations. Lastly, this set of circumstances is practically decisive in answering the question whether President Roosevelt interfered too early. It will appear from the following paragraphs that the President's hand was forced both by the French overtures and by the expression of a Japanese preference for American rather than French good offices.

On the occasion of his regular diplomatic reception on April 5th, Delcassé remarked to the Japanese Minister, Motono, that the war had been the subject of his earnest consideration and that according to the most reliable information in his possession regarding the intentions of the Russian Government, he was "firmly convinced" that it would be possible for him to bring Russia and Japan together with a view to peace negotiations provided Japan would agree to eliminate certain conditions inadmissible by Russia. Delcassé explained that Russia would find the cession of Russian territory or the payment of indemnity too humiliating to be considered. He added that he himself did not ask for the Japanese terms of peace and he believed that they had better be discussed only in direct negotiations between the belligerents. The fact that five days earlier, March 31st, the German Emperor had disembarked at Tangier and proclaimed his hostility toward France would appear to be sufficient reason for this sudden overture of Delcassé.[1]

This important information was immediately reported to Tokio and five days later Motono, upon instruction from his government, asked Delcassé if he could confirm his belief that Russia was sincere in her desire for peace. Delcassé replied that he "entertained a firm conviction of Russia's sincere desire for peace," provided Japan would not propose the humiliating conditions already mentioned. Motono stated that Japan was pleased to know that France was in favour of direct negotiations and pointed out that in this approach from Delcassé Japan was actually being asked to agree to certain conditions in advance of the direct negotiations. In other words, Russia, while entering upon the negotiations unpledged, was seeking to obtain a pledge from Japan.

The Japanese Government appears to have given a week to the consideration of the subject and then decided to lay the matter before President Roosevelt. On April 18th, eight days after the second Delcassé-Motono interview, Takahira conveyed the information above to Secretary Taft, who was in charge of diplomatic affairs while Roosevelt made his combined speech-making and hunting trip in the Southwest and in Colorado. Minister Takahira requested Secretary Taft to inform Roosevelt of the developments. The Japanese Government wished the President to know that it "had no intention to close the door to friendly offices exerted purely for the purpose of bringing the belligerents together." On the contrary, they felt that "it is not unlikely that the friendly good offices of

---

[1]André Tardieu, "France and the Alliances," pp. 168 ff., supplies a chronological description of the Moroccan incident which is very useful at this point.

some Power might be necessary," although they were firmly convinced that the peace itself must be made by direct negotiations. This was practically an invitation to Roosevelt to come forward.

The text of the telegram to President Roosevelt was as follows:

White House, Washington, D. C.,
April 18, 1905.

Hon. Wm. Loeb, Jr.,
 Secy. to the President,
  Glenwood Springs, Colo.

Secretary Taft asks that the following be submitted to the President soon as possible. It is sent at request of Japanese Minister who would be glad to have the President's views:

"Strictly confidential. Summary of a telegram from Baron Komura to Mr. Takahira. On April fifth on the occasion of his regular diplomatic reception Monsieur Delcassé told Monsieur Motoss [Motono], Japanese Minister to France, that the Japan-Russian situation has been the subject of his constant consideration and that according to the most reliable information in his possession regarding the intention of the Russian Government he is firmly convinced that it would be possible for him to bring Japan and Russia together with a view to peace negotiations, provided that Japan would consent to eliminate from the negotiations certain conditions humiliating to Russia, namely, cession of Russian territory and payment of money indemnity. Monsieur Delcassé said in addition that he disclaimed all desire to be informed of terms of peace because he believed it better that they be discussed directly between the belligerents. On April tenth Monsieur Motoss [Motono] informed Monsieur Delcassé under instructions that as to the subject of direct negotiations his views precisely coincided with those of the Japanese Government and further asked him if he could confirm his belief regarding Russia's desire for peace. Monsieur Delcassé assured Monsieur Motoss [Motono] that he entertained a firm conviction of Russia's sincere desire for peace, provided that Japan would not propose the conditions above mentioned. On April thirteenth Monsieur Motoss [Motono] informed Monsieur Delcassé in pursuance of instructions that as the Japanese Government believed as before stated that the terms of peace should be discussed directly between the belligerents they naturally found themselves unable to consent in advance to any reservation as to the nature of their demand, and futher that as Russia would claim to enter upon the negotiations unpledged to accept Japan's terms, so Japan must remain equally free to present such terms as she deems just and proper. Referring to the above statement Monsieur Delcassé simply remarked that he did not know what consequences this communication of the Japanese Government might have upon the date of the opening of the peace negotiations. Communicate the above to the President in the strictest confidence, explaining at the same time that the Japanese Government have no intention to close the door to friendly offices exerted purely for the purpose of bringing the belligerents together. On the contrary the Japanese Government fully recognize that it is not unlikely that the friendly good offices of some Power might be necessary, but they are firmly convinced as they understand the President to share the same conviction, that any departure from the rule of direct negotiation regarding all the terms of peace would be exceedingly unwise and contrary to general interests."

B. F. BARNES, *Asst. Secy.*

Roosevelt replied immediately that he likewise was convinced of the wisdom of direct negotiations "as matters stand at present," having in mind presumably the

Moroccan incident, but beyond that he did not commit himself.[1] He wired:

Glenwood Springs, Colorado,
April 20, 1905.

HON. WM. H. TAFT,
Secretary of War,
Washington, D. C.

In the Japanese matter inform the Japanese Minister that as matters are at present it seems to me distinctly best that there should be direct negotiations between the Japanese and the Russian governments regarding all the terms of peace. As to what those terms should be, neither I nor any one else can at the moment definitely advise; but I am clear that at the present time the negotiations should be directly between Russia and Japan and should include all the possible terms of peace; it being of course understood that Japan is adhering to her position of maintaining the Open Door in Manchuria and of restoring it to China.

As regards Morocco I have written.

THEODORE ROOSEVELT.

Roosevelt's reply reached Tokio on the 21st and drew a response four days later in the form of a despatch from Baron Komura to Minister Takahira which the latter was requested to have conveyed to the President. It seemed to indicate a Japanese anxiety for peace. Secretary Taft felt that the message was of sufficient importance to warrant Mr. Loeb in sending it by special messenger to

---

[1] It is perhaps unfair to judge Baron Kaneko's version of how President Roosevelt came into the mediation from the summary of the Kaneko recollections in the *Japan Weekly Chronicle*, May 1 and 8, 1924. The *Chronicle* makes Kaneko convey the impression that Roosevelt offered his good offices on his own initiative. This impression is not at all supported by the texts of the telegrams given above.

Roosevelt, who was off in the mountains near Colorado Springs.

The only condition which Roosevelt had attached to his first reply to Japan was that the Open Door in Manchuria and the return of the area to China ought to have Japanese assent. Komura now replied that "Japan adheres to the position of maintaining Open Door in Manchuria and of restoring that province to China." Japan was thus committed in advance to the only two conditions of peace about which Roosevelt had hitherto expressed any great concern. Komura now invited Roosevelt to give his views in regard to the next step which should be taken, or "the measures to be adopted by Japan in order to pave the way for the inauguration of such negotiations." "You will ask the Secretary of War," said Komura to Takahira, "to transmit the above to the President by telegraph." The message was:

White House, Washington, D. C.,
April 25.

HON. WM. LOEB, JR.,
    Secy. to the President,
        Glenwood Springs, Colo.

Following just handed me by Secretary of War for the President:

"Japanese Minister has just handed me the following from Japanese Minister for Foreign Affairs: 'Confidential telegram received by Mr. Takahira from Baron Komura on the 25th April. Referring to your telegram of the 21st instant transmitting the telegram of the President you are hereby instructed to convey to the President through the Secretary of War cordial thanks of the Imperial Government for his observation and at the same time to declare that Japan adheres to [t]he position of maintaining Open Door in Manchuria and of restoring that province to China. Further you will say that the Imperial Government, finding that the views of the President coincide with their own on the subject of direct negotiations, would be highly gratified if he has any views of which he is willing or feels at liberty to give them benefit in regard to the steps to be taken or the measures to be adopted by Japan in order to pave the way for the inauguration of such negotiation. You will ask the Secretary of War to transmit the above to the President by telegraph.' Seems to indicate Japanese anxiety to begin negotiations. Letter from Griscom to-day says Dennison of Japanese Foreign Office says they are anxious to effect peace through you. Japanese Minister asked that all his communications on the subject be kept secret because fear of jealousy of other Powers anxious to be intermediaries. Cassini has sulked ever since your departure. Would it be wise to suggest beginning through him or through Jusserand? Dispatch would show Japan willing to avoid naval battle and possibly to be less insistent on money indemnity." Secretary of War suggests that in his judgment this is worth special messenger and asks that you advise me when you receive this.

B. F. BARNES,
Assistant Secy.

The same day a letter from U. S. Minister Lloyd C. Griscom at Tokio brought the information that the Japanese Foreign Office, according to the statement of Mr. Dennison, its American adviser, was anxious to effect the peace through Roosevelt, and that it was really anxious for peace. Takahira asked Secretary Taft to keep all of the communications secret because of the fear of the jealousy of other Powers anxious to become the intermediaries. Mr. Taft added his personal comment that Count Cassini had been sulking ever since Roosevelt left Washington, that Japan would appear to be willing to avoid a naval battle, and was possibly less insistent than formerly upon a money indemnity. He suggested that it might be wise to initiate negotiations through M. Jusserand, the French Ambassador, rather than through Cassini.

It required two days to get a reply from the President, who stated to Secretary Taft that he was "a good deal puzzled" by the last telegram. He had, however, determined to cut short his vacation and would leave Colorado May 8th rather than on the 15th, being careful to conceal the fact that he was hastening to Washington on account of the peace negotiations. Roosevelt expressed the opinion that there should be no reservations on either side, and suggested that Cassini and Takahira be brought together, as a preliminary step, "for an absolutely frank talk." He instructed Taft to suggest this plan to Takahira, and if the latter approved, to act accordingly. If Takahira did not approve, Taft was to telegraph Roosevelt and also tell Japan that the President would take the matter up as soon as possible after his return, which would be a matter of ten days.

The text of this message follows.

Colorado Hotel, Glenwood Springs, Colorado,
April 27, 1905.
7:05 P.M.

Hon. Wm. H. Taft,
  Secretary of War,
    Washington, D. C.

Am a good deal puzzled by your telegram, and, in view of it and the other information I receive, I shall come in from my hunt and start home Monday, May 8th, instead of May 15th, as I had intended. This will be put upon the ground of general condition of public business at Washington so as to avoid talk about the Russian-Japanese matter. Meanwhile, ask Japanese Minister whether it would not be advisable for you to see [Cassini] from [*sic*] me and say that, purely confidentially, with no one else to know at all, I have on my own motion directed you to go to him and see whether the two combatants cannot come together and negotiate peace, and it seems to me it would be better as a preliminary to have an absolutely frank talk between the representatives of the two Powers without any intermediary at all. If Japanese Minister approves of this, act accordingly. If not, wire me and, at the same time, tell the Japanese Minister that I shall take the matter up as soon as possible after I return to Washington.

THEODORE ROOSEVELT.

If Roosevelt had been in Washington at this time where he could have replied promptly and, what is more important, where he could have studied at closer range the developments of the Moroccan incident, he might have succeeded in devising an introduction to the negotiations which would have hastened the peace by a month or six weeks. Out in Colorado he was at a great disadvantage. The Japanese Government replied that conversations with a man of Cassini's known character would probably serve no purpose. They stated that by the time Roosevelt reached Washington the Japanese would be prepared to place in his hand a plan agreeable to them, for the inauguration of the negotiations. In delivering this message Takahira went further and intimated to Secretary Taft that in his judgment the Japanese Government was "ridiculously cautious." Takahira believed that Japan wished to end the war without a naval battle.   While the American public sentiment would, in Takahira's judgment, warrant the demand for indemnity and territory, he felt that to obtain an indemnity from Russia would require so much more fighting that the expenses would probably consume any amount which Russia might eventually be made to pay.   Takahira wished that Roosevelt would advise Japan against asking for an indemnity and thought that such advice would "greatly strengthen the peace party" in Japan.

The communication from the Japanese Minister was as follows:

WHITE HOUSE, WASHINGTON, D. C.
May 2.

THE PRESIDENT,
Glenwood Springs, Colo.

Japanese Minister has just handed me the following dispatch:

"TAKAHIRA.   Your telegram of April 28th received.   You are hereby instructed to request the Secretary of War to telegraph to the President in the following sense:

"'Japanese Government appreciate very highly the President's message and his willingness to sacrifice the remainder of his well-earned holiday in the interests of peace.   Japanese Government entertain serious doubt whether the course of procedure that suggests itself to the President would contribute to the desired end.   In the first place, having regard to the known views and temperament of Count Cassini, Japanese Government cannot believe that his coöperation would tend to bring the belligerents together for the purpose of peace negotiations, nor can Japanese Government think that an interview between him and Mr. Takahira would be productive of any good result.   Japanese Government, however, gather from the

183

President's message that he is of opinion that the time has arrived when 'the question of negotiations for peace may be approached with some hope of successful issue. Japanese Government share that view and wishing themselves to contribute as far as possible to the desired result they hope they will be in a position to submit to the President after his return to Washington a plan of procedure which they believe may be followed with advantage and of which they will be gratified to have the benefit of his views.'

"BARON KOMURA."

Japanese Minister then intimated that his Government was in his judgment ridiculously cautious in not stating more fully the letter of exact purpose. He inferred that his government wished the war to close before a naval battle in order that Russia might make peace with honour. He said that he had advised his government that popular sentiment in this country would support the demand of an indemnity and territory, but he said as this would continue the war and perhaps consume all the indemnity he was not so certain now of the wisdom of demanding indemnity. He dwelt on the fact that you had not expressed opinion as to indemnity and territory as having much influence with his government, and suggested that if you would give your views in answer to this dispatch as to the wisdom of peace without indemnity or territory [it] would have a marked effect. He says that there are elements at home anxious to prolong the war and others in favour of peace and that your attitude would greatly strengthen the peace party. He said that in his view by taking Port Arthur and driving Russia out of Manchuria and gaining control of the railroad Japan had accomplished her whole purpose and peace ought now to come. These were his personal views but he gave them to throw light on the situation.

Saw Durand a second time after he had heard from Lansdowne. Lansdowne said that England did not intend to attack Germany and on the other hand did not fear an attack from

Germany, because she was not strong enough on the sea. He said that France had acted in a most conciliatory way toward Germany under the greatest provocation. He said that they in England were quite familiar with the vagaries of the German Emperor and understood how your anxiety might be aroused by his extraordinary suspicions and unfounded imaginings. He said that England was not going to do anything in Morocco; that she expected to leave action as to local conditions to France who was natural guardian of the peace of that country. Durand added in answer to my question in respect to the French proposals to the Sultan of Morocco that he did not know what they were: that France would probably not submit them to England as the latter had no doubt that no one of them would intrude on England's and other nations' right to the Open Door. This morning's dispatches show further explanation, confirmation, and support by the English Minister to Morocco of French proposals. Durand expressed gratitude for your interest. Communicated result of my interview to Speck.

TAFT.

Thus by the second of May, more than a month before the actual intervention of President Roosevelt took place, the Japanese Government had by its own choice taken the question of good offices out of the hands of Delcassé and given the opportunity to Roosevelt. Within a few days, of course, events in Europe transpired to make improbable that Delcassé would ever have been able to be of service. His resignation was being forced upon the French Government by Germany and took place June 6th.[1]

We are thus left only partially in doubt as to why no important advances toward peace were made between May 2d and June 6th. There were the two parties in

---

[1]Stuart, "French Foreign Policy," p. 189, and the entire Chap. VII, "The Fall of Delcassé."

Japan, one able to see that a fight for indemnity was not worth while, the other confident that Japan would eventually be able to exact compliance with the full list of terms. In Russia there was the inflexible determination not to yield either territory or indemnity, buoyed up by the hope that the approaching naval battle would place Russia in a more favourable military position. There is no evidence, at least none in the Roosevelt Papers, to indicate that Japan delayed the peace in order to watch the development of the Moroccan affair. It is obvious, however, that if Germany had declared war on France in May, as for a few days seemed at least possible, Russia would have been placed in a still more unfavourable position toward Japan. France would have been wholly unable to give further financial support to Russia. Russia would have been isolated except for Germany, and naturally the more willing to make peace and give attention to matters nearer home. It is of course possible that Japan was also taking time to weigh more carefully the possibilities of a Russian revolution.[1] At any rate, confidence returned to Japan and the delay would appear to have been completely justified by the victory in the battle of the Sea of Japan, May 26th–27th.

The German Emperor watched the situation closely and on May 19th referring again to the Paris plot which he had revealed in January communicated to Roosevelt through Sternberg the information that the Tsar was

---

[1]"That the Japanese had money distributed among Russian revolutionists of a certain grade and that considerable sums were laid out in this way is, I am bound to say, certain, just as German money has been circulated among them ever since August, 1914. I know the names of some of those who distributed it." Dillon, "Eclipse of Russia," p. 184; see also Rosen, "Forty Years of Diplomacy," Vol. I, p. 255. The late Baron Korff confirmed this assertion in a personal statement to the writer.

"most anxious" that Roosevelt rather than Anglo-French instruments be the means of initiating the peace negotiations. The Kaiser asserted that the Tsar did not wish to yield to Delcassé, and the Kaiser himself felt that for Delcassé to be the medium of communications would "mean a step nearer to the triple (or quadruple) alliance in the Far East." It is difficult to know how much credence could safely be given to such a report, but there is nothing to make it appear impossible. Thus, more than two weeks before Roosevelt actually undertook the task of bringing the belligerents together, not only Japan but Russia and Germany would appear to have selected him as peacemaker.

Roosevelt did not press matters. He had already conveyed to both sides his personal opinion that peace should be made.[1] On May 13th, in a letter to Cecil Spring-Rice which was largely devoted to the Moroccan question, he added:

To turn to matters of more immediate importance, I am of course watching to see what the Russian and Japanese fleets will do in Eastern waters. France has obligingly given the Russians a base, but she may have to take it away from them. The Russian fleet is materially somewhat stronger than the Japanese. My own belief is that the Japanese superiority in morale and training will more than offset this. But I am not sure and I wish that peace would come. Personally I wish that Japan had made peace on the conditions she originally thought of after Mukden was fought; as I pointed out to her government, a few months' extra war would eat up all the indemnity she could possibly expect Russia to pay. Just at the moment Russia was riding a high horse and would not talk peace.

---

[1]Bishop, Vol. I, p. 378, gives a letter addressed to John Hay April 2d, in which Roosevelt mentions having conveyed such views to both Cassini and Takahira, as well as to Sternberg, Durand, and Jusserand, presumably shortly after the battle of Mukden.

Eleven days later (May 24th), he wrote to Ambassador Meyer that the Japanese appeared to be perfectly confident and were giving no hint that they would abate their terms. Roosevelt said that if he were a Russian he would not agree to an indemnity or to a cession of territory.

The Russians, on the other hand [he continued], are very much elated and will advance nothing in the way of terms which the Japanese will even consider. So I guess there is nothing to do but to watch for them to fight it out.

"The Tsar is a preposterous little creature," Roosevelt had written to Hay several weeks before,[1] "as the autocrat of 150,000,000 people. He has been unable to make war, and now he is unable to make peace."

Contemporary Comment

"Calchas," "The War and the Powers," *Fortnightly Review*, March, 1904.
"It is clear that the first attempt at diplomatic intervention is likely to be made by France and Germany in concert, acting upon a common understanding with St. Petersburg as to the proposals to be put forward as a basis of peace." Predicts a congress at Washington or Paris on the model of the Berlin Congress of 1878.

Alfred Stead, "Japan and Peace," *Fortnightly Review*, June, 1905.
"The unique position of irresponsibility in international affairs occupied by the United States marked out the President as the most effective mouthpiece for international opinion. The reason for the peace movement is easily found. It is because of the growth of the 'German Peril' or rather the 'Kaiser Peril.'"

---

[1]Bishop, Vol. I, p. 379.

CHAPTER IX

Good Offices

THE battle of the Sea of Japan and the new impetus to the constitutional or revolutionary movement in Russia which followed the news of the Russian naval disaster materially altered the situation. The net effect was greatly to increase Japanese confidence.

The peace parleys, first introduced by M. Delcassé in Paris on April 5th, were never allowed by the Japanese entirely to lapse. The correspondence continued throughout May and on the last day of the month Japan formally and definitely asked President Roosevelt "directly and of his own motion and initiative to invite the two belligerents to come together for the purpose of direct negotiations."[1]

This was the action for which the President had been waiting patiently. For those who have regarded Roosevelt's intervention as either precipitate or uncalled-for by either party it may be observed that forty-one days had elapsed since the first overtures to him from Japan, and ten days had elapsed since the German Emperor had con-

[1]Takahira to Roosevelt, May 31, 1905, Appendix A, pp. 215-16.

There are no less than twenty-two official communications which are essential to an understanding of the part taken by President Roosevelt in the peace negotiations and the resulting treaty. To insert them in the text of the book might annoy rather than assist the reader as well as the student. They are therefore gathered as appendices to this and the following chapter. These two chapters therefore comprise both a narrative and a documentary record of the subject. It is hoped that the collection of the documents thus given at the end of the chapters will invite rather than discourage the reader. The documents do not lack the human and dramatic interest which characterizes the less formal correspondence.

veyed the information that Russia likewise desired that the first steps be taken by the President.

A second aspect of the case was disclosed in a telegram from Ambassador Meyer on June 2d. Hitherto Meyer had not taken the revolutionary movement in Russia very seriously. At least, he had not reported it as a probable important factor in making peace. Now he was evidently impressed. The criticism of the press directed at the Government was remarkable. Indignation and wrath were poured out upon the bureaucracy which was "alone held responsible for all misfortunes of war." There was a demand, not so much for peace as for the calling of a representative assembly. The ambassador thought the great mass of Russians regarded the war as futile, but he did not believe that the nation was "ripe for revolution"; it had been reported that at a palace conference one party favoured a continuance of the war for five years if necessary, while the other wished, at a proper time, to accept the good offices of Delcassé.[1]

The German Emperor watched the domestic disturbances in Russia. On the third of June he resumed his correspondence with the Tsar after a lapse of two and one half months, and candidly stated, though with some circumlocution, that the naval defeat had put an end to the chances of a Russian victory.[2] He invited the attention of the Tsar to the fact that President Roosevelt might be in a position to influence Japan to moderate her peace terms.[3]

---

[1]Meyer to Adee, June 2, 1905, Appendix B, p. 217.

[2]Levine, pp. 172-75.

[3]For the Kaiser's own account of how he broached the subject see Howe's "Meyer," p. 212. Practically all of Meyer's weekly letters to Roosevelt are printed in this volume, which becomes an important source not only for the close of the Russo-Japanese War but also for European politics in 1903-06.

GOOD OFFICES

The same day the German Government sent a message to Roosevelt through Sternberg that "in the interest of all concerned" the Emperor thought Russia ought to effect peace. The Kaiser was ready "to silently support any effort which you may feel inclined to make in the interests of peace." The next day the Emperor followed the message with another one through Ambassador Tower which betrayed signs of panic.[1] He considered the situation in St. Petersburg so serious that when the truth should become known in regard to the recent defeat, the life of the Tsar would be in danger. The Kaiser repeated that he was pointing out to the Tsar that President Roosevelt was the person to persuade Japan to make reasonable proposals for peace.

"This did not meet my views," explained Roosevelt to Lodge in a highly confidential letter of June 5th, "for I did not desire to be asked to squeeze out of Japan terms favourable to Russia." Meanwhile he had obtained from the Marquis of Lansdowne a somewhat non-committal memorandum which at least had the virtue that it interposed no objections to peace.[2] Roosevelt was now in an unassailable position. He would meet with no obstacles from England; France was then in convulsions over the Delcassé policy; the German Emperor was urgent; and Japan had definitely requested him to undertake the task of bringing the belligerents together.

In the two Lodge letters, June 5th and June 16th, President Roosevelt brought together nearly all of the important documents related to the efforts of the first two weeks

[1] Tower to Roosevelt, June 4, 1905; also letter of Tower to Roosevelt, June 9th, and Kaiser to Tower, June 4th, Appendix C, pp. 217-20.

[2] June 3, 1905, telegram from Marquis of Lansdowne, presumably delivered through the British Embassy. See pp. 210-11.

of June and added to them his own illuminating as well
as entertaining comments.   We shall follow the course of
events as far as possible through these two letters, placing
at the end of the chapter the documents which he included
in the letters as much for purposes of record, perhaps,
as for the information of his friend.[1]

I was amused by the way in which *they* asked me to invite the
two belligerents together directly on my own motion and initiative.   It reminded me of the request for contributions sent by
campaign committees to office-holders wherein they are asked
to make a voluntary contribution of ten per cent. of their
salaries.   It showed a certain *naïveté* on the part of the Japanese.
I then saw Cassini and made the proposition to him.   Cassini
answered by his usual rigmarole, to the effect that Russia was
fighting the battles of the white race (to which I responded by
asking him why in that case she had treated the other members
of the white race even worse than she had treated Japan); that
Russia was too great to admit defeat, and so forth and so forth.
However, I spoke to him pretty emphatically, and he said he
would communicate my views to his home government and find
out if they were agreeable to my request.   Meanwhile I had
been keeping in touch with Speck and Jusserand and suddenly
received an. indication of what the Kaiser was doing.   I sent
you a copy of his telegram in my last letter.   Partly because
of this telegram, and also partly because I could not be sure that
Cassini would really tell his home government what I had been
doing or Lamsdorff would tell the Tsar what I wished, I made up
my mind to have Meyer see the Tsar in person, and I sent him
the cable about which I wrote you in my last letter.

The instruction to Ambassador Meyer was to see the
Tsar personally and urge him to consent to direct negotia-

[1] These two letters form the basis for Chap. XXXI, Vol. I, of Bishop.

tions.[1] Meyer was to say for the President that he regarded the present contest as "absolutely hopeless" and
that to continue it could only result in the loss of all
Russia's possessions in eastern Asia. The President
offered, provided the Tsar was willing, to seek to get Japan's consent, "acting simply on his own initiative," and
he promised to keep absolutely secret the Tsar's assent
so that nothing would be made public until Japan also
agreed. If the two Powers would first approve privately
then he would openly ask both Powers to agree to a meeting. Roosevelt suggested some place between Harbin and
Mukden as suitable.

The manner in which Ambassador Meyer conveyed this
message to the Tsar was both dramatic and pathetic.[2]
It was the Tsarina's birthday. Only the fact that the
ambassador bore a message from the President would have
overcome Lamsdorff's jealous care that his sovereigns
should have a happy fête. Meyer wrote:

I arrived at Tsarskoë Selò shortly before two o'clock (June
6th), entered the Palace by a private entrance, and was taken,
without formality, to the waiting room adjoining the Emperor's
study. Promptly at two o'clock the door of the study was
opened and the Tsar came forward to meet me and received me
very cordially. I thanked His Majesty in your behalf for receiving me on such a day, saying I realized it was the birthday
of the Empress. He invited me at once to be seated near him at
his desk.

It was the first time that Meyer had seen the Tsar alone,
for either the Tsarina or Lamsdorff watched his audiences
with evident concern.

---

[1]June 5, Memo. for State Dept., Appendix D, pp. 221-22.
[2]This is described in Meyer's letter of June 9th, Howe's "Meyer," pp. 157-62.

ROOSEVELT AND THE RUSSO–JAPANESE WAR

Ambassador Meyer first delivered his message orally. The Emperor asked for time to consider, the very thing which Meyer wished most to avoid. Then the Ambassador took out the instruction and read it sentence by sentence. There was no reply. Meyer continued with as much tact as force. He played on the Emperor's conscience, on his vanity, and on his fears. He drew a parallel from history. He called attention to the internal affairs of the state, and he reminded him of the condition of Russia's credit. At length the Tsar yielded and then suddenly confessed: "You have come at a psychological moment; as yet no foot has been placed on Russian soil; but I realize that at almost any moment they can make an attack on Sakhalin. Therefore it is important that the meeting should take place before that occurs." Notwithstanding this evidence of eagerness, the Tsar wished above all else that the fact of his consent be kept secret until Japan's answer had become known.

My audience had already lasted an hour [wrote Meyer], and having gained his consent without any conditions other than those in your instructions, contrary to all customs I asked leave, before His Majesty made the move, to depart in order to cable at once to Washington, fearing that on further consideration the Tsar might make some changes in the plan. The Emperor then shook hands warmly and said with some feeling: "Say to your President I certainly hope that the old friendship which has previously existed and united the two nations for so long a period will be renewed. I realize that whatever difference has arisen is due to the press, and in no way to your government."

While the Emperor is not a man of force I was impressed with his self-possession.

GOOD OFFICES

The telegram from Meyer containing the Tsar's assent was received in Washington, June 7th.[1]

I then had a perfectly characteristic experience [wrote Roosevelt], showing the utterly loose way in which the Russian Government works. On June sixth, Cassini showed me a despatch from his government in which they declined my proposition; or rather did not answer it at all, but said that they would not ask either peace or mediation, but asked me to exercise a moderating influence on the demands of Japan, and to find out what these demands were. Of course, the telegram from Meyer directly contradicted the despatch to Cassini.

Cassini was not notified of this and insisted that Meyer had misquoted the Tsar and got his words wrong. I had this statement cabled over to Meyer, who got the authority of Lamsdorff to say that he had quoted the Tsar correctly and that his (Meyer's) despatch, which was shown to Lamsdorff, was an accurate account of what had been said. Cassini's words were that Meyer "might have misinterpreted or forgotten what the Emperor had said." He told this to Cal O'Laughlin, a very good little fellow, whom he has been using as a means of communicating with me, with Speck, and with Takahira, as regards these peace matters. Is not this characteristically Russian? Cassini also sent various other messages to me by O'Laughlin, including a protest against my seeing so much of the Japanese Minister and of the representatives of the neutral Powers. I told O'Laughlin that I regarded this protest as impertinent, and requested that Cassini would not repeat it. He also protested that I was trying to make Russia move too quickly, and was very indignant over my order interning the Russian ships at Manila, saying "This is not the time to establish new principles of international law." As you probably saw, I had declined to allow the Russian ships to make any re-

[1] Meyer to Secretary of State, June 7, 1905; Cassini to Roosevelt, June 6, 1905; Appendix E, see pp. 222-23.

pairs that were rendered necessary by the results of the battle, and then had them interned. I informed Cassini that it was precisely the right time to establish a new principle of international law, when the principle was a good one, and that the principle is now (?) established.[1]

The Tsar's assent to the invitation for peace negotiations having been confirmed and Japan's assent having been included in the formal request of May 31st, the way was now clear for the formal invitation which was made on June 8th, and given to the press two days later. It has been customary to take these identical notes as the starting point for a narrative of the intervention, a fact which no doubt gave rise to the impression that Roosevelt was acting hastily.

The notes of June 8th expressed the President's conviction that the time had come to make some efforts "in the interests of mankind" to end the "terrible and lamentable conflict."[2] The President accordingly urged the Russian and the Japanese governments "not only for their own sakes but in the interests of the whole civilized world, to open direct negotiations for peace with one another." The President offered to do what he could to arrange the preliminaries as to the time and place of meeting in case the two Powers were unable to effect these arrangements directly between themselves. The sole purpose of the offer was "to bring about a meeting which the whole civilized world will pray may result in peace."

[1]Following the battle of the Sea of Japan three Russian war vessels sought asylum at Manila. All three were in need of repairs. The American Government declined to permit the repairs to be made on the ground that such permission would virtually be allowing Russia to augment her naval force in a neutral port. This application of international law was not new. The vessels were interned June 8th, five days after their arrival. Moore's "Digest," Vol. VII, pp. 992-94.

[2]State Dept. to Meyer, June 8, 1905. Appendix F, pp. 224-25.

GOOD OFFICES

President Roosevelt's strategy would appear to have been to place the belligerents, with their consent, in a position where the further obstruction of negotiations by either party, or exorbitant demands, would immediately place the burden of reproach for the continuance of the war publicly upon the responsible party. No more skilful check on the war parties in both countries could have been devised. Even on September 5th, when the treaty was signed, Roosevelt still retained one last arrow in his quiver, and there is some reason for believing that he may have prepared it for use in case no other measures had succeeded in keeping the conference in session until the treaty was actually signed. He could have released to the press a considerable amount of correspondence, not all of it, but enough to locate clearly the guilt of the responsible parties.[1] Roosevelt, in his narrative of June 16th, continues:

Then Cassini must have been told by his government what had happened, for he called upon me and notified me that the Russian Government thanked me and adopted my suggestion. I am inclined to think that up to the time he had received the message which he then communicated to me, his government had told him nothing whatever as to their attitude toward peace.

Now occurred a rather exasperating incident.

Both governments had accepted.[2] The Japanese agreed to appoint plenipotentiaries "for the purpose of negotiating and concluding terms of peace." Cassini's verbal statement had been just as unreserved, but in the formal reply of June 12th Lamsdorff returned to his accustomed

[1]In the Roosevelt Papers one finds that a number of the important letters had been copied on the typewriter with a number of copies suitable for distribution to selected members of the press. These copies carry no indication as to their intended use.

[2]Text of Japanese acceptance. Appendix G, pp. 225–26.

ways of fogging the question with verbiage.[1] He stated that His August Majesty had found in the note a new proof of the traditional friendship which united the two countries, but he clearly failed to commit Russia to a peace conference. Lamsdorff wrote:

> With regard to the eventual meeting of Russian and Japanese plenipotentiaries, "in order to see if it is not possible for the two Powers to agree to terms of peace" the Imperial Government has no objection in principle to this endeavour if the Japanese Government expresses a like desire.

The words quoted in Lamsdorff's message were taken from Roosevelt's formal invitation and had the effect of distorting the proposition into something which might turn out to be very different from a sincere peace conference.

> This note [commented Roosevelt] is of course much less satisfactory than Japan's for it showed a certain slyness and an endeavour to avoid anything like a definite committal, which most naturally irritated Japan, while at the same time as it used the very words of my identical note it did not offer grounds for backing out of the negotiations. But Japan now started to play the fool. It sent a request for me to get a categorical answer from Russia as to whether she would appoint plenipotentiaries who would have full power to make peace, and hinted that otherwise Japan did not care for the meeting. Meanwhile Russia had proposed Paris for the place of meeting, and Japan, Chefoo.[2] Each declined to accept the other's prop-

---

[1]Text of Russian reply. Appendix H, p. 226.

[2]In this selection of places for the meeting one hardly knows whether to admire the cleverness of Russia or that of Japan more. Paris would have provided the setting most favourable for Russia to make use of European intrigue; Chefoo would have afforded Japan the opportunity to demonstrate in the very presence of China its defeat of the great Russian Empire, and would doubtless increase Japanese prestige in all eastern Asia even more than did the conference at Portsmouth.

osition. I then made a counter proposition of The Hague, which was transmitted to both governments. It was crossed, however, by a proposition from Russia that the meeting should take place in Washington.[1] Japan answered my proposition, positively declining to go to Europe and expressing its preference for the United States, as being halfway between Europe and Asia. Russia having first suggested Washington I promptly closed and notified both Japan and Russia that I had thus accepted Washington.

Meanwhile Roosevelt obtained from Cassini assurances that notwithstanding the evasive character of Lamsdorff's reply of June 12th, Russia intended to send plenipotentiaries clothed with full powers.

But no sooner were Japan's fears quieted than Russia again raised obstacles. Lamsdorff still clung to the idea that the conference could be held at The Hague notwithstanding Japan's refusal to go to Europe, and even after he had expressed a willingness for Washington in case Paris was rejected. This information was conveyed to Roosevelt in a telegram on the 16th and drew from Roosevelt a very forceful reply.[2] What was going on in St. Petersburg may best be described in the words of Ambassador Meyer himself, to whom belongs the credit of having forced Count Lamsdorff to retreat again:[3]

Yesterday and the day before I had two heated discussions with the Minister of Foreign Affairs. However, as we carry them on in French, it makes them seem always more polite. The fact that you cabled me the Lamsdorff instructions to

---

[1]In justice to Lamsdorff it ought to be stated that his suggestion of Washington was not quite so positive as Roosevelt's assertion of it. Lamsdorff, June 13th, still expressed a preference for Paris but remarked that Washington would be his next choice.

[2]Appendix I, pp. 226–29.

[3]June 18, 1905, Meyer to Roosevelt. Howe's "Meyer," pp. 167–70.

Cassini was a great assistance, because I could not get it out of him the day before, when he implied that Cassini had made a mistake and gone beyond his instructions. I said it was time that he recalled Cassini at once if the President could not rely on what he said. I could not make Lamsdorff realize that, after Washington had been decided upon, it was outrageous of him endeavouring to force you to reverse your action, your decision having been made on the instructions to Cassini and which I compelled him to acknowledge had been approved by the Tsar. Even then he said: "Why should we not reconsider, as The Hague is better for many reasons?" As it made no impression on him that Japan had refused and you had announced it to the world, I was obliged to tell him that in America when we gave our word we abided by it, and that if he did not decide to abide by Washington I should be compelled to carry it personally before the Emperor. This did not meet with his view at all, and he answered that it was not customary for the Emperor to give audiences weekly to an Ambassador.

I have discovered that the bureaucracy was not at all pleased that I was able to carry through so quickly with the Emperor the question of accepting your invitation; and as I have been up against them the last two days, I realize now how the Emperor is hampered and how much is kept from him.

In the end Lamsdorff gave way with his usual grace, and Cassini, in his final acceptance of Washington as the place of meeting, ascribed the entire trouble to the newspaper publication of rumours!

While this dispute was taking place President Roosevelt improved the opportunity to administer a wholesome rebuke to Japan.[1] He considered it "most unwise for Japan to hang back or raise questions" over the wording of a note.

---

[1]Appendix J, pp. 229–31.

GOOD OFFICES

He cautioned the Japanese that Japan had already won American public sentiment by its frank and straightforward conduct, and that this valuable support could easily be lost by needless haggling over non-essentials. He reminded Japan that the "force of events," once the two parties came together, would be a powerful factor in making peace.

Meanwhile [wrote Roosevelt, June 16th], I have been explaining at length to both Russia and Japan the folly of haggling over details. I have treated both Takahira and Cassini with entire frankness, saying the same things in effect to each, except that I have of course concealed from every one—literally every one—the fact that I acted in the first place on Japan's suggestion. I told Russia that it was nonsense for her to stick at trifles, but if the war went on she would lose all her possessions in eastern Asia and that the blow to her would be well-nigh irreparable; that while I had not sympathized with her at the outset I should be very sorry, because of my real regard for the Russian people and because of my regard for the interests of the world generally, to see her driven out of territory which had been hers for a couple of centuries; and that I hoped she would make up her mind that she would have to make concessions in order to obtain peace because her military position was now hopeless, and that however future wars might come out this war was assuredly a failure. To the Japanese I have said that if they made such terms that Russia would prefer to fight for another year, they would without doubt get all eastern Siberia, but that in my opinion it would be an utterly valueless possession to them, while they would make of Russia an enemy whose hostility would endure as long as the nation herself existed, and that to achieve this result at the cost of an additional year of loss of blood and money and consequent strain upon Japanese resources seems to me to be wholly useless. Japan now has

Port Arthur and Korea and the dominance in Manchuria, and I should feel that the less she asked for in addition the better it would be. I also told them that if I were in their place I should cheerfully have accepted Russia's proposition to go to The Hague, or for the matter of that to go to Paris, because I should have been only too glad to give Russia the shell as long as I kept the kernel. The latter expression, by the way, interested Takahira very much and I had to explain at some length what I meant.

In short, the more I see of the Tsar, the Kaiser, and the Mikado, the better I am content with democracy, even if we have to include the American newspaper as one of its assets— liability would be a better word. . . . I should not be surprised if the peace negotiations broke off at any moment. . . .

The significant aspect of Roosevelt's policy during the middle of June was that he plainly believed that he was intervening to prevent Russia from being driven out of all eastern Asia. This was not only the argument which he put forward to the Russian Government but also the one which he repeated many times to his closest personal friends.[1]

While President Roosevelt sought to avoid the unpleasant rôle assigned to him by the German Emperor and the Tsar of squeezing favourable terms out of Japan, he was none the less impressed with the fact that the peace parleys might easily be wrecked if Japan put forward exorbitant demands. As in Russia, so in Japan there was a war party as well as a peace party. Minister Takahira had already disclosed the fact that he belonged to the latter.[2] The official memorandum of June 3d from Japan,[3] while

[1]Roosevelt took this position in July in his interviews with Baron Rosen ("Forty Years of Diplomacy," Vol. I, p. 260).

[2]See p. 184.

[3]Appendix A, p. 215.

vague, had seemed to intimate that the moderates were still in control of the Japanese councils. The memorandum stated that

the demand to be formulated by Japan will only be commensurate with the original objects to be obtained, and even in the sequel of the decisive battles of Mukden and the Japan Sea, she has no intention of demanding anything excessive. . . . The demand for territorial cession will be limited to Sakhalin and the indemnity to be demanded will be moderate and reasonable. . . .

As late as June 11th Minister Takahira betrayed to Sternberg that he had some doubts as to the indemnity. "Do you think we are entitled to an indemnity?" he asked.[1] It was repeatedly stated, on the other hand, both to Ambassador Meyer in St. Petersburg and through the Russian representatives elsewhere, that Russia would not consent either to cession or indemnity. There was prospect of a deadlock, unless Japan could be induced to reduce her terms.

The radical party in Japan, led by such men as Count Okuma, was gaining ground. "It is really very interesting," observed the *China Review* (June 7, 1905), "to note the absolute unanimity with which politicians, press, and public alike in Japan view the certainty of their retention of Korea and Manchuria. . . ." The *Review* then gave a summary of a recent article by Count Okuma in the *Taiyo* in which he had pointed out how Japan might pay for the war in Korea and Manchuria and asserted that Japan must take such a course in these two regions as would bring sufficient compensation for war losses. On June

[1]Sternberg to Roosevelt, June 11, 1905.

28th the Constitutionalist (*Seiyukai*) and Progressive (*Shimpoto*) parties in Japan both passed resolutions relative to the coming conference for peace. Neither party's declaration could be very assuring to Roosevelt.[1]

The Constitutionalist party declared:

Yet the acquisition of territory, the receipt of an indemnity, and the definite solution of all questions regarding Korea and Manchuria that relate to the future security of the rights and interests of our Empire and the preservation of the permanent peace of the Far East, must, in compliance with the Imperial Rescript declaring war, be effected.[2]

The Progressive party, then not in power and led by Count Okuma, was more specific and less modest in its demands:

If therefore peace is now to be reëstablished we must demand an indemnity sufficient to cover the loss that we have sustained, the cession of territory important enough to guarantee the peace of the Far East, and the prohibition of any military enterprises at points that menace our national safety. Korea is already under our protection and our actual power in Manchuria is recognized by the Powers. It is therefore reasonable to demand that Russia abandon her privileges in Korea and Manchuria and be prevented from interfering in our enterprises there. As China's inability to defend herself has often been the cause of trouble to her neighbours, Russia must at this juncture be required to abstain from any undertaking likely to menace the Chinese frontiers, thus removing the possibility of international complications in this connection.

[1]Griscom to Hay, June 29, 1905, enclosed in Adee to Barnes, July 18th.

[2]Text of Imperial Rescript, pp. 145–46. The purpose of the war was declared to be, to effect the security of Japanese imperial interests by the preservation of the integrity of Korea and by driving Russia out of Manchuria.

GOOD OFFICES

The Japanese Government was slow in formulating the terms to be demanded at Portsmouth, but they were increased with each week of delay.

The rapid maturing of the revolutionary movement in Russia at the end of June and in July appeared to be a happy circumstance for Japan.

In the last days of June the sailors and some of the officers on the *Knyaz Potemkin* at Odessa mutinied and took possession of the ship. The ostensible cause was a dispute over the rations, but it soon became known that it was an actual expression of a revolutionary movement which was also showing itself in strikes at Lodz, Libau, and in many industrial centres. Ambassador Meyer telegraphed (July 3d):[1]

I have believed heretofore that revolution in Russia [is] improbable but events of the past week have altered conditions and aspects. Increasing strikes; the disturbances in Lodz; the arousing by the Socialists of both the marines in Libau [and] the sailors in Odessa to a successful mutiny show progress made by revolutionists. There is general dissatisfaction among the people over last mobilization; [it is] felt that these troops will refuse to act in case of disturbances. Should Japan refuse armistice and inflict severe defeat on Russian Army [it is] impossible to foretell what conditions and events might follow, due to the state of mind of the people and the incompetency of the Government.[2]

---

[1] Meyer to Secretary of State, July 3, 1905; see also Meyer's letters of July 1st and 8th in Howe's "Meyer," pp. 173–75.

[2] Russia had requested Roosevelt to ask Japan for an armistice. After some delay, in spite of Roosevelt's arguments in its favour, Russia's request was refused. The fact, however, that Japan did not follow up this favourable opportunity and make a further attack on Russia in Manchuria appears to have revealed to Roosevelt for the first time that the Japanese Army was not in as favourable condition as had been supposed. See Roosevelt to Kennan, Oct. 15, 1905, below, p. 282.

Minister Takahira conveyed to Roosevelt the information
July 8th, which had reached him from the Japanese representative at Berlin, who had his information from the
St. Petersburg correspondent of the *Vossische Zeitung*,
that Russia was no longer in a position to question either
the cession of territory or the indemnity. At this time
the odds were all in favour of Japan, and as early as June
29th even Cassini had admitted to Mr. O'Laughlin that
Japan had the luck of the devil. The Russian plenipotentiaries would have to make concessions which would
otherwise be refused while the very compliance with
Japanese demands would serve as a still further club in
the hands of the revolutionists in Russia.[1]

At some time previous to the opening of the conference
at Portsmouth President Roosevelt came into possession
of the formal statement of Japan's terms of peace. The
exact date is not very important for they are summarized
here[2] to be contrasted with the rather vague and timid
proposals which had been discussed early in June. There
were thirteen articles. They included, among the more
important items not previously mentioned, the following:

> Japan to restore Manchuria to China "subject to
> the guarantee of reform and improved administra-
> tion."
> The transfer and assignment to Japan of the lease of
> the Liaotung Peninsula, as well as the Harbin-Port
> Arthur railway.

---

[1] J. C. O'Laughlin to Roosevelt, June 29, 1905. Roosevelt had already credited O'Laughlin with
being a messenger very useful to Cassini (see p. 195) but he had omitted to state that the messenger was probably even more useful to the President.

[2] Printed in full, Appendix K, pp. 231-32.

The cession of Sakhalin and the appurtenant islands.

An indemnity sufficient to cover the actual expenses of the war.

The dismantling of Vladivostok and the admission of a Japanese consul.

The limitation of Russian naval strength in the Extreme East to . . . tons.

The surrender to Japan of all interned Russian war vessels which had sought asylum in neutral ports in consequence of injuries received in battle.

Full fishing rights along the coasts, bays, harbours, inlets, and rivers in the Japan, Okhotsk, and Bering seas.

These demands, it will be seen, went far beyond even the extreme programme of the Progressive party of June 28th. While it did not break faith with the preliminary promise which Japan had made to Roosevelt April 25th, to respect the integrity of China, it did place restrictions upon the return of Manchuria to China which would permit Japan to exercise after the signing of the peace more influence than she had been able to exercise in Korea from 1898 to the beginning of the war, and almost as much as was included in the Japan-Korea protocol of February 23, 1904.

The German Emperor intimated to Roosevelt that both France and Great Britain, particularly the latter, desired the approaching peace negotiations to fail in order to give these two Powers an opportunity to come forward again with their suspected plan of January, 1905, and then to demand compensations which would amount to the dismemberment of China. On July 8th, the Kaiser, then on his memorable cruise in the North Sea, transmitted to Ambassador Tower a letter, parts of which were forwarded to the President.[1]

So far as I am informed [wrote the Kaiser] all the Powers on the Continent hope fervently that the President may succeed and lend their help. There is but one Power, not on the Continent, which I am afraid will hold aloof and create difficulties even for the great work that the President is so ardently pursuing for the benefit of the whole world.

Ambassador Tower, whose relations to the Emperor appear almost childlike, believed that he was able to define more specifically the exact character of the plot with which England was thus being charged. Prince von Bülow, returning from a conference, also memorable, with the Kaiser on July 12th, handed to Tower a pencilled note of the Kaiser's in which the Emperor specifically charged:

. . . if the disinterested mediation of the President failed, we have every reason to expect that Delcassé's plan of indemnifying Belligerent and Mediator at the expense of China may be tried on again.

This statement, thought Tower, made clear the Emperor's solicitude. Of course, Bülow confirmed this fear of his august sovereign and repeated that England would greatly prefer to end the war in this manner by advancing her own interests at the same time.

Bülow added

in the strictest confidence that the German Emperor is constantly in close personal correspondence with the Emperor of Russia.

---

[1] July 13, 1905, Tower to Roosevelt. Given in full, Appendix L, pp. 233-35.

Naturally; for it was during this cruise in the Imperial yacht that the Kaiser met the Tsar at Björkö, and signed with him the treaty of July 23d, which, if ratified, would have broken the Dual Alliance and ranged Russia on the side of Germany in the war of 1914–18.[1]

President Roosevelt, too little informed about domestic conditions in Russia, and too trustful of the Kaiser's good faith, confessed again that he was bewildered. To Spring-Rice, with whom he had been in frequent and earnest correspondence, urging upon England the necessity of helping to get Japan to moderate her terms of peace, he wrote July 24th:

There is one thing I am a little puzzled at, and that is why, excepting on disinterested grounds, the German Emperor should want Russia and Japan to make peace; he has done all he could to bring it about. Of course, it may be that he fears lest a continuation of the war result in the internal break-up of Russia and therefore an impetus to the German revolutionary movement. France has a very obvious motive in seeing peace made.

It would be a pleasure to find that always our hero pierced the obscure machinations of the Kaiser and Bülow and then in true heroic fashion took the necessary steps to thwart them. It must be our purpose, however, to hold true to the facts as they existed, always resisting the temptation to pride in the wisdom which comes after the event. Roosevelt is here revealed as having failed to measure the cunning of the German Foreign Office. It may be observed in extenuation of this lapse of judgment that the Marquis of Lansdowne and the British Govern-

---

[1] S. B. Fay, "The Kaiser's Secret Negotiations with the Tsar," pp. 66 ff.

ment itself were supplying some of the evidence which misled the President.

At the beginning of the negotiations in June, Roosevelt appears to have assumed as a matter of course that he could count on England, the ally of Japan, to contribute its influence to moderate the Japanese peace terms—the great obstacle to peace. He had been disappointed at the result. His failure to appreciate the really desperate character of the existing European situation, as well as his unwillingness to credit the Kaiser with other than a "jumpy" policy and a desire to humiliate Delcasse simply opened the door to speculations and at length to the conclusion—formed, however, a month before the receipt of the Kaiser's letter—that Great Britain really did not want peace.

England was travelling a very narrow line between its alliance with Japan and its entente with France. The end in view was an understanding with Russia which is now the more fully justified by what we know to have been taking place at Björkö at this very time.

We have here reached a point of obscurity in the British policy which cannot be easily explained or justified, and therefore we contribute merely to its definition by recording the correspondence.

On June 3d, the British Embassy submitted to the President a memorandum from Lansdowne as follows:

His Majesty's Government have not received any indication whatever of the terms of peace which Japan will now expect and I fear it would be useless for us to express an opinion based upon conjectures.

In the view of His Majesty's Government it would be better

to reserve our judgment until more is known of the recent maritime catastrophe and of the temper and expectations of both belligerents.

On June 15th, while the President was in the midst of his troubles both with Japan and with Russia over the place of meeting and the appointment of envoys with full powers, he put into a telegram to Ambassador Whitelaw Reid in London rather more of his irritation than usually appears in a telegram or in a state paper. He directed the Department of State to send the following message:

The President desires you to find out whether the English Government really does wish for peace or not.

Lansdowne replied through Reid the next day stating that he "had heard unofficial rumours and persons were hinting that England might not so much want peace at the moment as other things." He would gladly send assurance that would neutralize such intimations. It would be absolutely abhorrent to England if any course of hers should prolong the bloodshed. On the other hand, it would be a different thing to attempt exerting pressure about terms, especially when he did not know what the terms were to be. Lansdowne also confirmed the impression, already entertained in Washington, that the sudden removal of Sir Mortimer Durand to his summer residence, just at the time when the effort of Roosevelt to bring the belligerents together was at its most difficult point, was with the express purpose of avoiding any involvement of the British Government in the negotiations.[1]

Less than a week later Reid had a confidential con-

[1]Reid to the Department of State, June 15, 1905.

versation with King Edward at Ascot (June 22, 1905), which did not simplify the mystery. The King expressed the opinion that Russia was likely to be beaten again and that the Japanese would probably take Vladivostok. He did not share Roosevelt's desire to prevent this and suggested that it might be a good plan for Japan to take Vladivostok and thus provide herself with a token of magnanimity which she could return to Russia during the conference. "Wouldn't that ease the final settlement?" whispered the King in Reid's ear.[1]

This conversation served only to confirm the President's opinion that, after all, England did not really desire peace. He intimated as much to Spring-Rice. The latter then stepped into the breach and had an interview with Lansdowne with a special view to the transmission of the Foreign Minister's statements to Roosevelt. As a part of his exposition of British policy in the summer of 1905 he said, paraphrasing Lansdowne's statement:[2]

The object of England was [is] to see peace established and above all a durable peace—a peace which would be satisfactory to both Russia and Japan and create a state of things in Asia which would preclude the outbreak of another war whether in the East, the South, or the West. The sooner peace is established, the better for us—provided that the peace in question has the guarantees of stability—i. e., leaves no intolerable wrong behind it, demanding revenge.

From this paragraph one may infer that Lansdowne doubted Roosevelt's ability at that time to bring a durable peace.

---

[1] Bishop, Vol. I, p. 396.

[2] Spring-Rice to Roosevelt, undated, but about July 10, 1905.

GOOD OFFICES

Other paragraphs of the letter shed light on the peculiar international situation as viewed from London.

Our treaty with Japan [continued Spring-Rice], which is now in force and remains in force as long as the war lasts, binds England not to allow a hostile combination against Japan. England must not only observe the letter but the spirit of this treaty. Whatever our momentary or practical interests, our duty (and with our duty our chief and main interest) is to be absolutely and resolutely true to our plighted word.

England could not, continued the writer, ask Japan to give up what she might think necessary for her national well-being.

Lansdowne invited the President to keep him informed and to tell him frankly if the time came when England could be of direct assistance in the peacemaking.

In speaking in general terms of our relations with Japan, [continued Spring-Rice] he pointed out that from the very first our political interest had been to prevent the war which would not only expose us to great dangers of loss in Asia itself, but would seriously imperil our good understanding with France which is the most popular event in modern times in England. But the English Government, while kept fully informed, abstained from offering advice or exercising pressure on Japan because we did not think ourselves justified in trying to make Japan abandon what she thought were her interests in Asia because they conflicted with ours in other parts of the world. Great pressure was brought to bear on us in this direction: but like your government, we thought that Japan must be left to judge of her own vital interests and defend them as best she could, relying, as to other Powers, upon the plighted word of England. As a result we all but lost our agreement with

France; but it would have been worse if we had broken our word; on which the value of any agreement with England depends.

As the war went on we were constantly in danger of complications with Russia or of difficulties with France at a time when, owing to the losses of the S. African war, peace and recuperation were of vital necessity to us—and the financial situation became more and more alarming. At the present moment interests of every sort and description urge us to do all in our power to promote peace. If Russia is excluded from the Pacific she must seek an exit for her energies elsewhere—in Persia, Afghanistan, or in the Near East. And besides this it is a very narrow policy which sees in the ruin of Russia the interest of England.

It is difficult to resist the conclusion that President Roosevelt had been wrong in his interpretation of British policy. England desired peace but Lansdowne, having watched Roosevelt through the first stages of the Moroccan crisis, and having observed his willingness to assist the Kaiser out of an impossible position by urging on France the international conference, had little confidence that the President understood Europe well enough to make a durable peace in the Far East. Certainly no fact was brought forward in this letter which adequately explained why Lansdowne with all propriety might not have expressed to Japan his disapproval of some of the demands which were being advanced. One comes to feel that perhaps the Kaiser was not wholly wrong in his assertions that France and England would have been glad themselves to be the peacemakers.[1]

---

[1] Since the above was written I have the following information from my good friend, Professor A. L. P. Dennis, who has discussed this subject with some of those who were, in 1905, members of the permanent staff of the British Foreign Office: It is asserted that while the Marquis of Lansdowne did not wholly trust President Roosevelt's diplomatic skill at the time, there is no basis whatever for the Kaiser's assertion that England was joining in a plot to partition China. England did not attempt to delay the peace negotiations. It is stated, on the other hand, that the Foreign Office was completely ignorant of the dire necessity for Japan to make peace.

APPENDIX A

Count Komura to Minister Takahira, May 31, 1905.
Transmitted to Roosevelt by Takahira

With reference to your telegram of the 18th of May, you are hereby instructed to say to the President that Japan's signal naval victory having completely destroyed the force upon which Russia confidently relied to turn the tide of the war, it may be reasonably expected that the Government of St. Petersburg will turn now its attention to the question of peace. The Japanese Government still adhere to the conviction that the peace negotiations, when they come, should be conducted directly and exclusively between the belligerents, but even in such case friendly assistance of a neutral will be essential in order to bring them together for the purpose of such negotiation, and the Japanese Government would prefer to have that office undertaken by a neutral in whose good judgment and wise discretion they have entire confidence. You will express to the President the hope of the Japanese Government that in [the] actual circumstances of the case and having in view the changed situation resulting from the recent naval battle, he will see his way directly and entirely of his own motion and initiative to invite the two belligerents to come together for the purpose of direct negotiation, and you will add that if the President is disposed to undertake the service, the Japanese Government will leave it to him to determine the course of procedure and what other Power or Powers, if any, should be consulted in the matter of suggested invitation. You will ask the President whether in his opinion the Japanese Government can, with a view to facilitate the course, [?] advantageously take any other or further action in the matter, and you will make it entirely clear to the President that the Japanese Government have no intention by the present communication [?] to approach Russia either directly or indirectly on the subject of peace.

Confidential Memorandum from Minister Takahira, June 3d

You are hereby instructed to express to the President our thanks for the steps which he has taken in the interest of peace. You will say to him that the Japanese Government believe he has very clear appreciation of their present disposition as well as the principles by which they have been guided throughout the struggle. But even at the risk of repetition they will restate their attitude. The war, from Japan's point of view, is essentially and exclusively one of self-defence. It has never, so far as she is concerned, possessed any element of self-aggrandizement. Accordingly, the demands to be formulated by Japan will only be commensurate with the original objects to be attained, and even in the sequel of the decisive battles of Mukden and the Japan Sea, she has no intention of demanding anything excessive. Her territorial and financial demands will be found to be wholly consistent with that attitude. The demand for territorial cession will be limited to Sakhalin and the indemnity to be demanded will be moderate and reasonable, containing nothing of a consequential or exemplary nature.

. . . .

The above is in answer to my report on the conversation of the President on the night of the 3d May [June?] (Saturday).

T [akahira].

GOOD OFFICES

APPENDIX B

St. Petersburg (Received June 2, 1905, 8:55 P.M.)

ADEE,
Washington.

Seventy-one. St. Petersburg for the first time since war commenced really moved by fleet's defeat. Fearless criticism of press here rather remarkable. Indignation and wrath is poured out freely upon Bureaucracy, which is alone held responsible for all misfortunes of war. Press calls for Russian people themselves to say what should be done rather significant. No universal cry for peace, but for immediate assembling of representation. Believe great mass of Russians realize war is futile. Nation may not be ripe for revolutionists. Naval disaster in the first instance causing rising will not occur again. This government will bring about further reforms, therefore radicals and liberals receive news of defeat with concealed relief. Important conference imperial palace. It is rumoured that one party wished United States to be used to inform Japan that if large money indemnity was demanded Russia would arrange to drag war along for five years; another element wanted nothing done for the present, but at proper time use only good offices of France through Delcassé. This information concerning conference not from official source.

MEYER.

APPENDIX C

Tower to Roosevelt

June 4, 1905.

MR. PRESIDENT:

The German Emperor has asked me to say to you that he considers the situation in Russia so serious that, when the truth is known at St. Petersburg in regard to the recent defeat, the life of the Tsar will be in danger, and the gravest disorders likely to occur. The Emperor of Germany has written to the Tsar, therefore, urging him to take immediate steps toward peace. The Emperor said to me: "I called his attention to the fact that the Americans are the only nation regarded by the Japanese with the highest respect, and that the President of the United States is the right person to appeal to with the hope that he may be able to bring the Japanese to reasonable proposals. I suggested to the Tsar to send for Meyer and charge him with a message to President Roosevelt, or to empower me to put myself in direct communication with the President. Please inform the President privately, from me personally, of the steps that I have taken, which I hope will be for the benefit of the world."

TOWER.

9 June, 1905.

MR. PRESIDENT:

The telegram which I sent to you in cipher last Sunday, the 4th instant, was prompted by the German Emperor, who has arrived at the conclusion that peace ought to be made between Russia and Japan and believes that you can accomplish a declaration of peace better than any one else in the world. On Sunday morning the Emperor wrote me a personal note, with his own hand, expressing his views and describing the step which he had taken toward the Emperor of Russia to induce him to consider the question of coming to terms with the Japanese. He told him that, as the American nation is the one held in highest respect in Japan, you "would be the right person to appeal to in the hopes that you may be able to bring the Japanese down to reasonable proposals." This message went to the Tsar on Saturday, June 3d.

The Emperor sent his note to me by an orderly who was directed to give it to me personally, and who put it into my hand as I was coming out of the door of the Cathedral where I had gone to attend a service in connection with the Crown Prince's wedding. I sent word to the Emperor that I should communicate his wishes to you immediately; and, hurrying home, I despatched my telegram to your address. I have made a copy of the full text of the Emperor's note, which I have the honour to enclose to you herewith in order that you may obtain from it a fuller understanding of his purpose than I could convey in my cipher telegram. I had a personal interview of some duration with him later in the day, during which he discussed at length the situation in Russia.—He looks upon the continuation of the war, from the Russian side, as hopeless. The people are strongly opposed to it, they will not sustain it longer, and unless peace is made they will kill the Tsar. He told me that he knows this danger to be imminent. He thinks that there is everything to be feared from the result of the Tsar's death at this moment— an infant heir to the throne—a long regency under a Grand Duke who, however personally agreeable, is little better than a child himself and sure to be surrounded by conspiracy and unscrupulous intrigue—a condition of things not only disastrous to the Empire of Russia but dangerous for the rest of the world. The Emperor said to me: "Peace must be made at once! I have told him to consult his army in the field and then to take steps without delay—I have offered him the alternative, either of communicating with President Roosevelt through Meyer in St. Petersburg, or of authorizing me to put myself into communication with the President for him."

> I have the honour to be,
> Mr. President,
> Your obedient servant,
> CHARLEMAGNE TOWER.

ROOSEVELT AND THE RUSSO–JAPANESE WAR

[*Copy.*]

Strictly Confidential.

Berlin, Schloss,
4/VI, 1905.

DEAR MR. TOWER:

The situation created by the annihilation of the Russian fleet in the Korean Straits is clearly to be defined by the expression "loss of the Command of the Asiatic Waters." It is to be feared that the news will—when published at Petersburg—create such a commotion that grave disorders, even revolution, are to be expected, if not attempts on the Zar's life. For he is looked upon as the instigator of the prolongation of the war *quand même*, which the Russian nation is decided to end. Considering the grave dangers to all of us, which might arise in case something serious happened to H. I. M., I have written him a letter counselling him to open negotiations for Peace. At the same time I drew his attention to the fact that America was the *only* nation which is regarded by the Japanese with highest respect, and that the head of the American People would consequently be the right person to appeal to, in the hopes that he will be able to bring the Japanese down to reasonable proposals. I therefore suggested to H. I. M. to send for Meyer and charge him with a message to President Roosevelt, or to empower me to put myself into communication with the President in H. I. M. name. Please *privately* inform the President directly by cipher from me personally of this step I have taken which I hope will be for the benefit of the world.

Ever yours truly,

(*Signed*)   WILLIAM
I. R.

APPENDIX D

Roosevelt to Meyer, June 5, 2:20 p.m., 1905

Memorandum for despatch to be sent by the State Department:

Ambassador Meyer will at once call on His Majesty the Tsar and say that he does so by personal direction of the President to urge upon His Majesty the desirability of his consenting to the request of the President to have representatives of Russia meet with representatives of Japan to confer as to whether peace cannot now be made. The President speaks with the most earnest and sincere desire to advise what is best for Russia. It is the judgment of all outsiders, including all of Russia's most ardent friends, that the present contest is absolutely hopeless and that to continue it can only result in the loss of all Russia's possessions in East Asia. To avert trouble, and, as he fears, what is otherwise inevitable disaster, the President most earnestly advises that an effort be made by a direct interview without intermediary between Russian and Japanese plenipotentiaries, to see if it is not possible for them to agree as to terms of peace. The President believes it would be better for the representatives of the two Powers to discuss the whole peace question themselves rather than for any outside Power to do more than endeavour to arrange the meeting—that is, to ask both Powers whether they will not consent to meet. After the meeting has been held it will be time enough, if need be, to discuss suggestions as to the terms from any outside friend of either party. If Russia will consent to such a meeting the President will try to get Japan's consent, acting simply on his own initiative and not saying that Russia has consented, and the President believes he will succeed. Russia's answer to this

221

request will be kept strictly secret, as will all that has so far transpired, nothing being made public until Japan also agrees. The President will then openly ask each Power to agree to the meeting, which can thereupon be held. As to the place of meeting, the President would suggest some place between Harbin and Mukden; but this is a mere suggestion. The President earnestly hopes for a speedy and favourable answer to avert bloodshed and calamity.

APPENDIX E

Meyer to Secretary of State, June 7, 1905

London (?) (Received June 7, 1905, 4:30 P.M.)

SECRETARY OF STATE,
    Washington.

The Emperor assured me yesterday afternoon that he was convinced that his people did not desire peace at any price and would support him in continuing the war rather than have him make what would be considered dishonourable terms.

The Emperor, however, authorized me to say that he accepts and consents to the President's proposition, as cabled to me with the understanding that it is to be kept absolutely secret, and that the President is to act on his own initiative in endeavouring [*sic*] obtain the consent of Japanese Government to a meeting of Russian and Japanese plenipotentiaries, without intermediary, in order to see if it is not possible for them to agree to terms of peace. It is of the utmost importance that Tsar's answer and acceptance are to be kept absolutely secret as well as all that has so far . . . nothing being made public until Japan also agrees. The President will then openly, on his own initiative, ask each Power to agree to a meeting. The Emperor said that as yet no foot has been placed on Russian soil, that he realized that Sakhalin could be attacked very shortly, therefore important to get Japan's consent at once before attack is made. The Tsar desired me to inform him at the earliest possible moment of Japan's answer. He assured me he had the greatest confidence in the President, and that he hoped to see the old friendship return which had formerly existed between the two countries, and that he realized that any change which had come about was due to the press and not to the governments.

MEYER.

Count Cassini to Roosevelt

Strictement confidentiel.

Ambassade Impériale de Russie,
Washington, le 6 juin 1905.

MONSIEUR LE PRÉSIDENT:

J'ai l'honneur de Vous transmettre ci-joint la copie d'un télégramme que je viens de recevoir à l'instant même de St. Pétersbourg comme réponse à la démarche que j'ai faite après l'entrevue que Vous avez bien voulu m'accorder.

Me tenant à Votre disposition pour toute communication que Vous voudriez bien me faire à ce sujet je Vous prie d'agréer l'assurance de ma plus haute considération.

CASSINI.

MONSIEUR ROOSEVELT
    etc.   etc.   etc.

Copie d'un télégramme de S. E. Mr. le Comte Lamsdorff à S. E. Mr. le Comte Cassini, en date de St. Pétersbourg le 6 juin, 1905

Vous êtes invité à remercier Monsieur le Président Roosevelt de sa démarche qui est hautement appréciée en Russie. Dans les circonstances actuelles le Gouvernement Impérial ne peut demander ni la apix, ni une médiation. Mais si une Puissance, amicalement disposée pour la Russie, pouvait exercer une influence modératrice sur les exigences du Japon et faire connaître ses vues, une pareille action contribuerait certainement à la pacification désirée. Les vraies négociations de paix ne pourront cependant être entamées que lorsque les termes proposés par le Japon seront établis. Comme Vous le savez, le Gouvernement Impérial ne pourra jamais consentir à des conditions blessantes pour la dignité de la Russie.

APPENDIX F

Roosevelt to Meyer, June 8, 1905

MEYER,
   American Ambassador,
   St: Petersburg, Russia.

Inform the Tsar's Government that Japan has consented to the proposal. Then present to the Russian Government the following despatch, which is identical in terms with one that is being sent to Japan. When this despatch has been received by both governments it will be made public in Washington.

"The President feels that the time has come when in the interest of all mankind he must endeavour to see if it is not possible to bring to an end the terrible and lamentable conflict now being waged. With both Russia and Japan the United States has inherited ties of friendship and good will. It hopes for the prosperity and welfare of each, and it feels that the progress of the world is set back by the war between these two great nations. The President accordingly urges the Russian and the Japanese governments not only for their own sakes, but in the interest of the whole civilized world, to open direct negotiations for peace with one another. The President suggests that these peace negotiations be conducted directly and exclusively between the belligerents; in other words, that there may be a meeting of Russian and Japanese plenipotentiaries or delegates, without any intermediary, in order to see if it is not possible for these representatives of the two Powers to agree to terms of peace. The President earnestly asks that the Russian Government do now agree to such meeting, and is asking the Japanese Government likewise to agree. While the President does not feel that any intermediary should be called in in respect to the peace negotiations themselves he is entirely willing to do what he properly can if the two Powers concerned feel that his services will be of aid in arranging the preliminaries as to the time and place of meeting. But if even these preliminaries can be arranged directly between the two Powers, or in any other way, the President will be glad, as his sole purpose is to bring about a meeting which the whole civilized world will pray may result in peace."

(The same instruction, *mutatis mutandis*, was sent to U. S. Minister Griscom in Tokio.)

APPENDIX G

Griscom to Secretary of State, June 10, 1905

Tokio.

Minister for Foreign Affairs has handed me the following answer to the despatch embodied in your telegram of the 8th instant:

"The Imperial Government have given to the suggestion of the President of the United States, embodied in the note handed to the Minister for Foreign Affairs by the American Minister on the 9th instant, the very serious consideration to which, taking into consideration its source and its import, it is justly entitled. Desiring in the interest of the world as[1] well as and in the mutual interest [of] Japan the reëstablishment of peace with Russia on terms and conditions that will fully guarantee its

---

[1]Text apparently mangled in transmission or decoding.

stability, the Imperial Government will, in response to the suggestion of the President, appoint plenipotentiaries of Japan to meet plenipotentiaries of Russia at such time and place as may be found to be mutually agreeable and convenient for the purpose of negotiating and concluding terms of peace directly and exclusively between the two belligerent Powers."

GRISCOM.

APPENDIX H

Meyer to Secretary of State, June 12, 1905

The following note is just received from the Foreign Office, which I transmit in full:

"I did not fail to place before my August Majesty the telegraphic communication which your excellency has been pleased to transmit to me under instructions of your government. His Majesty, much moved by the sentiments expressed by the President, is glad to find in it a new proof of the traditional friendship which unites Russia to the United States of America, as well as an evidence of the high value which Mr. Roosevelt attaches even as His Imperial Majesty does to that universal peace so essential to the welfare and progress of all humanity.

"With regard to the eventual meeting of Russian and Japanese plenipotentiaries, 'In order to see if it is not possible for the two Powers to agree to terms of peace,' the Imperial Government has no objection in principle to this endeavour if the Japanese Government expresses a like desire."

APPENDIX I

Meyer to Secretary of State, June 16, 1905

Your cable of 15th received. While at Foreign Office, yesterday, Lamsdorff informed me that he had cabled Cassini, Washington, that morning, that The Hague would be most acceptable to Russia as a place of meeting. I told him that I had received word, confidentially, that the President is doing what he properly can to get both governments to agree upon The Hague. On returning to the Embassy I cabled what Lamsdorff had said . . . this morning, in compliance with your instructions. I informed Lamsdorff that the President, before the receipt of my cable and in accordance with the statement of the Russian Government made to him through Cassini, Washington, that Washington, D. C., as the place of meeting would be agreeable to Russian Government, the President had notified Japanese Government that Washington, D. C., [would be?] named as the place of meeting, this being agreeable to both Russia and Japan, it is too late now for the President to reverse his action and that such a course would doubtless not be acceptable to Japan.[1] Lamsdorff acknowledged that Cassini, Washington, had received the above instructions but claims that he cabled Cassini, Washington, in reply to his cable about The Hague before he was informed of any final decision as to Washington; that The Hague was preferable to them for many reasons, that they desired it instead of Washington on account of the distance, that Washington was also undesirable on account of the summer heat and the fact that they were changing ambassadors. I called his attention to the fact that the negotiations as to the meeting place had been carried on through his ambassador at Washington, and asked him if he would read me his cable instructions to Count Cassini, Washington, D. C., on this matter. This he however avoided. I assured him that I considered it extraordinary procedure on Russia's part to endeavour to force the President to reverse his action after having taken such action on a favourable representation from their ambassador as to Washington for a place of meeting; also that I believed it might be a serious and embarrassing matter if they now continued to press for The Hague. Lamsdorff then said he would have to

[1]Meaning clear but text apparently garbled in transmission or decoding.

consult with the Emperor and that he would cable Cassini, Washington.

Roosevelt to Meyer, June 16, 1905

MEYER,
   American Ambassador,
      St. Petersburg.

You will please immediately inform Count Lamsdorff that I was handed by Ambassador Cassini a cable from him dated June 13th which ran as follows:

"As regards the place of the proposed meeting its choice is of only secondary importance since the plenipotentiaries of both Russia and Japan are to negotiate directly without any participation by third Powers. If Paris, so desirable for many reasons, encounters opposition, then the Imperial Government gives the preference to Washington over all other cities, especially since the presence of the President, initiator of the meeting, can exercise a beneficent influence toward the end which we all have in view." Accordingly, after having received word from Japan that she objected to The Hague, and before I received any notification whatever about The Hague from Russia, I notified Japan that Washington would be the appointed place and so informed Ambassador Cassini. I then gave the same announcement to the public. It is of course out of the question for me to consider any reversal of this action and I regard the incident as closed, so far as the place of meeting is concerned. If Count Lamsdorff does not acquiesce in this view you will please see the Czar personally and read to him this cable stating to Count Lamsdorff that you are obliged to make the request because of the extreme gravity of the situation. Explain to Count Lamsdorff and if necessary to the Tsar that I am convinced that on consideration they will of their own accord perceive that it is entirely out of the question for me now to reverse the action I took in accordance with the request of the

Russian Government, which action has been communicated to and acquiesced in by Japan, and has been published to the entire world.

THEODORE ROOSEVELT.

APPENDIX J

Memorandum for the Japanese Government given by the President to Minister Takahira, June 14, 1905

The President regrets that Japan did not feel able to accept The Hague as the President suggested, but in accordance with Japan's wishes he has notified Russia that Washington will be the place of meeting. Russia will accept Washington, although of course she would have preferred The Hague. The President most strongly urges the inadvisability of requesting a categorical answer on the lines of the Japanese despatch received to-day (June 14th). The President would much have preferred if Russia's answer to his identical note had been couched in the same language that was used in the Japanese note, but the Russian note used the President's own language, which language had been submitted by the President to the Japanese Government before he used it, and it would put both the President and, in his opinion, the Japanese Government in a false and untenable position if the Japanese now refuse to meet, in spite of the fact that the Russian answer uses the exact language of the President's request. Moreover, the President feels most strongly that the question of the Powers of the plenipotentiaries is not in the least a vital question, whereas it is vital that the meeting should take place if there is any purpose to get peace. If there was no sincere desire to get peace, then the fact of the plenipotentiaries having full powers would not in any way avail to secure it. But if, as the President hopes and believes, there is a real chance for peace, it makes comparatively little difference what the formal instructions to the plenipo-

229

tentiaries may be. It is possible, of course, that an agreement may not come, but the President has very strong hopes that if the meeting takes place it will be found that peace can be obtained. The President has urged Russia to clothe her plenipotentiaries with full powers, as Japan has indicated her intention of doing. But even if Russia does not adopt the President's suggestion, the President does not feel that such failure to adopt it would give legitimate ground to Japan for refusing to do what the President has, with the prior assent of Japan, asked both Powers to do.

June 16, 1905.

GRISCOM,
    American Minister,
        Tokio.

The President has informed Minister Takahira that he considers it most unwise for Japan to hang back or raise question over the wording of the Russian note about the sending of delegates to the peace conference. For Japan to now hang back will create a most unfortunate impression in this country and in Europe. At present the feeling is that Japan has been frank and straightforward and wants peace if it can be obtained on proper terms, whereas Russia has shown a tendency to hang back. It will be a misfortune for Japan in the judgment of the President if any action of Japan now gives rise to the contrary feeling. Moreover, in the President's judgment there is absolutely nothing to be gained by such action on the part of Japan. No instructions to the plenipotentiaries would be of any avail if they did not intend to make peace. But if, as the President believes, the force of events will tend to secure peace if once the representatives of the two parties can come together, then it is obviously most unwise to delay the meeting for reasons that are trivial or of no real weight. The President regretted that Japan would not accept The Hague as the place of meeting but in accordance with Japan's wishes he has arranged for the meeting to take place in the United States. The President has the assurance of the Russian Ambassador that the Russian plenipotentiaries will as a matter of course have full power to conclude a definite treaty of peace, subject to the ratification of the home government, but even if this were not so the President feels that it would be most unwise for Japan now to withdraw from the meeting, especially in view of the terms in which the President's identical note was couched, and he also feels that if the meeting can be secured the really important step toward obtaining peace will have been taken, without any reference to the exact form in which the plenipotentiaries receive their instructions. Communicate this to the Minister for Foreign Affairs.

[THEODORE ROOSEVELT.]

APPENDIX K

Statement of Japan's Terms of Peace

I.   Russia to acknowledge that Japan possesses in Corea paramount political, military, and economical interests and Russia to engage not to obstruct or interfere with any measures of guidance, protection, and control which Japan finds it necessary to take in Corea;

II.   Russia to evacuate Manchuria within a specified period and to relinquish all territorial advantages and all rights of occupation and all preferential and exclusive concessions and franchises in that region in impairment of Chinese sovereignty or inconsistent with the principle of equal opportunity;

III.   Japan to restore to China Manchuria subject to the guarantee of reform and improved administration;

IV.   Japan and Russia reciprocally to engage not to obstruct any general measures common to all countries which China may take for the development of the commerce and industries of Manchuria;

V. Russia to transfer and assign to Japan the lease of the Liaotung Peninsula;

VI. Russia to assign to Japan the Harbin-Port Arthur railway;

VII. Russia may retain and work Trans-Manchurian railway subject to the condition that the same is to be employed exclusively for commercial and industrial purposes;

VIII. Russia to cede to Japan Sakhalin and the appurtenant islands;

IX. Russia to pay to Japan an indemnity sufficient to cover the actual expenses of war;

X. Vladivostok to be dismantled and to be made essentially a commercial port and Japan to have the right to station a consul there;

XI. The naval strength of Russia in the Extreme East hereafter not to exceed —— tons;

XII. Russia to surrender to Japan as lawful prizes all vessels of war which sought asylum in neutral ports in consequence of injuries received in battle and were there interned;

XIII. Russia to grant to Japanese subjects full fishery rights along the coasts and in the bays, harbours, inlets, and rivers of her possessions in the Japan, Okhotsk, and Bering seas.

GOOD OFFICES

APPENDIX L

Tower to Roosevelt

13 July, 1905.

MR. PRESIDENT:

The letter which I addressed to the German Emperor to enclose to him a copy of your letter to me of the 24th of June—as I had the honour to report to you in my letter of July 6th—reached him on board the *Hohenzollern*, off the coast of Schleswig-Holstein, on the 7th instant, and he telegraphed to me from Flensburg, on the 8th: "Best thanks for letter. I perfectly agree with the President's views. I have done my utmost energetically to second his action in every manner. So far as I am informed, all the Powers on the Continent hope fervently that the President may succeed, and lend their help. There is but one Power, not on our Continent, which I am afraid will hold aloof and create difficulties even for the great work that the President is so ardently pursuing for the benefit of the whole world."

I had no definite explanation of this suspicion, evidently of England, which the Emperor intimated in his despatch, nor could I determine whether he referred to some specific step upon the part of the British Government, with which he was acquainted, or whether this was to be regarded as merely indicating the general lack of confidence in the policy of England which, as you well know, Mr. President, plays so important a part in the political movements of Germany to-day.

I hoped to obtain in some way a probable explanation of it, at least, before communicating it to you through the mail bag which leaves here for Washington to-morrow; and I am glad to be able now to indicate to you what it is that disturbs the Emperor's mind.

A few days after the copy of your letter of June 24th reached the Emperor, the Chancellor of the Empire went to the North

Coast to confer with him, aboard the *Hohenzollern.* He returned to Berlin yesterday, and I had a long interview with him at his house last evening. Prince Bülow opened the conversation with me by saying that he wished to assure me that your letter had given the Emperor the greatest pleasure. He had read it to him soon after his arrival on the *Hohenzollern,* expressing, as he did so, not only his personal satisfaction but his complete accord with your views as to the question of peace between Russia and Japan.

The Chancellor handed me a pencil memorandum which he said he had made the day before, from the Emperor's dictation, as follows: "The Emperor wishes Prince Bülow to tell Mr. Tower once more how heartily he sympathizes with the diplomatic action of the President regarding the termination of the Japanese war. Germany is directly concerned in that matter, for, if the disinterested mediation of the President failed, we have every reason to expect that Delcassé's plan of indemnifying Belligerent and Mediator at the expense of China may be tried on again. But, on the other hand, it is only natural that those parties who consider this latter plan as the superior one should do their best to prolong the war."

This makes clear the Emperor's solicitude. I asked Prince Bülow whether that was what the Emperor meant when he said in his telegram to me: "There is but one Power, not on our Continent, which I am afraid will hold aloof and create difficulties." To which the Chancellor replied that it was. He added that M. Delcassé had formed a plan by which peace was to be made between Russia and Japan through the mediation of France and England, and that, under it, an arrangement was contemplated by which not only Russia and Japan were to obtain portions of China but that France and England were also to be indemnified by Chinese territory, as a price of their intervention; a course which, he said, would lead to the destruction of Chinese sovereignty and the disruption of the Chinese Empire.

GOOD OFFICES

The Emperor has reason to believe that England would greatly prefer to end the war in this manner, by advancing her own interests at the same time; and this is the source of his anxiety lest something shall happen to interrupt the course of events as they are now taking shape under your guidance. Prince Bülow added, in the strictest confidence, that the German Emperor is constantly in close personal correspondence with the Emperor of Russia, urging him to support your efforts and using the strongest arguments to encourage him to accept such terms as it may be possible for him to accept from the conference which you have called together in America.

Though, whilst the Chancellor consented to my writing this to you, he pointed out the extreme danger which would arise from its being disclosed; for, said he, if it were to become known in Russia that foreign influence is being brought to bear, the Russian Emperor—surrounded as he is by the intrigues of his court and the bitterness of party strife which make it difficult at present for him to act—would then have the whole country against him to such an extent that it might be impossible for him even to formulate a plan.

In connection with the German Emperor's earnest wish to see a successful issue from the present negotiations for peace, Prince Bülow assured me again, as he has done frequently heretofore, that the policy of Germany in regard to China is precisely in accord with that of the United States.

He declared in the most solemn manner that Germany wishes the preservation of the integrity of China, the Open Door, and equal rights in China for the commerce of the whole world.

I have the honour to be,

Mr. President,

Your obedient Servant,

CHARLEMAGNE TOWER.

To the PRESIDENT
Washington.

CHAPTER X

The Peace of Portsmouth

TO REVIEW the minor events from the middle of June until the first session of the peace conference at Portsmouth, August 10th, forms no essential part of our study, for it throws no peculiar light upon President Roosevelt's share in the peace. A few details are sufficient.

The most important peace treaty previously negotiated by Japan was at Shimonoseki in 1895. At that time China had attempted to trick Japan by first sending representatives without full powers and it was only the persistence of the Japanese military pressure which finally compelled the Chinese Government to send Li Hung-chang as plenipotentiary.[1] It had been the usual experience of Japan in her dealings with the Western Powers to find that in the negotiations the latter conveyed a more or less studied affront by delegating the negotiations to diplomats far below the first rank.[2]

In 1905, therefore, Japan was particularly alert to safeguard Japanese national dignity. Many efforts were made to find out in advance of the announcement who the Russian envoys were to be in order that Japan might act accordingly. Japan did not care to appoint her most distinguished statesmen unless she were sure that Russia would do likewise. The attitude of St. Petersburg was

---

[1]"Am. in East. Asia," p. 501.

[2]For example, in the treaty revision conferences, *ibid.*, Chap. XXVII.

still such as to foster the suspicions which had been so well merited for several years. Russia looked down upon Japan. Russian statesmen did not regard the task of peacemaking as one likely to confer honour or lead to other preferments at the hand of the Tsar. It was only after the failure of several selections that the Tsar at last was compelled to appoint M. Witte as the first Russian plenipotentiary—Witte, the man who had steadily opposed and criticized the very policy which had brought Russia to its unhappy pass.[1] The associate was Baron Rosen, the newly appointed Russian Ambassador at Washington, who had been designated, late in May, to replace Cassini, but who did not arrive until July. Rosen was regarded both in Russia and in Japan, where he had served as Russian Minister, as an amiable though not very strong man, but Witte had the respect and admiration of the Japanese.[2]

Had Witte's appointment been made immediately rather than after several others had avoided the task it is possible that Japan would have appointed Marquis Ito. Ito was a true statesman with moderate views and ambitions for his country. His presence at Portsmouth would doubtless have materially altered the result. It would have been, however, quite beneath Japan's dignity to appoint Ito and then find that at the conference he was confronted by men of less rank and dignity. Consequently, Baron Komura, who had been Minister for Foreign Affairs during the war, and Mr. Takahira, the Japanese Minister in Washington, became the Japanese representatives.

[1]Howe's "Meyer," pp. 170 ff.; Rosen, "Forty Years of Diplomacy," Vol. I, p. 257.

[2]Baron Sternberg stated to the President in a letter, June 11, 1905, that Takahira had intimated to him that the Japanese Government would like to have General Kuropatkin and Witte appointed as envoys.

ROOSEVELT AND THE RUSSO–JAPANESE WAR

During the conference Witte and Komura were pitted against each other, the associate plenipotentiaries taking very little part. The result was unfortunate, for Komura does not appear to have shared Marquis Ito's wisdom or moderation, and was certainly not the kind of a man to establish the most favourable relations with Witte. Baron Komura should have been quite at home in the United States for he had studied at Harvard and spoke English, while Witte had that supercilious contempt for America which was so common in the courts of the Continent and was especially marked in Russia. It happened quite otherwise. Witte fully realized that Russia had utterly lost the confidence of Americans, and above all that Lamsdorff had failed to appreciate the value of the newspaper in shaping public opinion. As we have already pointed out, Russia had possessed a much better case against Japan, at least in Korea, than was generally known in the West, and if the facts about Japanese penetration in Manchuria had been exploited in the papers as widely as the Russian aggressions, public opinion on the war would have been much more sharply divided. Japan had won a victory in the press of England and the United States. Having won, however, Japan utterly failed in preparing public opinion for its terms of peace. Witte studied the technique of handling the newspapers with consummate wisdom and attached to himself Dr. E. J. Dillon, the St. Petersburg correspondent of the *Daily Telegraph* (London), who performed the duties of a highly proficient publicity agent.[1]

Japan had built up an opinion that she was fighting for

[1] "Eclipse of Russia," p. 299; Witte's "Memoirs," p. 137; Korostovetz, pp. 21–22; Rosen, Vol. I, pp. 266–67.

the independence of Korea and the return of Manchuria to China. She had presented herself as an unoffending David attacked by a brutal Goliath and possessed of no purpose save to battle for justice and right. The facts hardly supported this extreme claim and it was the task of Japan, if we may view the situation somewhat cynically, as soon as the peace conference was agreed upon, to prepare public opinion for the truth. This would have been easier had Japan been more candid with the public at an earlier date. It was extraordinarily difficult in the summer of 1905. To make it worse, it does not appear to have been recognized by Baron Komura as of any importance. Japanese "publicity," to use a term not then in vogue, suffered an inglorious defeat at Portsmouth.

Washington, in the month of August, would not have proved a very satisfactory place for a conference. The President selected Portsmouth, New Hampshire, where the Government possessed a navy yard and ample conveniences, while the presence of a large summer colony and hotel accommodations made the choice the more reasonable. Newport was rejected on the ground that in the social life which would surround the plenipotentiaries the Japanese might experience some unpleasant discrimination in contrast to the Russians.

It is sufficient to state that the reception of the envoys by the American Government, their visits to the President at Oyster Bay, and their presentation to each other, were accomplished with perfect tact. All the delicate problems of diplomatic rank and precedence were solved satisfactorily and the delegates were set down at Portsmouth ready for work without any untoward incident. Every slightest detail of the procedure was considered in advance by the President and it must have been with no little sense of relief that Roosevelt learned of the actual opening of the conference on August 9th.[1]

FACTORS FAVOURING PEACE

It was to the advantage of none of the neutral Powers that the war be continued. All the Powers most directly interested had reasons to desire peace. France, so recently threatened by Germany in Morocco and not yet out from under the shadow, greatly wished that Russia might be freed to perform her functions under the Dual Alliance. While M. Witte was in Paris on his way to America he had been informed that although French financial support would be available for the payment of an indemnity, no more war loans could be obtained, and Witte himself confessed that the Russian finances were in a very bad condition.[2]

Germany wanted peace because the purpose to weaken Russia had already been achieved, and because the Kaiser and German autocracy feared the spread of the Russian revolution. England does not appear to have been disturbed by the revolution, but no British interests would be served by the continuance of a war with such uncertainty as to its results. England likewise desired peace, though for no such urgent reasons as France and Germany.

The American people wished for peace not so much because of any direct national interest in the Far East as because war seemed horrible and the conflict in Manchuria had been bloody and costly in human life to a degree hitherto unknown. Once the plenipotentiaries were

---

[1]Bishop, Vol. I, pp. 404–05.
[2]"Memoirs," p. 292.

gathered at the peace table, American public opinion could be counted on to demand peace, and would be turned heavily against whichever power obstructed the conclusion of a treaty. President Roosevelt reckoned on this situation.

The decisive factor was President Roosevelt himself. He was not squeamish about the bloodshed and he was no pacifist. He had no vain ambition to be a peacemaker. This alluring rôle, which few statesmen are able to push aside when presented, does not appear to have seemed especially attractive to him. There is no trace in even his most personal letters from December, 1904, to July, 1905, that he entered upon his work to bring the belligerents together with any personal motive. He did not shrink from a public service, and when the opportunity was placed in his hand out in the mountains of Colorado he welcomed it, though with no great expectations of success. On July 27, 1905, Roosevelt wrote to Lloyd C. Griscom:

. . . Before you receive this the peace negotiations I suppose will have come to an end and I rather think they will end in failure. The Russian Government have jumped from one side to the other, but I do not think they are yet in a frame of mind to accept the consequences of their defeat. If anything could have added to the unfavourable impression I already had of them it would be their conduct during these peace negotiations. They have been unable to make war and now they cannot make peace. They strike me as corrupt, tricky, and inefficient. . . .

There was nothing ignoble or selfish in Roosevelt's efforts. However, once the consent of the belligerents to peace parleys had been obtained the President assumed a grave personal responsibility. From that moment he had a large personal stake in making peace. Failure would render him ridiculous in his time and in history. England did not appear to be coöperating. The German Emperor was frequently whispering that both France and England expected him to fail and were merely waiting to step in and make a profit out of his failure. Even in the United States there was no lack of critics who for partisan or other reasons freely predicted failure. Even though President of the United States, Roosevelt was placed somewhat in the position of a young man who still has his reputation to make. Lastly, M. Witte had no confidence that peace could be made and frequently let it be known that he expected the conference to break up after the briefest of efforts.[1] The Portsmouth Conference presented a challenge, the greatest challenge he had ever accepted, to a man of determination who did not easily accept defeat.

Two other factors making for peace we mention here and elaborate later. Both Russia and Japan required peace. Russia had evidently consented to the Delcassé overture in April. Japan had asked for negotiations. The Tsar had betrayed his eagerness. At the beginning of the conference neither Russia nor Japan correctly appraised these factors. Each calculated on the other's more exigent need. The revolutionary movement in Russia was promising from the Japanese standpoint, while Russia had always cherished the belief that in the end she could win by wearing out Japan. This had been the opinion in Europe. Cassini frequently expressed it in Washing-

---

[1]Howe's "Meyer," pp. 186, 189–90, 194; Korostovetz, pp. 22, 28. However, see Dillon's "Eclipse of Russia," p. 301, for assertions which make one wonder whether Witte's repeated statements were not a pose, and that his primary purpose was not to come to a complete understanding with Japan, even to an alliance.

THE PEACE OF PORTSMOUTH

ton. As the summer of 1905 wore on, indications were not
lacking that Japan had already reached the limit of her
resources. The Portsmouth Conference was commonly
likened in the cartoons and the metaphors of the correspondents to a poker game in which neither party held
satisfactory hands. It was a game of bluff. Peace was, in
fact, almost inevitable. One side or the other was bound
to give way—if not at the moment, then within a very
brief period.

EARLY SESSIONS OF THE CONFERENCE

There were twelve sessions of the conference and a few
private conversations between Witte and Komura. There
were twelve items in the Japanese peace terms as presented. Eight of these demands were practically disposed
of in the first eight sessions which mark a definite phase of
the proceedings. The last four sessions may be described
almost as a new conference in which President Roosevelt
had become, though not actually present, a dictator.
The first eight sessions present some aspects of peculiar
importance, for they foreshadowed the trend of Far
Eastern politics. A review of these negotiations becomes
a preface to the next ten years of Far Eastern history and
also affords a background essential to a definition of the
broad outlines of Roosevelt's Far Eastern policy.[1]

---

[1]Considering the fact that the sessions of the conferences were secret, at the request of Japan, we
are in possession of a surprising amount of published documents and sources covering nearly all the
phases of the discussions and issues. In addition to the memoirs of Witte and Rosen and Doctor
Dillon's book we have the diary of M. Korostovetz: "Pre-War Diplomacy" (London, 1920).
The latter acted as secretary and interpreter to M. Witte. This unpretentious little volume,
while sometimes inaccurate in details, is, on the whole, when compared with the other sources,
reliable. Bishop's "Roosevelt," Howe's "Meyer," and a chapter in Melville E. Stone's "Fifty
Years a Journalist" (N.Y., 1922) supply all of the essential correspondence. The Japanese Foreign
Office published in 1906 "Protocoles de la Conférence de Paix entre le Japon et la Russie." The

243

ROOSEVELT AND THE RUSSO–JAPANESE WAR

Upon the exchange of credentials at the first sitting of the conference it developed that, notwithstanding Japan's expressed fears that Russia would not send envoys clothed with full powers, the authority of Witte and Rosen was greater than that of Komura and Takahira. The latter were empowered to negotiate subject only to the ratification of the Japanese Government, while Witte had full authority to conclude a treaty. It was therefore agreed at the second sitting, August 10th, that the credentials of the Russians should not be interpreted as conferring greater powers than those possessed by the Japanese envoys.[1]

At the second session Japan presented her terms of peace. They were substantially the same as those already given to Roosevelt,[2] with the exceptions that the demand for the dismantling of Vladivostok had been omitted, and the word "indemnity," at Roosevelt's suggestion, was not used. It was felt that Russia might find the term even more wounding to her dignity than the payment of the expense of the war under a more euphonious name. This expedient was a failure. The terms discussed and tentatively settled in the first eight conferences, up to and including Friday, August 18th, were as follows:

Russian Government likewise published the Protocols in French in a so-called "Orange Book." Many of the Russian counter-drafts of articles which were rejected are omitted from the Japanese edition of the Protocols. For this reason these publications must be used with caution and checked with Korostovetz. The only important records now missing are the letters which passed between the Japanese Foreign Office and their plenipotentiaries at Portsmouth as well as the letters between Baron Kaneko and Marquis Ito. A comparison of all these records, one with the other, and in turn with the Roosevelt Papers, leads to the discovery of no mystery, and one feels justified in the assumption that all the important facts relating to the conference are available for study. The Roosevelt Papers add very little in the way of new facts and are chiefly valuable at this point for the help they yield to an interpretation of the information already known.

In appendices at the end of the chapter we have collected all the important documents relative to Roosevelt's intervention.

[1] "Protocoles," p. 3.

[2] Chap. IX, Appendix J, pp. 231–32.

THE PEACE OF PORTSMOUTH

(1) Peace and amity between Russia and Japan.

(2) Japan's place in Korea.

(3) The evacuation and restoration of Manchuria.

(4) The freedom of China to take measures to develop the commerce and industry of Manchuria.

(5) The transfer of the leased area from Russia to China, subject to the consent of China.

(6) The transfer of the greater part of the southern section of the Chinese Eastern railway and the mining concessions to Japan, Russia retaining the Chinese Eastern railway, that is, the segment of the trans-Siberian system in northern Manchuria which provided a short cut to Vladivostok and a spur to the south as far as Kuanchengtze.

(7) Mutual engagement not to exploit the Manchurian railways for strategical purposes.

(8) Agreement to enter into a separate convention for the regulation of railway services.

Only a single phase, though an important one, of these negotiations need detain us.

In presenting the demands upon which these terms were based it became necessary for Japan to reveal again its purpose in Korea and Manchuria just as this purpose had been disclosed in the negotiations with Russia which preceded the outbreak of hostilities. For this revelation Japan had not prepared the public. In the Japanese terms relative to Korea and Manchuria there was a marked absence of phrases which would in any way tend to limit Japan's future sphere of action. There was no mention of the independence of Korea, and there was the qualifying phrase with reference to Manchuria that it was to be returned to China "subject to the guarantee of reform and improved administration."[1] The reservation with reference to Manchuria was particularly significant because the necessity for reform and improved administration in Korea had been the ground upon which Japan had urged its right to intervene in the peninsula in 1894, and that intervention had already led, in spite of many setbacks, to a substantial Japanese protectorate. Was, then, Japan planning a similar achievement in Manchuria, notwithstanding the promises which had been made directly to President Roosevelt on May 25th[2] that Manchuria would be restored to China?

M. Witte was quick to see the weakness in the Japanese position. Following the presentation of the Japanese demands the Russian delegation held a conference to discuss the terms.[3] M. Witte had no sentimental attachment to the Emperor of Korea nor did he care anything about the integrity of China, but both might be made into useful pawns. Having been wholly out of sympathy with the Russian political aggression in the East, he was quite willing to arrange a peace which would serve the purpose of keeping Russia out of temptation in the future. Witte proposed a bold stroke. It seemed to him feasible to accept the evident ambitions of Japan and even to go further. He suggested that it would be wise to propose to Japan an alliance in which Russia would engage to "insure" Japanese interests, not only in Korea, where they were already secure, and not merely in Manchuria, but also elsewhere in China. The plan seemed especially

---

[1] Article III, see Appendix J, p. 231; "Protocoles," p. 6.
[2] See p. 180.
[3] Korostovetz, pp. 56–58, 68, 75.

reasonable to him because he was aware that England and Japan had already been negotiating for a new alliance.[1] Witte even went so far as to suggest the idea to Komura and also presented the plan to Count Lamsdorff, who did not favour it. Komura likewise did not encourage it, although he did not close the door to further conversations. Had Marquis Ito been in Komura's place, the result might have been different.[2]

Having failed to secure the necessary support for this plan, which was proved within a few years to be premature rather than impractical, Witte contented himself with using the facts merely to embarrass his opponents according to approved diplomatic practice. On August 12th, he secured from Komura the admission that the independence of Korea no longer existed *"dans sa plenitude,"* and Witte good-naturedly agreed to omit from the article all reference to the sovereignty of Korea, but Japan consented, on the other hand, to take no measures against the sovereignty of the Empire without the consent of the Korean Government.[3]

In the case of Manchuria, Witte contented himself with a re-phrasing of the articles so that Japan and Russia would mutually agree to evacuate "completely and

---

[1] The second Anglo-Japanese alliance was signed in London, August 12th, only two days after this subject was discussed at Portsmouth. It is possible that the signing of the alliance and the presentation of the Japanese demands at Portsmouth, which took place on the same day, were not unrelated to this scheme. Marquis Ito had long favoured an agreement with Russia and had preferred it to an agreement with England in 1902 (Hayashi, p. 143). In 1905, however, an agreement between Japan and Russia would probably have been more unwelcome in London than it was five years later when England helped to bring it about.

[2] Witte's "Memoirs," p. 176; Korostovetz, p. 68.

[3] "Protocoles," p. 10. The Russian counter-draft of the article on Korea, which is omitted from th : Protocoles printed by the Japanese Government, is given in Korostovetz, p. 61. It contained the sentence: "It is also understood that the taking of such measures by Japan must not impair the sovereign rights of the Emperor of Korea." The text of the Russian reply to the first Japanese demands is given in *Harper's Weekly*, September 16, 1905, pp. 1334 ff.

simultaneously" and to restore "entirely and completely to the exclusive administration of China" all portions of Manchuria with the exception of the leased area, which by the provisions of another article (Art. V) were to be transferred subject to the consent of China. Then a separate article was added to the treaty (Art. IV) in which Japan and Russia reciprocally engaged "not to obstruct any general measures common to all countries, which China may take for the development of the commerce and industry of Manchuria"—very different provisions from the qualification that Japan would return Manchuria to China subject to reforms and improved administration.[1]

We may record here a personal opinion, based not so much on specific statements of Roosevelt as on a general review of his discussions together with the policy of Secretary Hay, that the American Government in 1905 would have acquiesced in the proposed Japanese policy in Manchuria just as it had accepted the new order in Korea. And we may add that there had been nothing in Japanese policy up to that time, with the possible exception of rumoured brutal conduct of Japan in Korea since the opening of the war, and some recent trade discriminations in Manchuria which were just becoming known, which offered any certain indication that Manchuria would not be better off under reforms and an administration supervised by Japanese than under the corrupt and impossible Manchu dynasty.

Japan, however, was now to reap the harvest of having broken faith, not with any Western government, but rather with a sympathetic public which had been led to look upon Japan's struggles with Russia as purely de-

---

[1] "Protocoles," pp. 17-19.

fensive and altruistic. This ensuing loss of public confidence became an important factor in the final conclusion of peace.[1]

THE INTERVENTION OF PRESIDENT ROOSEVELT

A few glimpses at the way in which President Roosevelt at Oyster Bay kept in touch with the proceedings of the conference at Portsmouth reveal again his fondness for irregular communications. Perhaps one may more properly call it his preference for effective methods. The Department of State was utilized only occasionally. Notwithstanding the appointment of Elihu Root in July to the place made vacant by the death of John Hay, Roosevelt continued to be his own Secretary of State so far as the relations with the peace conference were concerned. Third Assistant Secretary of State Herbert H. D. Pierce was at Portsmouth representing the Department and in charge of the arrangements for the conference. Through him on two or three occasions President Roosevelt communicated with the Russian plenipotentiaries. The correspondence with foreign governments was conducted partly through the Department of State, but many urgent communications were sent from or received at Oyster Bay. Regular diplomatic channels were used very little.

At Portsmouth there was "Cal" O'Laughlin, a newspaper representative already referred to.[2] O'Laughlin

---

[1] Korostovetz wrote in his diary, August 27th (p. 102): "During the day I went out walking and had a chat with Thompson [Associated Press representative]. He told me that the Japanese were uneasy at the course the negotiations had taken. They were alarmed at sympathy going over to our side, as they had shown their cards by letting it be seen that their real aim in continuing the campaign was not the independence of China and Korea but selfish designs." One is reminded of Roosevelt's remark, previously quoted, that the Japanese were "utterly selfish."

[2] See p. 195.

had succeeded in placing himself in the same relation to the Russian plenipotentiaries that he had held with Count Cassini. By frequent letters and then by means of a telegraphic code which he devised for the purpose, O'Laughlin kept the President informed not only as to the Russian deliberations but also as to the general prospects. He rendered important service. Other correspondents made contributions from time to time. Melville E. Stone of the Associated Press was in close touch with the President and was prepared to render an even more important service than was in the end required.[1] Lastly, Baron Kaneko remained in New York and by messenger, letters, and almost daily visits to Oyster Bay, supplied Roosevelt with the news from the Japanese point of view. Kaneko worked in perfect coöperation with Komura at Portsmouth, through whom his messages to Tokio were relayed. Ambassador Meyer was the only member of the American diplomatic corps who was called upon to render important service.

In the course of the sittings on Wednesday, Thursday, and Friday (August 16th–18th) it became apparent that Russia and Japan were in almost hopeless disagreement over the questions of indemnity and the cession of Sakhalin. Other disputed questions, the fisheries, the limitation of Russian naval strength in the Pacific, and the surrender of interned Russian naval vessels in neutral ports, could easily be settled if only the two important points could be taken care of. At Friday's sitting Witte and Komura had a personal conference in which a compromise was offered. Komura immediately telegraphed this fact

[1] On August 28th, the day before the final agreement, Korostovetz records in his diary (p. 103) that Thompson of the Associated Press told him that "the papers have been instructed to write to the effect that Russia will be acting unwisely if she declines Japan's last terms."

to Kaneko and asked him to "ask the President to wait for the outcome of this compromise before he takes a decisive step."[1]

Komura's message through Kaneko reached Oyster Bay too late. The President had already, after a conference with Kaneko, decided to intervene.

From Ambassador Meyer the President received the information on Friday (August 18th) that the Tsar had reaffirmed his purpose not to make peace unless the demands for territory and indemnity were dropped.[2] Roosevelt was prepared to support the Japanese in both these demands.[3] From Baron Sternberg he learned that preparations were already under way in Paris and London to rescue the conference by Anglo-French mediation, or to take it out of Roosevelt's hands in case he failed.[4] Such a message could hardly fail to put him on his mettle. He determined to approach the Russian Government directly. To Assistant Secretary Pierce he telegraphed (August 18th):

See Witte at once and present this message from the President and get an immediate answer from him.

---

[1]Korostovetz, p. 86, states that Witte represented that Komura offered the compromise. Komura stated that Witte made it. Komura wrote to Kaneko (Kaneko to Roosevelt, August 19, 1905): "To-day the Russian Envoy proposed a compromise in regard to Sakhalin and reimbursements; therefore you are requested to ask the President to wait for the outcome of this Compromise before he takes a decisive step. Moreover, the Compromise is to be kept a strict secret for the present."

This compromise, according to Korostovetz was that Sakhalin was to be divided and instead of indemnity Russia was to pay Japan for its retrocession. Korostovetz states that he saw Komura hand to Witte a paper, on which he infers that this compromise was outlined. Witte had already outlined such a compromise to Rosen ("Forty Years of Diplomacy," Vol. I, pp. 263-64).

[2]Howe's "Meyer," p. 195.

[3]August 16, 1905, Roosevelt to Pres. Charles W. Eliot: ". . . I think I can get the Japanese to abandon two of the proposed articles. But there will have to be some indemnity under some name, and it is madness for the Russians to expect the Japanese to give up Sakhalin, which they have taken."

[4]Appendix A, p. 265.

ROOSEVELT AND THE RUSSO-JAPANESE WAR

"To M. Sergius Witte: I earnestly request that you send either Baron Rosen or some other gentleman who is in your confidence to see me immediately so that I may through him send you a strictly confidential message."[1]

Baron Rosen visited Sagamore Hill on Saturday and as a result of his conference carried back to Portsmouth the outline of a proposed compromise which the President requested to have transmitted to the Tsar as a personal suggestion of the President's. Roosevelt proposed that Russia agree to the division of Sakhalin. In view of the fact that Japan was now in possession of nearly all of the island, he suggested that Russia might with propriety buy it back from Japan for a sum to be fixed after a commission of neutrals had reviewed the facts. Roosevelt argued that such a procedure would allow time for passions to cool, and would prevent the breaking up of the conference. The delay thus obtained, urged the President, would operate in Russia's favour.[2]

Notwithstanding the fact that the Russians resented this interference, O'Laughlin was able to telegraph on Sunday that, although the Tsar was adopting an unyielding attitude, Witte "earnestly recommended concessions." O'Laughlin suggested that direct pressure on the Tsar through Ambassador Meyer would reinforce Witte's argument.

---

[1] See Rosen, Vol. I, pp. 269–70, for Rosen's account of this message.

[2] This proposition, which was made on Saturday, August 19th, bears such a striking resemblance to the plan outlined to Roosevelt in the following telegram from O'Laughlin that one wonders whether Roosevelt's plan was not based on the information supplied to him from Portsmouth. O'Laughlin telegraphed in cipher, August 19th: "As you are probably aware, Sakhalin and indemnity principal questions; others said to be capable of adjustment. Russians talking earnestly about dividing Sakhalin, retaining northern portion, which valueless. Japan holding southern portion where fisheries, agriculture. Such compromise possible. Russians insist won't pay indemnity though might pay something for part Sakhalin, prisoners and other like expenses. Best Japanese opinion five hundred millions minimum."

THE PEACE OF PORTSMOUTH

The President approved of the suggestion for he was never quite sure that the Russians would transmit his messages as he gave them. Therefore, on Monday he cabled to Meyer to see the Tsar personally and deliver him a personal communication.[1]

If Peace is not made now and war is continued [wrote Roosevelt] it may well be that, though the financial strain upon Japan would be severe, yet in the end Russia would be shorn of those east Siberian provinces which have been won for her by the heroism of her sons during the last three centuries. The proposed peace leaves the ancient Russian boundaries absolutely intact. The only change in territory will be that Japan will get that part of Sakhalin which was hers up to thirty years ago. As Sakhalin is an island it is, humanly speaking, impossible that the Russians could reconquer it in view of the disaster to their navy; and to keep the northern half of it is a guarantee for the security of Vladivostok and eastern Siberia for Russia. It seems to me that every consideration of national self-interest, of military expediency, and of broad humanity makes it eminently wise and right for Russia to conclude peace substantially along these lines, and it is my hope and prayer that Your Majesty will take this view.

Two days later, Wednesday, August 23d, the President supplemented this message with another explaining more in detail how Russia would not be committed to the payment of an unreasonable sum, for the amount would be submitted to a commission to pass on.[2] In the earlier telegram he had used the phrase "a substantial sum," for the amount to be paid for the return of Sakhalin to Russia.

---

[1] Text in full, Appendix B, pp. 265–67.
[2] Text, Appendix C, p. 267.

The plan was designed to save Russia's face and its success depended, of course, entirely on how badly Russia desired peace.

From the nature of the messages to the Tsar it might be inferred that the President had become an attorney for the Japanese. Such, however, was far from the fact.[1] Witte was known to have approved of the division of Sakhalin, and to have favoured the payment of a substantial sum in lieu of an indemnity. Roosevelt was merely seeking to help the proposition along. Now he turned his attention to the Japanese.

After a conference with Baron Kaneko, who appears to have accepted his views and to have reflected the moderate policy of Marquis Ito, the President addressed to Kaneko a personal letter which was designed for transmission to Tokio and for the ultimate view of the Emperor. It was a sharp letter, phrased so as to provoke reflection.[2]

I think I ought to tell you [wrote Roosevelt] that I hear on all sides a good deal of complaint expressed among the friends of Japan as to the possibility of Japan's continuing the war for a large indemnity.

He warned the Japanese that in such a case there would be a shifting of public opinion which might influence the

---

[1]Since the publication during the Institute of Politics at Williamstown in August, 1924, of the terms of the agreement between Count Katsura and President Roosevelt several editorial writers both in this country and abroad have argued that the President must have been guilty of bad faith toward Russia at Portsmouth in view of the previous agreement with Japan. In the light of the acts presented above we do not see how the charge of bad faith can be supported. Roosevelt's mediation between Japan and Russia ended in June when he secured the consent of both Powers to the peace conference. At Portsmouth, there was no resemblance to technical mediation. At no point in the negotiations was Roosevelt acting as other than an outsider anxious to see peace restored. He did not mediate: he intervened.

[2]Text, Appendix D, pp. 268-69.

settlement. He stated that Russia had absolutely refused to pay a large indemnity. (Japan was then asking $7,000,000,000.) Moreover, argued Roosevelt with much force, a continuance of the war would eat up as much indemnity as could ever be exacted and then Japan would still have to pay for the expenses already incurred. The war was costing more than $1,000,000 a day.

Ambassador Meyer experienced difficulty in conveying the President's message directly to the Tsar. The bureaucracy, already much annoyed at Roosevelt's direct appeal in June, took precautions this time. The message was sent in a code which the Foreign Office could read.[1] Meyer had reason to believe that the delivery of the message was delayed so that the Foreign Office would have time to consider it and coach the Tsar as to the answer.[2] The Ambassador did not succeed in reaching the Tsar until Wednesday afternoon (August 23d). The latter appeared to be already familiar with the nature of his errand and quickly expressed his determination not to pay indemnity or surrender territory. Meyer argued with him for two hours and at length he agreed to the division of Sakhalin and the payment of a "substantial sum" for the return to Russia of the northern part.[3] As for the payment of indemnity, whatever the name might be, the Tsar would not consider it. He was well aware that

---

[1]Nearly a year earlier the code book at the American Embassy had come into possession of the Russian Government, and when Meyer arrived in April, he found that the Government had been intercepting the correspondence of the Embassy. After that the usual method was to send the messages by way of Berlin, whence they were carried into Russia by courier, but in this instance Roosevelt was too impatient to admit such delays.

[2]Howe's "Meyer," pp. 197-202, Meyer to Roosevelt, August 25, 1905.

[3]Text of Meyer's report to Roosevelt, Appendix E, pp. 270-71.

the Japanese needed money, and he was equally aware that there was no precedent for the payment of indemnity under such conditions. Russia was not in the condition of France in 1870, nor of China in 1895. "The Japanese are making claims not based alone on victories," he said, "but as though they were at the gates of my capital. Why have they not attacked the army for nearly four months?" This was a pertinent question. As soon as the interview was over Meyer cabled that the Tsar would pay a "substantial sum" for the northern half of Sakhalin, and for the care of prisoners in Japan, but would make no other concessions.[1]

Russia had offered her most favourable terms. Meanwhile Roosevelt, through Kaneko, sent a second message to the Emperor of Japan in which he reiterated his arguments and appealed to Japan to take Sakhalin and relinquish all demands for indemnity.[2] He concluded with an impassioned appeal to which Japan would be by no means insensible, for Japan desired above many other objects to be respected and well regarded among the nations. Roosevelt urged:

The civilized world looks to her (Japan) to make the nations believe in her, let her show her leadership in matters ethical no less than in matters military. The appeal is made to her in the name of all that is lofty and noble, and to this appeal I hope she will not be deaf.

It is strange language to find in diplomatic records.

---

[1]Meyer's report and Roosevelt's second message (August 23d) crossed. Meyer was thus confused and sent an inquiry to Oyster Bay which drew from Roosevelt still further elaboration of his arguments. The text of this exchange of telegrams is given as Appendices F and G, pp. 271–74.

[2]Text, Appendix H, pp. 274–75.

THE PEACE OF PORTSMOUTH

The Peace Conference resumed its sessions on Wednesday the 23d. In the afternoon Witte made a tentative proposition for Japan to retain all of Sakhalin and to drop entirely the demand for indemnity. Komura refused.[1] Thus Japan was manœuvred into exactly the position against which the President had warned both Kaneko and Komura. Japan now appeared to be willing to resume the war for the sake of money. At the next sitting, Saturday, the 26th, Witte had another private conversation with Komura in which he proposed the division of Sakhalin and no indemnity. This was less than had been proposed tentatively three days before. Witte stated that he had orders to break off the negotiations if Komura continued to insist upon indemnity.[2]

The news of the formation of the second Anglo-Japanese Alliance which had been signed on August 12th was reported in the papers on Friday the 25th. Roosevelt had been made aware through Sir Mortimer Durand, by instruction from the Foreign Office, that the negotiations had been in progress and he knew the nature of the terms. For some reason the announcement of its conclusion had been held back. According to information from German sources, the British Government had caused the delay. But the publication on Friday might be taken as the reply of the Foreign Office to an appeal which Roosevelt had directed to Durand on the preceding

---

[1] Korostovetz, pp. 96–97.

[2] The day before Witte had intimated to two responsible journalists, who interviewed him together, that Russia might be willing to pay as much as from two to three hundred millions for the half of Sakhalin. The next day he categorically denied having given this intimation, but one inclines to the belief that he did make it and that on Saturday Witte felt so confident of victory that he was not even willing to offer Komura as much as on the preceding Wednesday. H. H. D. Pierce to Roosevelt, August 25, 1905.

257

Friday. In this way the British Government rendered substantial though exclusively indirect support to the President.[1]

On Friday the President had addressed his second appeal to the Tsar.[2] He reminded the Emperor that the Japanese were already in possession of Sakhalin, so that in giving up the island Russia was actually surrendering no territory. The Japanese proposed to retrocede to Russia the northern half of the island and would agree that the amount of money to be paid by Russia to redeem it could be settled by further negotiations. Roosevelt again suggested provisional arbitration. He warned the Tsar that if these terms were rejected Japan might resume the war and take all of eastern Siberia. "Such a loss to Russia," wrote Roosevelt, "would in my judgment be a disaster of portentous size, and I earnestly desire to save Russia from such a risk."

The situation at Portsmouth on Sunday, August 27th, was distinctly worse than a week earlier. Notwithstanding the appeals of the President, Russia was unmoved and between the middle and the end of the week had shown a disposition to increase rather than reduce her demands. Now Russia would not divide Sakhalin and Witte at least would favour no payment of money whatever, although the Tsar had agreed to a "substantial sum." The only quarter from which concessions could be expected was

---

[1] August 18, 1905, Roosevelt to Durand; also Sternberg to Roosevelt. On September 5th Durand wrote to the President: "[Lansdowne] also asked me to let you know privately that the agreement between England and Japan, the substance of which I communicated to you when I was at Oyster Bay, was signed not long afterwards. His Majesty's Government felt that by promptly concluding this agreement, and thereby relieving Japan of all apprehension of vindictive action on the part of Russia in the future, they would make it easier for Japan to moderate her demands, and they believe that their action had the result they anticipated."

[2] Roosevelt to Meyer, August 25th, Appendix G, pp. 272-74.

Japan, and the Japanese were still holding out for a large payment of money.

The Japanese envoys in Portsmouth and Baron Kaneko in New York were in despair. Witte had been ordered to break off the negotiations on Monday if the demand for money was continued; Kaneko appears to have keenly felt the weakness of the Japanese position, but Komura may have been more obdurate. Roosevelt felt that he could do nothing more.

Baron Kaneko then appealed to Melville E. Stone. The latter suggested a request to the Kaiser to use his good offices with the Tsar.[1] Notwithstanding some embarrassing delays the message to the Kaiser was sent on Monday.[2] With the approval of the Japanese envoys, the proposition was submitted to the German Emperor that peace could be obtained if Russia would pay a sum to be determined by a neutral commission for the return of the northern half of Sakhalin. This sum would take the place of all indemnity. In order to commit the Japanese to this proposition Mr. Stone, with the approval of the President, released the information to the press on Monday evening that Japan would waive the indemnity. The significance of this appeal through the Kaiser was that the Japanese had been publicly committed to waiving the indemnity. It produced no effect on the Tsar.

By this time St. Petersburg was thoroughly convinced that Japan had no choice, because of her financial straits, but to make peace. Russia would not now promise even the "substantial sum." Meyer cabled August 28th:

[1] "Fifty Years a Journalist," pp. 287–90. Stone's account is partially supported by the Roosevelt Papers, but the significance of the action would appear to have been not wholly as Stone understood it.

[2] Text, Appendix I, pp. 275-76.

ROOSEVELT AND THE RUSSO–JAPANESE WAR

Situation as it appears here, Russia absolutely decided not to pay any war indemnity. In this respect apparently supported by the press, the people, and even the peasants. Each country would like peace, yet Russia feels that Japan's financial condition is such that in the long run she will be ruined financially unless she makes peace. Japan evidently thought that Russia, on account of her internal troubles, could be forced into paying war indemnity. Issue, as recognized in Russia, has come down to a question of money, which will strengthen the war party throughout Russia.

The envoys had a sitting on Tuesday, August 29th, which had been postponed from the day before with Witte's approval, notwithstanding the orders of the Foreign Office to break off the negotiations on Monday. Witte felt that it would be a great mistake for Russia to refuse to listen to the last proposition from Japan. In the conference on Tuesday, Witte assumed the aggressive and handed to the Japanese a note in which Russia refused categorically to pay the 1,200,000,000 yen which had been demanded, and then offered to cede to Japan the southern half of Sakhalin on condition that the northern part remain in the possession of Russia without any compensation.[1]

He further warned the Japanese that this was the last concession which Russia would make. It was not as much as the Tsar had consented to seven days earlier.

The scene can best be described by an eyewitness:

Absolute silence reigned for a few seconds. Witte, as usual, kept tearing up the paper that was lying beside him. Rosen smoked his cigarette. The Japanese continued to be enigmatic.

[1]Text, Appendix J, pp. 276–77; Korostovetz, pp. 107–08.

THE PEACE OF PORTSMOUTH

At last Komura, in a well-controlled voice, said that the Japanese Government, having for its aim the restoration of peace and the bringing of the negotiations to a successful conclusion, expressed its consent to Russia's proposal to divide Sakhalin in two, without indemnity being paid. Witte calmly replied that the Japanese proposal was accepted and that the line of demarcation of Sakhalin would be reckoned the fiftieth degree.[1]

At the last minute Baron Komura had been stricken with weakness. If he had held out he probably could have obtained all of Sakhalin for Japan. This at least was the firm conviction of President Roosevelt. To Cecil Spring-Rice he wrote (September 1st):

I think the Japanese gave up more than they need to have given up when they returned the northern half of Sakhalin, which I am confident I could have obtained for them—or at least which I think I could have made Russia redeem for a small sum of money. But on the whole I think it was all right, and I think the peace is just to Russia and Japan, and also good for England and the United States.

The Associated Press despatch on the afternoon of the 29th, describing the reception of the news and containing an interview with M. Witte, is sufficiently vivid to be worthy of preservation. It contains statements of the Russian plenipotentiary which have an important place in the historical record. We use it with purely verbal changes.

Mr. Witte, accompanied by Baron Rosen, came to the hotel for luncheon. There was a wonderful demonstration upon their

[1]Korostovetz, p. 108.

arrival. A great crowd had collected under the porte cochère of the annex where the Russians were quartered and when their automobile drew up, the air was torn with frantic cheers. Hats were thrown into the air. Mr. Witte, as he stepped out of the motor car, seemed quite overcome. Too full for utterance, he could only grasp and shake the hands that were extended to him. Baron Rosen also was equally moved and received the congratulations of the crowd in silence. For about five minutes the two plenipotentiaries were kept upon the porch listening to the incoherent praises of the hotel guests. "Do you pay indemnity?" was the universal interrogation.

"*Pas un sou* [not a sou]," was the response.

Forcing his way to the door Mr. Witte encountered the members of the Russian mission who rushed forward to shake his hand. Briefly in Russian he gave them the joyful tidings. Then as he started up the stairs, the newspaper correspondents clamoured for information. "What have you done? How is it settled?" they cried.

"We pay not a kopek of indemnity," he replied as he turned at the landing halfway up the stairs. "We get half of Sakhalin, that is the agreement in a nutshell."

The Associated Press correspondent accompanied Mr. Witte to his room. The ambassador had been quite overcome by the great ovation he had received and the intense strain he had been under. He threw himself into his armchair and after a few minutes to "pull himself together" he began to speak slowly and deliberately, almost as if he were talking to himself.

"It seems incredible," he said. "I do not believe that any other man in my place would have dared to hope for the possibility of peace on the conditions to which we have just agreed. From all sides, from President Roosevelt down to my own friends in Russia, I received up to the last moment, even this morning, urgent representations that something should be paid to Japan." At this point Mr. Witte, who was still labouring under excitement, again almost lost control of himself. He paused a moment.

Then he went on: "The Japanese wanted to take our interned ships and I have not consented. The Japanese wanted to limit our naval power in the Far East and I have not consented. The Japanese wanted war indemnity, or reimbursement for the cost of the war, aye, demanded it, and I have not consented. The Japanese wanted the Chinese Eastern Railway, south of Harbin, but I gave them only the railway in the possession of their troops south of Chengchiatum. The Japanese wanted the Island of Sakhalin and I refused it, agreeing, however, at the last moment to cede the southern half and then only because I was commanded by my Sovereign to yield and obeyed. Not only do we not pay so much as a kopek but we obtain half of Sakhalin now in their possession. At this morning's meeting I presented my written proposition which was the Russian ultimatum. It was accepted by the Japanese. I was amazed. Until I was in the conference room I did not think that would happen. I could not anticipate such a great and happy event.

"It was a psychological crisis. I had made up my mind not to strike out a letter of the ultimatum I submitted. So far as I was concerned it was ended. But I could not tell how it would work on the Japanese mind. It was a complete victory for us."

In giving out such an interview Witte again exhibited his surpassing cleverness. Was it indeed such a great Russian victory?

It does not seem to me [wrote the President to George Harvey, September 6th] that the Japanese are wise in letting everybody talk as if they had got the worst of it. They have won an astonishing triumph and have received a remarkable reward. They have secured control of Manchuria and Korea. They have Port Arthur and Dalny, and the south half of Sakhalin. In destroying the Russian Navy they have made themselves a formidable sea power—one which, in the Pacific, is doubtless a match for any nation save England. Under such circumstances, it seems to me that they are very unwise, because they could not get an indemnity to which they had no real title whatever, to make it appear as if the terms of peace were utterly unsatisfactory.

To an extraordinary degree it had been a newspaper battle. Japan had won the first victories between 1900 and 1904 when she had convinced the world that Russia was threatening to take Korea as well as Manchuria. She had won again during the war by a censorship of the press and personally conducted tours of the battlefields which favoured the release of tales of heroism and suppressed or retarded the spread of other narratives less flattering. Yet now at the end, although Japan had won the material victory, she lost the battle for public opinion not only in Portsmouth and in the United States, but what was more serious, in Japan, where a disappointed populace raged.

APPENDIX A

Sternberg to Roosevelt, August 18th

The German Ambassador at Paris wires: "The Foreign Office has given out the news that during the last days an exchange of ideas has taken place between Paris and London to the effect that in case of failure of the Portsmouth Conference an attempt is to be made to merely cause an interruption. England and France then are to offer their good services to bring the conflict to an end ["]. It is firmly believed here that England and France will not wait for a dissolution of the Conference, but will take advantage of the first hitch so as to place themselves in your position.

APPENDIX B

Roosevelt to Meyer, August 21, 1905

Oyster Bay, N. **Y.**

MEYER,
 American Ambassador.
  St. Petersburg.

Please see His Majesty personally immediately and deliver following message from me:

"I earnestly ask Your Majesty to believe that in what I am about to say and to advise I speak as the earnest well-wisher of Russia, and give you the advice I should give were I a Russian patriot and statesman. The Japanese have, as I understand it, abandoned their demands for the interned ships and the limitation of the Russian naval power in the Pacific, which conditions I felt were improper for Russia to yield to. Moreover, I find, to my surprise and pleasure, that the Japanese are willing to restore the northern half of Sakhalin to Russia, Russia, of course, in such case to pay a substantial sum for the surrender of territory by the Japanese, and for the return of Russian prisoners. It seems to me that if peace can be obtained substantially on these terms it will be both just and honourable, and that it would be a dreadful calamity to have the war continued when peace can be thus obtained. Of the twelve points which the plenipotentiaries have been discussing, on eight they have come to a substantial agreement. Two, which were offensive to Russia, the Japanese will, as I understand it, withdraw. The remaining two can be met by an agreement in principle that the Japanese shall restore, or retrocede, to Russia the northern half of Sakhalin, while Russia of course pays an adequate sum for this retrocession and for the Russian prisoners. If this agreement can be made the question as to the exact amount can be a subject of negotiation. Let me repeat how earnestly I feel that it is for Russia's interest to conclude peace on substantially these terms. No one can foretell the result of the continuance of the war and I have no doubt that it is to Japan's advantage to conclude peace. But in my judgment it is infinitely more to the advantage of Russia. If peace is not made now and war is continued it may well be that, though the financial strain upon Japan would be severe, yet in the end Russia would be shorn of those East Siberian provinces, which have been won for her by the heroism of her sons during the last three centuries. The proposed peace leaves the ancient Russian boundaries absolutely intact. The only change in territory will be that Japan will get that part of Sakhalin which was hers up to thirty years ago. As Sakhalin is an island, it is, humanly speaking, impossible that the Russians should reconquer it in view of the disaster to their navy, and to keep the northern half of it is a guarantee for the security of Vladivostok and eastern Siberia for Russia. It seems to me that every consideration of national self-interest, of military expediency, and of broad humanity, makes it eminently wise and right for Russia to conclude peace substantially along these lines, and it is my hope and prayer that Your Majesty may take this view.

"THEODORE ROOSEVELT."

APPENDIX C

Roosevelt to Meyer, August 23, 1905

Oyster Bay, N. Y.

MEYER,
   St. Petersburg.

Make clear to His Majesty that if my suggestion is adopted, then the whole question of what reasonable amount is to be paid for the retrocession of northern Sakhalin, and for the return of the Russian prisoners, will remain a subject for further negotiations, so that the acceptance in principle, of the terms I have suggested, would not commit the Russian Government to any particular sum of money, and above all would not in any way commit Russia to pay any amount which would be exorbitant or humiliating. Please send this supplementary cable to His Majesty at once and further explain that I of course cannot be sure Japan will act on my suggestions, but that I know she ought to, and that if Russia accedes to them I shall try my best to get Japan to accede to them also.

APPENDIX D

Roosevelt to Kaneko, August 22, 1905

Oyster Bay, N. Y.

MY DEAR BARON KANEKO:

I think I ought to tell you that I hear on all sides a good deal of complaint expressed among the friends of Japan as to the possibility of Japan's continuing the war for a large indemnity. A prominent member of the Senate Committee on Foreign Relations, a strong pro-Japanese man,[1] has just written me:

"It does not seem to me as if Japan could possibly afford to continue the war merely for a money indemnity. I should not blame her if she broke off on the issue of obtaining the island of Sakhalin. But if she renews the fighting merely to get money she will not get the money and she will turn sympathy from her in this country and elsewhere very rapidly. I am bound to say I do not think her case for indemnity a good one. She holds no Russian territory except Sakhalin, and that she wants to keep."

I think your government ought to understand that there will be at least a very considerable sentiment in America among men who have hitherto been favourable to the Japanese along these lines. The willingness to retrocede the northern half of Sakhalin gives a chance to get some money in addition to that which is justly due for the Russian prisoners, but I do not think that anything like the amount advanced by Japan as what she wants—that is, six hundred millions—should be asked or could possibly be obtained. You know how strongly I have advised the Russians to make peace. I equally strongly advise Japan

---

[1] Senator Lodge.

not to continue the fight for a money indemnity. If she does, then I believe that there will be a considerable shifting of public opinion against her. I do not believe that this public opinion will have any very tangible effect, but still it should not be entirely disregarded. Moreover, I do not believe that the Japanese nation would achieve its ends if it continued the war simply on the question of the indemnity. I think that Russia will refuse to pay and that the general sentiment of the civilized world will back her in refusing to pay the great amount asked, or anything like such an amount. Of course, if she will pay, then I have nothing to say. But if she will not pay, then you would find that after making war for another year, even though you were successful in obtaining East Siberia, you would have spent four or five hundred million dollars additional to what has already been spent, you would have spilled an immense amount of blood, and though you would have obtained East Siberia you would have obtained something which you do not want, and Russia would be in no condition to give you any money at all. She certainly could not give you enough money to make up for the extra amount you would have spent. Of course my judgment may be at fault in this matter, but this is my judgment, speaking conscientiously from the standpoint of the interest of Japan as I see it. Moreover, I feel of course that every interest of civilization and humanity forbids the continuance of this war merely for a large indemnity.

This letter is of course strictly confidential, but I should be glad to have you cable it to your home government, and hope you can do so. If cabled at all, it should be done at once.

Sincerely yours,
THEODORE ROOSEVELT.

APPENDIX E

Meyer to Roosevelt, August 23, 1905

St. Petersburg.

The Tsar received me in Peterhof at 4 P. M. Said he would welcome peace which he believed to be honourable and lasting, but reiterates that Russia will not pay any war indemnity whatever. In that, his conscience tells him he is right and he feels sure he has the support of the nation. Appreciate that their naval arm has been cut off, but still has an army which has endurance, opposed to the Japanese army, which latter army is thousands of miles from St. Petersburg. He added, "if necessary I will join the army myself and go to the front." Claims that it should not be forgotten that the Japanese commenced hostilities, that they now have obtained all that they went to war for and a great deal more. He is unwilling to pay a substantial sum for half of Sakhalin as it would be interpreted as a war indemnity differently expressed. He said "I should prefer to lose territory temporarily than to humiliate the country by paying a war indemnity as though a vanquished nation. Russia is not in the position of France in 1870." The Tsar told me he had received yesterday telegram from German Emperor urging peace, read me his reply in which he said peace was impossible if Japan insisted upon any war indemnity. Closeted with the Emperor two hours, at the end of which time he informed me of the terms on which he would conclude peace. Acceptance of the eight points substantially agreed upon by the plenipotentiaries at Portsmouth, [no ?] payment of war indemnity but a liberal and generous payment for care and maintenance of Russian prisoners but not such a sum as could be interpreted for a war indemnity, withdrawal of Japan's claims for interned ships and limitation of naval power in the Pacific, Russia to possess north half of Sakhalin while Japan to retain southern half (that portion which formerly belonged to Japan). The Emperor instructed me to express his thanks and full appreciation to the President for the efforts that he had made in behalf of peace.

MEYER.

APPENDIX F

Meyer to Roosevelt, August 24, 1905

St. Petersburg.

Notify President that his second cable has been forwarded to Tsar. Let me know if his was sent before or after the arrival of mine. I discussed for two hours with Tsar yesterday Sakhalin and payment of substantial sum for north half. Tried to commit him to maximum amount he would be willing to pay. Emperor repeatedly stated that he had given his word publicly not to pay war indemnity of any kind or surrender Russian soil. It was only after I got him to acknowledge that lower half of Sakhalin had been, like Port Arthur, merely temporary Russian territory that he agreed to a division of Sakhalin. I think, moreover, that by negotiation Russia might consent to pay land value for north half of Sakhalin on same basis as Alaska was sold to us. Discussed it with Tsar (after he absolutely refused to pay substantial sum) but he said, "How can the value be ascertained?" Shies at it and fears Russians would consider any payment dishonourable. Claims he must act according to his conscience in this matter. Can you advise me of probable amount of money Japan has now on deposit in United States?

MEYER.

APPENDIX G

Roosevelt to Meyer, August 25, 1905

Oyster Bay, N. Y.

MEYER,
St. Petersburg.

My second cable was forwarded after the arrival of your first. Japan has now on deposit in United States about fifty million dollars of the last war loan. I do not know whether she has more. Please tell His Majesty that I dislike intruding any advice on him again, but for fear of misapprehension I venture again to have these statements made to him. I of course would not have him act against his conscience, but I earnestly hope his conscience will guide him so as to prevent the continuance of a war when this continuance may involve Russia in a greater calamity than has ever befallen it since it first rose to power in both Europe and Asia. I see it publicly announced to-day by Count Lamsdorff that Russia will neither pay money nor surrender territory. I beg His Majesty to consider that such an announcement means absolutely nothing when Sakhalin is already in the hands of the Japanese. If on such a theory the war is persevered in no one can foretell the result, but the military representatives of the Powers most friendly to Russia assure me that the continuance of the war will probably mean the loss not merely of Sakhalin but of eastern Siberia, and if after a year of struggle this proves true, then any peace which came could only come on terms which would indicate a real calamity. Most certainly I think it will be a bad thing for Japan to go on with the war, but I think it will be a far worse thing for Russia. There is now a fair chance of getting peace on honourable terms, and it seems to me that it will be a dreadful thing for Russia, and for all the civilized world, if the chance is thrown away. My advices are that the plenipotentiaries at Portsmouth have come to

THE PEACE OF PORTSMOUTH

a substantial agreement on every point except the money question and the question of Sakhalin. Let it now be announced that as regards these two points peace shall be made on the basis of the retrocession of the northern half of Sakhalin to Russia on payment of a sum of redemption money by Russia, the amount of this redemption money and the amount to be paid for the Russian prisoners to be settled by further negotiations. This does not commit the Russian Government as to what sum shall be paid, leaving it open to further negotiation. If it is impossible for Russia and Japan to come to an agreement on this sum, they might possibly call in the advice of, say, some high French or German official appointed by or with the consent of Russia, and some English official appointed by or with the consent of Japan, and have these men then report to the negotiators their advice, which might or might not be binding upon the negotiators. This it seems to me would be an entirely honourable way of settling the difficulty. I cannot of course guarantee that Japan will agree to this proposal, but if His Majesty agrees to it I will endeavour to get the Japanese Government to do so likewise. I earnestly hope that this cable of mine can receive His Majesty's attention before the envoys meet to-morrow, and I cannot too strongly say that I feel that peace now may prevent untold calamities in the future. Let me repeat that in this proposal I suggest that neither Russia nor Japan do anything but face accomplished facts and that I do not specify or attempt to specify what amount should be paid, leaving the whole question of the amount to be paid as redemption money for the northern half of Sakhalin to be settled by further negotiation. I fear that if these terms are rejected it may be possible that Japan will give up any idea of making peace or of ever getting money, and that she will decide to take and to keep Vladivostok and Harbin and the whole Manchurian railway, and this of course would mean that she would take East Siberia. Such a loss to Russia would in my judgment be a disaster of portentous size, and I earnestly desire to save Russia from such a risk. If peace is made on the terms I have mentioned, Russia is left at the end of this war substantially unharmed, the national honour and interest saved, and the results of what Russians have done in Asia since the days of Ivan the Terrible unimpaired. But if peace is now rejected, and if Japan decides that she will give up any idea of obtaining any redemption money or any other sum, no matter how small, the military situation is such that there is at least a good chance, and in the estimate of most outside observers a strong probability, that though Japan will have to make heavy sacrifices she will yet take Harbin, Vladivostok, and East Siberia, and if this is once done the probabilities are overwhelming that she could never be dislodged. I cannot too strongly state my conviction that while peace in accordance with the suggestions above outlined is earnestly to be desired from the standpoint of the whole world and from the standpoints of both combatants, yet that far above all it is chiefly to Russia's interest and perhaps to her vital interest that it should come in this way and at this time.

THEODORE ROOSEVELT.

APPENDIX H

Roosevelt to Kaneko, August 23, 1905

Oyster Bay, N. Y.

MY DEAR BARON KANEKO:

In supplement to what I wrote you yesterday, for the consideration of His Majesty the Japanese Emperor's envoys, let me add this.

It seems to me that it is to the interest of the great empire of Nippon now to make peace, for two reasons: 1, self-interest, 2, the interest of the world, to which she owes a certain duty. Remember, I do not speak of continuing the war rather than give up Sakhalin, which I think would be right, but of continuing the war in order to get a great sum of money from Russia, which I think would be wrong. Of course you may succeed in getting it, but in my judgment even this success would be too dearly paid for, and if you failed to get the money, no additional humiliations and losses inflicted on Russia would repay Japan for the additional expenditure in blood, in money, in national exhaustion.

1. It is Japan's interest now to close the war. She has won the control of Korea and Manchuria, she has doubled her own fleet in destroying that of Russia, she has Port Arthur, Dalny, the Manchurian railroad, she has Sakhalin. It is not worth her while to continue the war for money, when so to continue it would probably eat up more money than she could at the end get back from Russia. She will be wise now to close the war in triumph, and to take her seat as a leading member at the council table of the nations.

2. Ethically it seems to me that Japan owes a duty to the world at this crisis. The civilized world looks to her to make peace, the nations believe in her, let her show her leadership in matters ethical no less than in matters military. The appeal is made to her in the name of all that is lofty and noble, and to this appeal I hope she will not be deaf.

With profound regard, sincerely yours,

THEODORE ROOSEVELT.

APPENDIX I

Oyster Bay, N. Y.
August 27, 1905.

HIS MAJESTY,
WILLIAM, Emperor of Germany.

Peace can be obtained on the following terms: Russia to pay no indemnity whatever and to receive back north half of Sakhalin for which it is to pay to Japan whatever amount a mixed commission may determine. This is my proposition to which the Japanese have assented reluctantly and only under strong pressure from me. The plan is for each of the contending parties to name an equal number of members of the commission and for them themselves to name the odd member. The Japanese assert that Witte has in principle agreed that Russia should pay something to get back the north half of Sakhalin and indeed he intimated to me that they might buy it back at a reasonable figure, something on the scale of that for which Alaska was sold to the United States.

These terms which strike me as extremely moderate I have not presented in this form to the Russian Emperor. I feel that you have more influence with him than either I or any one else can have. As the situation is exceedingly strained and the relations between the plenipotentiaries critical to a degree, immediate action is necessary. Can you not take the initiative by presenting these terms at once to him? Your success in the matter will make the entire civilized world your debtor. This proposition virtually relegates all the unsettled issues of the war to the arbitration of a mixed commission as outlined above, and I am unable to see how Russia can refuse your request if in your wisdom you see fit to make it.

THEODORE ROOSEVELT.

APPENDIX J

Communication made by the Plenipotentiaries of Russia in the Session of August 29, 1905

La notice présentée par les Plénipotentiaires du Japon à la Séance du 23 août et formulant en quatre points la proposition de restaurer à la Russie la partie nord de Sakhaline moyennant une somme de 1,200,000,000 yens—a fait l'objet de la plus sérieuse considération de la part du Gouvernement Impérial de Russie.

En réponse à cette notice les Plénipotentiaires de Russie ont l'honneur d'informer les Plénipotentiaires du Japon que le versement de toute somme excepté celle pour l'entretien des prisonniers de guerre étant contraire à l'une des principales bases exposées par la Russie lors de l'ouverture des négociations, le Gouvernement Impérial de Russie se voit dans l'impossibillité de consentir à la proposition précitée.

Les Plénipotentiaires de Russie ont également présenté à la Conférence des raisons très sérieuses pour démontrer l'importance pour la Russie de la possession de toute l'île de Sakhaline.

Toutefois Sa Majesté l'Empereur, afin de donner un nouveau témoignage de son sincère désir de contribuer au rétablissement de la paix en Extrême Orient, consent à céder au Japon la partie sud de l'île de Sakhaline, à condition que la partie nord reste en la possession de la Russie, sans aucune compensation. Il est bien entendu que la Japon devra dans ce cas garantir la liberté de navigation dans le détroit de Lapérouse et s'engager à ne prendre aucune mesure militaire dans la partie de Sakhaline occupée par lui.

En présentant ce projet à la considération des Plénipotentiaires du Japon, les Plénipotentiaires de Russie ont l'honneur de déclarer, sur l'ordre de leur Auguste Maître, que ce projet forme la dernière concession que la Russie puisse faire dans le but unique d'arriver à une entente.

CHAPTER XI

Roosevelt and His Critics

PRESIDENT ROOSEVELT did not escape the usual lot of peacemakers. Although the signing of the peace treaty was greeted with almost world-wide joy, within a short time Roosevelt found himself being severely criticized by both Japanese and Russians and by their friends, respectively. He was accused of having robbed both Japan and Russia of the benefits of the advantageous positions, respectively, which the two Powers were assumed by their friends to have occupied at the opening of the Portsmouth Conference.

The partisans of Japan were almost bitter toward the treaty. One of the first critics of the President to appear in print was Professor Paul S. Reinsch of the University of Wisconsin, and subsequently American Minister at Peking in the Wilson administration. Under the caption, "An Unfortunate Peace," in the *Outlook*, September 16, 1905, he charged that the peace was inconclusive, that Russia had not been sufficiently curbed, and that the terms of the treaty would impose upon Japan crushing burdens of military preparation for the next struggle with Russia which he regarded as certain to come. Professor Reinsch appears to have thought that the Kaiser was responsible for what he regarded as the Russian victory at Portsmouth. He wrote:

Much as we must desire peace at all times, we cannot escape the conclusion that such a peace at this time was unfortunate, as it immediately revives all the dangerous ambitions of Russia, and gives the autocracy the power to reëstablish its police rule and hold fast to its reactionary traditions.

If we ask ourselves the question, how was such a peace possible, after such uninterrupted successes and decisive victories on the part of Japan? the only possible explanation is that in the hour of need Russia was powerfully backed by her friends, especially by the German Government, while the allies and friends of Japan were lukewarm in their support. The German Government evidently realized an unusual opportunity to strengthen its power.

Professor Reinsch's comment was an interesting illustration of how a comprehensive knowledge of the history of modern European politics, plus a complete ignorance of the immediate facts, might lead one astray in the interpretation of contemporary politics. He, and a great many others, had been misled by the news of the meeting of the Kaiser and the Tsar in the Björkö Sound July 23d. The secret treaty was unknown and Professor Reinsch appears to have assumed, very naturally, that the influence of the Kaiser at that time had been directed toward stiffening the determination of his brother autocrat.[1] The Kaiser had not been supporting Russia in the war with Japan since the first of June. President Roosevelt had been rather mystified by the generous support which the German Emperor had given him. He was quite unable to get Professor Reinsch's point of view, and the mistaken

---

[1] For the meeting at Björkö and the Russo-German Treaty of Alliance which the Tsar was subsequently forced to repudiate, see Sidney B. Fay, "The Kaiser's Secret Negotiations with the Tsar," pp. 65 ff.

interpretation of the way in which the treaty had been made provided the President with an opportunity to express himself in one of his characteristic letters. He wrote:[1]

It is astonishing to me that a man with the reputation of Reinsch, who professes to teach in a great university, should make statements such as he did in his letter to you—statements which are not merely recklessly untruthful but utterly foolish. Instead of the Kaiser backing up Russia the Kaiser loyally did everything he could to make Russia yield far more than she did, and Great Britain entirely declined to try to bring pressure upon Japan, which Germany and France attempted to bring upon Russia. In other words Reinsch got his facts exactly inverted and you are quite welcome to tell him so. Both Seaman and Reinsch betray an ignorance equal to that of the Tokio mob.[2]

In the same vein, George Kennan, then in Tokio, had prepared an article on September 17, 1905, which was published under the caption, "The Sword of Peace in Japan."[3] He described the riots in the capital which broke out as soon as the terms of the treaty were made known in Japan.[4] He alluded to the way in which the hopes of the Japanese populace had been built up, showing that even the more intelligent classes had much sympathy

---

[1]September 20, 1905; to Elbert F. Baldwin of the *Outlook*.

[2]Louis F. Seaman had published in the same number of the *Outlook*, September 16, 1905, pp. 115-16, an article taking the same position as Reinsch, namely, that Russia had escaped too easily.

[3]*Outlook*, October 14, 1905.

[4]Bertram Lenox Simpson makes the reception of the news of the peace terms in Japan and the ensuing riots the starting point for his review of the Far East in 1907. B. L. Putnam Weale, "The Truce in the East and Its Aftermath" (N.Y., 1907), Chap. I.

with the disappointment of the mob, a sympathy which he shared. Kennan concluded:

It seems to me that it would have been much better—for Russia as well as for Japan—if President Roosevelt had waited until the close of this campaign before he suggested a peace conference. Marshal Oyama, by that time, would probably have defeated General Linevich; the Liberal party in Russia, by that time, might have acquired real power and control; and both events would have made for permanent peace. As it is, the Tsar and the bureaucracy, freed from the pressure and apprehensions of war, may withdraw even the shadowy concessions which they have made to the Russian Liberals, and the Japanese people, dreading another war as a sequel to this peace, are filled with dissatisfaction.

This article and criticism drew from President Roosevelt a long letter which, after rereading, the President decided not to send. The letter, none the less, contains his answer to the charge, and reveals a new phase of the subject. President Roosevelt was aware of the fact that Japan was in urgent need of peace. The letter is therefore rather startling when compared with his repeated assertion that Japan would probably be able in the course of another six, eight, or twelve months to drive Russia out of all east Siberia as far west as Lake Baikal. He wrote (October 15th):

I have just received your letter and the book of photographs, both of which were very interesting. I had seen most of the photographs already. I very much like your first article on Korea, in the *Outlook*, but at present I wish to write you as to your article called "The Sword of Peace in Japan." As far as I am concerned it is of exceedingly little importance what any one says about the peace negotiations. My object in bringing them was not my own personal credit or even the advancement of this country, but the securing of peace. Peace was secured. Personally I believe that the credit of this country was greatly increased by it, and as far as I am personally affected I have received infinitely more praise for it than in my opinion I deserve, and I have not been very greatly concerned as to whether I was praised or blamed. But you are writing as a man supposed to know the facts at first hand. Your writings will be read here and in Japan, and while you may not do much damage to America you may do some to Japan if you get your facts crooked. They are crooked in this article. You say that it seems to you that "it would have been much better both for Russia and Japan if President Roosevelt had waited until the close of this campaign before he had proposed a peace conference." What I am about to say is for your information and not for the public. I acted at the time I did at the written request of Japan, and when Japan made the request I explained to the Japanese Government that in my judgment she would not get an indemnity, and she asked me to bring about the peace meeting with full knowledge of the fact that in my opinion she neither deserved nor would get an indemnity. You say that Marshal Oyama, if I had waited, would probably have defeated General Linevich. Your guess is probably as good as any one else's, and no better. Personally I should make the same guess, but the ugly fact remains that after winning the battle of Mukden Marshal Oyama, instead of being able to press his demoralized foe, had let four months and over go by without being able to strike him, and that the Russian Army had recovered its morale, was in good position, was reinforced, and was very anxious to be allowed to try the chances of another battle before peace was declared.

As I say, I personally think you are right in your guess, and I took this view in my communications with the Russians; but it is not a matter about which any one can be sure. The parallel you draw between what has happened to Russia and an imaginary case of what might happen if we were engaged in a war with Germany is thoroughly misleading, if only from the simple fact that in drawing it you are ignorant that it was not the "suggestion of an outsider" but the immediate need of Japan, and the earnest wish of the Japanese Government (expressed in writing) which brought about the peace conference. Your fancied analogy would have to be corrected by supposing that every serious American statesman knew that America would be terribly exhausted by further war, and that, if she could retain what she had gained, peace was urgently necessary; while there was nothing she wanted which it was possible for her to gain by further war. It is simply nonsense for any one to talk of the Japanese being in a position to demand an indemnity. No nation that does not give up anything ever gets an indemnity in such circumstances or ever could get it unless the other nation was hopelessly frightened. In recent times no sensible nation has made such a request. Moreover, your whole comparison is vitiated by the fact (which, my dear Mr. Kennan, it is extraordinary that you do not know) that the prime motive influencing Japan to wish peace was not any one of those that you give, but her great personal interest in obtaining peace on the very terms that finally were obtained and at that very time. You were on the ground. There may be reasons why you do not choose to make public the fact; but if these reasons do not exist, it is extraordinary that you should not know the fact, that the headmen of many villages and country communities in Japan were notifying the Government that they could not spare any more of their young men; that if more of their young men were drawn for the army the ricefields would have to be partially abandoned and a partial famine would ensue, and that, moreover, the little savings of their people had all been exhausted. I believe that Japan was partly influenced by proper motives of humanity and by the desire to have the respect of the nations as a whole, and that this feeling had its weight in influencing the Japanese states-men who knew the facts to disregard the views held by the Tokio mob and which are substantially the views set forth by you.

But the main factor in influencing Japan was undoubtedly the fact that to go on with the war meant such an enormous loss, such an enormous cost to her, that she could not afford to incur it save from dire need. For example, you speak about her not having obtained the north half of Sakhalin Island. She had not reduced to possession this north half of Sakhalin, and there were Russian forces still there, a fact of which you do not seem to be aware. But this is not important. It may interest you to know, again for your own private use, the following facts. Do what I could I was unable to get the Tsar to yield more than the south half of Sakhalin. On the point of honour he insisted on keeping the comparatively valueless northern half. So far from advising the Japanese to give up on the question of Sakhalin, I explicitly told and wrote them that in my judgment they would be justified in fighting for Sakhalin. I did not appreciate quite how urgent their need of peace was. They, as I think, with eminent propriety, went a little beyond what I advised and made peace without getting the northern half of Sakhalin. I had told them all along that to fight for an indemnity merely would forfeit the respect of everybody whose respect was worth having, and would be an act of wicked folly, for it would mean, at the very best, at least another year of war, and mortgaging the future of Japan for a generation to come, while they would get nothing of any value to them. They would certainly not get any money, and if, as I thought was likely, they conquered East Siberia, they would get what they ex-plicitly assured me that they did not want and what would cost them an immense amount to administer; while there would be always the risk that some reverses would occur, in which case the damage done to Japan might well be irreparable.

The above are the facts. They are for your private informa-tion. I do not intend to make public any of the details about this peace, because the Japanese have asked me not to make public those details which they think would in any way embarrass them, and I am anxious to do what they desire. But I do intend, privately, to keep intelligent observers sufficiently enlightened to prevent their going wrong. I think it is wise that a man of your standing who is supposed to speak with knowledge, should, for his own information merely, know what the facts are, and thereby avoid taking a position as wholly mistaken as you have taken in the part of your article to which I have referred.

Let me repeat. The peace negotiations were entered into by me at the instance of Japan. The treaty of peace was finally made by Japan because it was greatly to her interests to make it then, and in the shape in which it was made. Japan was not entitled to an indemnity, and in my judgment it is so absurd to suppose that she was entitled to an indemnity as to mark the man making the claim as either utterly ignorant of the facts or not competent to pass upon the facts. Japan gained everything she was entitled to. She was entitled to much and she gained much. It would have been (from the standpoint of her own interest) criminal, as well as foolish to the last degree, for her to continue the war under these circumstances, and she owes a great debt of gratitude to her statesmen who disregarded the feelings of the mob at home and of their well-meaning but most ill-advised counsellors abroad who desired her to take any other course. The peace was made on practically exactly the terms on which it should have been made. It was for the interest of Japan; it was for the interest of Russia; it was for the interest of the world.

In a postscript the President quoted the text of the Japanese request of May 31st for his good offices. He added:

This information is given to you confidentially. Dr. Abbott knows it. So do two or three other people—Secretary Root,

Secretary Taft, Senator Lodge. I do not know for certain the exact reasons why Japan does not wish that it be made public; but of course I take for granted that it is because the Japanese Government feels that it might hurt them with their people at home and might have a bad effect upon their prestige abroad.

This hypothesis appears to have been correct. In view, therefore, of the fact that the Japanese Government was allowing blame to be placed on President Roosevelt which more properly belonged to themselves, the President struck rather a high note of magnanimity when he added, "I think the Japanese Government has behaved very well."

Now comes a very human touch in the correspondence. President Roosevelt thought over the letter he had written and the next day decided not to trust it to the mails. Instead, he contented himself with writing to Dr. Lyman Abbott of the *Outlook* enclosing the letter to Kennan and adding some further comments. This letter to Doctor Abbott (October 16, 1905) may well be treasured by all lovers of President Roosevelt as an example of the largeness of his devotion to duty and his magnanimity:

Yesterday I wrote enclosing you a copy of a letter I sent to Kennan. On second thought I think it best not to send this letter lest by some accident it should go astray in the mail. The Japanese are very anxious that it should not be publicly known that they took the initiative. When Kennan comes back I shall show him the letter, or you can show him the copy that you have. Meanwhile I do not know that it is worth while to write him. I do not care a rap for the fact that I am evidently supposed by the wild pro-Japanese people like Kennan, as well as by the ignorant Japanese themselves, to have pushed Japan into a disadvantageous peace. It does not hurt me to have Kennan think this; and though in some ways it is perhaps hardly just for Japan to think it, yet I am inclined to think that less damage comes from letting Japan and the pro-Japanese think it than from causing the Japanese Government any humiliation in the matter. I think that the Japanese behaved very well and I want to help them. I should like to have their good opinion; but I am much less anxious to get their good opinion than I am anxious to give them real help.

Kennan is a very good man, but he gets carried away. In his account of the siege of Port Arthur, for instance, while what he said about the Japanese soldiers was true, he left some very important things unsaid. Either he did not know or did not repeat certain incidents which happened there which showed that the Japanese soldiers, like other soldiers, are human. For instance, I know at first hand that one Japanese regiment behaved so badly—refusing to advance even when the officers cut down the men—that they had to be withdrawn and set to making roads. I know another regiment that behaved well, which, nevertheless, under great strain, broke as almost any regiment might break, and bolted from a Russian counter attack, many of the Japanese soldiers leaving their rifles and everything else behind them as they ran. The official report of this was ludicrously false.

This does not destroy the value of Mr. Kennan's observations; but we must take into account that he makes errors. . . .

I respect Mr. Kennan and admire him. I would not say anything behind his back that I would not say to his face, and you are quite at liberty to show him this letter when he comes back. If you choose you can briefly inform him that he had better be sure whether or not Japan wanted the peace conference held at the time it was called, and whether or not it was primarily from underlying self-interest that she made peace as she did, before he makes any more comments on the subject.

ROOSEVELT AND THE RUSSO-JAPANESE WAR

ROOSEVELT AND THE RUSSIAN REVOLUTION

The criticisms of both Reinsch and Kennan grew not more out of their Japanese sympathies than out of their utter dislike of the old Russian autocracy. This leads us to examine the other charge, namely, that by causing the war to come to an end President Roosevelt really was the means of bolstering up the Russian bureaucracy when it was about to yield to the constitutionalist party.

The point at issue is whether President Roosevelt's intervention at Portsmouth on August 18th was a factor in the defeat of the Russian reform movement of 1904–06.

The chronological course of the Russian movement, briefly summarized with a view to comparing the dates with the events of the peace negotiations, is as follows:[1]

Nov. 19–21, 1904. Zemstvo Congress met and issued a request for general reforms, calling for judicial changes: freedom of religion, speech, press, assembly, meeting, association; extension of local self-government and the calling of a national assembly.

Dec. 25, 1904. Imperial Edict, promising reforms.

Jan. 22, 1905. "Bloody Sunday." This event marked a broadening of the reform movement. Until then it had been in the hands of the Zemstvo and the professional classes. Now the proletariat was drawn in and it became an economic as well as a political movement. The next twelve months were characterized by great agrarian and industrial unrest and very many strikes. A third element appeared

---

[1] The following summary is taken from Sir Bernard Pares, " Russia and Reform" (London, 1907), Part IV, Chap. I, pp. 487 ff.

in the dissatisfactions of many alien nationalities within the Russian Empire, such as the Poles, Letts, Ests, Tartars, Cossacks, and Lithuanians.

Mar. 3, 1905. Imperial Edict, promising to "invite. the worthiest persons, invested with the confidence of the people and chosen from the population, to share in the preparation and discussion of legislative proposals. The Emperor invited "views and proposals" for that purpose.

June 4, 1905. Congress at Moscow, composed of the "Union of Unions," and led by Professor Milyukoff. This meeting marked the growing industrial character of the movement and revealed its increasing complexity. While its actions were influenced by the crushing naval defeat in the Sea of Japan, the sentiments expressed were still moderate. A series of Imperial Edicts, April 30th, May 14th, and a subsequent one on July 8th, granted a measure of reform in religious and agrarian matters.

June 19, 1905. The Tsar met a deputation of fourteen from the Zemstvo Congress, the spokesman being Prince Trubetskoy. The Tsar reaffirmed his intention to call a national assembly.

July. 19, 1905. General Congress of Zemstvo and the Four Councils, reflecting the increasing confusion as well as discontent throughout the country.

Aug. 19, 1905. Imperial Decree, proposing a scheme for a Parliament of extremely limited powers —much less than the General Congress had expected. A Duma without legislative powers was promised. It was to be composed of members selected in such a way as to eliminate as far as possible the classes most disaffected. The workingmen were not enfranchised at all.

Sept. 8, 1905. Universities made autonomous.

Sept. 25, 1905. Another congress of Zemstvo and the Four Councils: many formidable strikes in September and October.

Oct. 30, 1905. The Tsar signed the first Russian Constitution.

May 10, 1906. Meeting of the First Duma. Between September and May the Government had been gradually acquiring control of the situation and was able to adopt increasingly repressive measures. The last two months of 1905 were characterized by atrocious persecutions and bloody executions, especially among the Siberian exiles. Upon Witte's return from Portsmouth he was placed at the head of the Government and succeeded at the close of the Algeciras Conference in securing a loan in Paris and London. Thus strengthened financially and no longer entangled in the Far East, the Russian Government felt strong enough to dissolve the Duma by imperial decree July 21, 1906. So far as immediate success was concerned the reform movement had been a failure. Beginning as a moderate reform led by patriotic members of the professional and relatively privileged classes it had passed by rapid stages into a more and more revolutionary movement in which economic purposes increasingly threatened to overshadow merely political measures.

President Roosevelt derived his information about Russia mainly from four sources: Spring-Rice, Am-

bassador Meyer, the Russian Embassy in Washington, and
the public press. He relied mostly upon Spring-Rice and
Meyer. So far as the Roosevelt Papers reveal, Spring-
Rice had little or nothing to say about the Russian
revolutionary movement. It is, therefore, in the reports of
Ambassador Meyer that we find the information upon
which the President chiefly depended in reference to the
Russian domestic situation. References in Meyer's letters and telegrams to the revolutionary movement are very
meagre. An embassy has always been an extremely poor
place from which to study a revolution.

Up to April 20th, when the Japanese Government first
intimated to President Roosevelt that his good offices
would be desired in the establishment of direct peace
negotiations, the despatches from the American Embassy
in St. Petersburg appear to have contained nothing which
would have made it appear likely that the revolutionary
movement would mature in such a form as to make it a
factor in the peace settlement. Mr. Meyer replaced
Robert S. McCormick as Ambassador in April and
immediately took the ground that the revolutionary
movement was as yet unimportant. In his memorable
interview with the Tsar on June 6th in which the ambassador secured the consent of the Emperor to peace
negotiations, Meyer expressed to the Tsar his conviction
that if Japan demanded unreasonable terms or excessive
indemnity the Russian Government would have the
almost united support of the people in resisting.[1] In the
same interview the ambassador gave as his opinion that
there would be no revolution in Russia.

It was not until early in July that Ambassador Meyer

[1]Howe's "Meyer," p. 159.

began to report any alarm as to Russian domestic conditions. By that time the arrangements for the Peace Conference had been fully perfected. The mutiny in the Black Sea fleet at the end of June, and the spread of industrial disturbances at Lodz and Libau led Meyer to cable to the Department of State (July 3d):

> I have believed heretofore that revolution in Russia [is] impossible but events of the past week have altered conditions and aspects.

He reported that if the Japanese Army were to advance and inflict another severe defeat on the Russian Army it would be impossible to foretell what conditions and events might follow, owing to the state of mind of the people and the incompetency of the Government.

This telegram was preceded by a letter,[1] in which he described the provoking measures of the bureaucracy.

> The Emperor no sooner makes an advance or a step in the right direction [wrote Meyer] than immediately its force is weakened by a communication to the press from the Foreign Office, or obstacles are put up by the Bureaucracy in the way of dilatory tactics . . . when the Emperor, on the 19th of June, received the Committee of Fourteen, representatives of different parts of Russia, the Tsar declared his firm intention to summon a national representative assembly. He also said: "I hope from this day forward that the relations between me and my people will enter upon a new phase." All this was modified in St. Petersburg when printed and the text of the speeches altered so as to conform with less advanced ideas, the bureaucracy not relishing the tenor of the Peterhof speeches.

---

[1]Meyer to Roosevelt, July 1, 1905, Howe's "Meyer," pp. 173-74.

Meyer felt that the Tsar, while honest and well-intentioned, was surrounded by reactionary and untrustworthy advisers. The ambassador concluded with the characteristically American opinion that what was needed was primary schools, trial by jury, freedom of the press, and a national representative assembly. The illiteracy he found to be the great obstacle to better government and he felt that it would take a generation of elementary education to raise the standard of citizenship.

Early in August, Meyer recorded in his diary:[1]

. . . the reformers and so-called revolutionists would prefer to see peace postponed for a while, because they think that in the present condition of affairs they can force the calling of a national assembly, and at a very early date. On the other hand, if peace was [sic] declared, it would postpone the assembly and the needed reform.

Four days later Meyer cabled that the reformers now appeared so sure of success that they were even urging the Tsar to make peace.[2] In his report to the President on his interview with the Tsar on August 23d, in which the Emperor agreed to the division of Sakhalin and the payment of a "substantial sum," the ambassador wrote:[3]

There is no doubt that the feeling in Russia has gained ground, that it has come down to a question of indemnity, or a matter of rubles, as they say here, all other points being settled or in such state that they can be solved. In one of my previous letters I stated that when it came down to a matter of rubles, there can

---

[1]August 3d, Howe's "Meyer," p. 190.
[2]August 7th, *Ibid.*, p. 191.
[3]*Ibid.*, p. 201.

be no question as to Russia's patriotism. . . . Now the war party here are in a fair way of winning over the people by showing that if a war-indemnity has to be paid, it will have to come out of them and will prove a heavy extra burden, which in the end will only be used against them and the country by the Japanese.

This is substantially all that Ambassador Meyer, according to his letters to the President, his despatches and telegrams to the Department, and his diary, appears to have known about this remarkable popular movement. If the Peace of Portsmouth had depended upon the condition of the Russian Revolution we should have to admit that the Ambassador's ignorance would have been deplorable. Clearly even the one American ambassador in Europe in whose reports President Roosevelt placed great confidence had given too little attention to an important political event about which his government should have been better informed. President Roosevelt in turn gave only the most casual consideration to the subject, so little that he seems to have been under the impression that Tolstoi was the spokesman of the reformers. However, the situation as presented to him amounted to this: the continued Japanese pressure for an indemnity was consolidating the Russian people behind the bureaucracy. On the other hand, the failure of Witte at Portsmouth would still further discredit the one strong statesman who occupied a moderating position between the autocracy and the revolutionary movement. When the Japanese accepted Witte's ultimatum on August 29th, Witte was suddenly rescued from his place of no influence in his government and sent back to become its head. At the same time the treaty took the pressure off Russia and permitted an opportunity for the Tsar to carry through the reforms which he had promised. As for the revolutionary leaders, Roosevelt had hardly more confidence in them than in the bureaucracy.[1] To J. St. Loe Strachey he wrote (September 11, 1905):

> Now I hope that Russia will move, no matter how sluggishly and haltingly, forward on the path of self-government. Of course, she is cursed almost as much by her reformers as by her oppressors. Tolstoi's last articles really do not rise to the dignity of drivel, and the people whose purpose is mere aimless destruction cannot be anything but a curse. If the peace negotiations give Witte, no matter how undeservedly, prominence in his country, good will come; for although his frank rejection of ethical considerations is to me appalling, still he does see that Russia cannot take a great place in the 20th Century if she adheres to the spirit and the methods of Ivan the Terrible.

It may be granted that the Tsar would have been less able to crush the revolution if the war had continued with another series of Japanese victories. It is not so clear that a decisive Russian victory in the autumn of 1905 would have helped the reformers. It would have been quite as likely to increase the prestige of the bureaucracy and give it added life. Our inquiry, however, does not turn on this speculative question of whether Japan or Russia could have won the next engagement in Manchuria, nor does it depend on speculations as to how defeat or victory might have influenced the course of events in Russia.

What would have happened if President Roosevelt had not intervened at Portsmouth on August 18th? Would the war have continued? This seems to us extremely

---

[1]Witte and Rosen held opposite views as to the effect of the continuance of the war upon the Revolution. "Forty Years of Diplomacy," Vol. I, p. 268.

improbable. From the beginning of April until the close of the Portsmouth Conference the choice was not between war and peace but between peace by the good offices of Roosevelt and peace by the good offices, mediation, or intervention of the Powers. Peace by the latter method would probably have meant a settlement more favourable to Russia than the one obtained by Witte. It would doubtless have taken the form of a support to the Russian bureaucracy. It might have precipitated a world war. Under these circumstances it seems to us that, while President Roosevelt was ill informed and working blindly, he could hardly have taken a different course if he had known all the facts.

On the other hand, if we assume that Russian victories would have followed the resumption of hostilities, what about the effect of such victories on political conditions in the Far East? Russian policy in north China had become intolerable and was a direct menace to American political and commercial interests. We must not fall into the error of supposing that Russian domestic reform would have been necessarily followed by reform in foreign policy. Historically there would appear to be no relation between constitutional government and abstinence from territorial aggression. Russia, under a constitutional government, having crushed Japan in the Far East, would have been as much of a menace to American interests as the old autocracy in 1898–1903.

Surely one could hardly have expected President Roosevelt, faced by all the uncertainties of 1905, to gamble in human blood by permitting the war to continue even if he had had it within his power to do so. We shall feel the force of this conclusion even more when we turn to a discussion of the probabilities of victory if the war had continued.

PROBABILITIES OF VICTORY IF THE WAR HAD CONTINUED

With the passing of years popular opinion on the relative advantages of Russia and Japan at the end of August, 1905, has altered. Few now entertain the opinion advanced by Mr. Kennan and inferred by Professor Reinsch that Japan was robbed of an even greater prospective victory. A contrary opinion is common. It is believed by many that Japan was so exhausted at the end of May that only the restoration of peace saved her from collapse or ultimate severe defeat at the hands of Russia. Unquestionably, Japan was in a very serious plight. The financial condition was alarming. The total war expenditures are estimated to have been practically $1,000,000,000 aside from interest paid during the period of the war. About 90 per cent. of this huge sum was supplied from loans either domestic or foreign.[1] More than half of the war expenses were paid for with foreign loans which were floated in London, New York, and to a very limited extent in Berlin.[2] These loans were secured by the customs receipts and the tobacco monopoly and were obtained at high rates of interest. Out of a total of nearly 725,000,000 yen[3] borrowed abroad nearly 27,000,000 yen went as commission to the bankers. Nominally, the rates of interest were 6 and 4½ per cent., but actually they were greater, for the bonds sold much below par. In the fiscal year 1902–03 the total revenue from taxation was

---

[1]Ushisaburo Kobayashi, "War and Armament Taxes of Japan" (N.Y., 1923), p. 29.

[2]Gotaro Ogawa, "Expenditures of the Russo-Japanese War" (N.Y., 1923), p. 65.

[3]The par value of a yen is $0.49⅔.

about 46,000,000 yen. At the close of the war the national indebtedness had increased from 600,000,000 to 2,400,000,000 yen with an interest charge of 110,000,000 yen a year.[1] By 1907 the Japanese were paying 7.273 yen per capita for war taxes and no less than 53 per cent. of the total tax revenue was being devoted to the payment of the cost of the war.[2] When it is remembered that the per-capita income of Japan in 1905 was probably not much in excess of 30 yen a year, one comes to realize how the war was devouring Japanese resources.

The Japanese statesmen were well aware of the condition in which they found themselves in the summer of 1905. The war was costing approximately $1,000,000 a day. Japan had to her credit about $50,000,000 in New York and perhaps three times that amount in London, but it was admitted that further foreign loans were improbable. It was this desperate financial situation which made Baron Komura at Portsmouth so obdurate about the payment of an indemnity. As early as July 31st Baron Kaneko had written to President Roosevelt:

My own opinion is that the payment of the actual cost of the war by Russia is absolutely necessary for the successful conclusion of the peace, because the public sentiment in Japan is strongly demanding a far larger amount of indemnity than that which is contemplated by our Government. Besides, the people in Japan are insisting on the cession of Vladivostok and its adjoining territory, which our Government is not contemplating to demand. Under such circumstances, it is almost impossible for us to bring the negotiations to a successful conclusion without having the actual war expenses defrayed by Russia.

---

[1]Kobayashi, *op. cit.*, p. 28; Ogawa, pp. 68, 252.

[2]Kobayashi, *op. cit.*, p. 41.

And apart from all these, I feel that without the payment of the cost of the war by Russia, we can hardly manage our national finance and economy after the war, which has already been a great strain upon our national economy. To these points Baron Komura entirely agreed with me.

The condition of Japanese finances became a subject for investigation by foreigners in the spring of 1905. In an article written in May but not published until the last of August, Thomas F. Millard presented figures to show that Japanese credit was already so nearly exhausted that no further foreign loan of any considerable size would be possible.[1] At about the same time as the publication of the Millard article, M. Gaston Dui of the *Écho de Paris* published a report on Japanese finances which was alleged to have been prepared by a French banker in Japan who brought it to Europe and presented it to the Tsar through the French Ambassador at St. Petersburg.[2] The banker concluded his review of Japanese finances with the assertion:

Without an indemnity Japan is ruined. It will not be possible to keep up her industries. Her merchant marine, which lives only by subsidies and bounties, will be unable to hold its own. . . . The payment of an indemnity would render Japan terribly strong. Without an indemnity she is ruined.

This report appears to have been received at St. Petersburg on or about August 18th.[3] Probably it accounts for the fact that there was in the last week of the peace negotia-

---

[1] Thomas F. Millard, "Financial Prospects of Japan," *Scribner's Magazine*, September, 1905, pp. 369–79.

[2] London *Times*, August 22, 1905.

[3] Howe's "Meyer," p. 204.

tions a perceptible retirement on the part of Russia as to the extent of the concessions she would make to Japan. But if Russia was in such an advantageous position that she was justified in expecting a victory over Japan, why did she not go on with the war? Why had she made so little advance in the previous four months?

Likewise Japanese man power was becoming exhausted. Out of a total productive male population of about 10,000,000, approximately 2,000,000 were put at some form of war service, more than half of this number being in the army. It is officially stated that no less than 999,868 went to the front. The losses were 60,068 killed in battle, 21,879 died of disease, to which must be added 29,000 more who were dismissed for ill health or other disabilities.[1] That President Roosevelt was aware of this exhaustion we learn from his letter, already quoted, to Mr. Kennan. We also learn that the President did not fully appreciate until August 31st, when Baron Komura abruptly accepted Witte's ultimatum, how very desperate the Japanese situation had come to be. Nevertheless, he repeated his conviction, as late as 1913,[2] that Japan stood a good chance of driving Russia out of Siberia if the war had continued.

It is a purely speculative question in which, as Roosevelt wrote to Kennan, one guess may be as good as any other. We do not believe that the most exhaustive research will be able to give a definite answer, for, while the Japanese situation was bad, the Russian situation was also bad,

---

[1] Ogawa, *op. cit.*, pp. 29, 113-14; see Putnam Weale, "The Truce in the East and Its Aftermath," p. 168, for a table of Japanese casualties which would appear to place the losses considerably higher.

[2] Theodore Roosevelt, "An Autobiography" (N.Y., 1913), p. 583.

and there were many contingencies and imponderables on both sides.

The Paris bankers had told Witte on his way to America that he could expect no more loans from France to continue the war, and according to Rosen, when Witte reached New York he was in despair.[1] Added to this Russia had a revolution on her hands, while the Japanese people were still loyal. There was a prospect of European intervention. Russia had greater reserves of man power, but she had lost control of the sea and between her and the battlefields of Siberia there was but a single-track, broken-down railway. The Dual Alliance, partly because of the Moroccan crisis and partly because France had not favoured the war to begin with, was worthless. On the other hand, the Anglo-Japanese Alliance held fast and British influence was of much importance in Paris in August, 1905, and it was not likely to be exerted in favour of Russia. It is absurd to suppose that one can strike a balance between such uncertain factors and predict what would have been the result of another year of war.

Are we not forced to the conclusion that according to the judgment of their own respective leaders, neither side believed that it could resume the war with any prospect of success?[2]

---

[1]"We had exhausted all our means and had lost our credit abroad. There was not the slightest hope of floating either a domestic or a foreign loan." Witte's "Memoirs," p. 135; see also, *ibid.*, pp. 78, 162; Rosen, "Forty Years of Diplomacy," Vol. I, pp. 263–64.

[2]There is still another possibility which at the time was considered by no one but which now appears very probable. The continuation of hostilities might have resulted in a decisive victory for neither Russia nor Japan. The effect of further warfare, therefore, might have been greatly to promote the democratic movement in Russia and, perhaps, to create one in Japan. See S. A. Korff, "Russia's Foreign Relations," Chap. IX. The whole question, however, still remains purely speculative, for it is reasonably clear that the failure of Roosevelt to effect peace at Portsmouth would have been followed by a more effective European intervention.

ROOSEVELT AND THE RUSSO–JAPANESE WAR

The most compromising charge—compromising if it could be sustained—that was brought against President Roosevelt was that he not only betrayed Korea but was even false to a treaty obligation to the Korean Emperor.

Shortly after the inauguration in 1905 Dr. H. N. Allen, U. S. Minister at Seoul, was replaced by Edwin V. Morgan. The recall of Doctor Allen is frequently cited as an indication of the policy which President Roosevelt was about to adopt. Dr. Arthur J. Brown writes, by way of explaining the reason for the recall of Doctor Allen, that the latter was an old and loyal friend of these unfortunate people and "could not tell the Koreans that his government would not observe its treaty obligations."[1] The inference is that Doctor Allen was spared the embarrassment and that Mr. Morgan was selected to convey this extraordinary message. Doctor Brown also intimates that Doctor Allen was recalled at the request of the Japanese Government. Such charges, unanswered, constitute a shameful blot on American history. Fortunately, there is material with which to answer them. Of the "good offices" clause in the American treaty with Korea we have already written. The recall of Doctor Allen can be very easily explained.

Dr. H. N. Allen went to Korea in 1883 as a missionary physician. His hospital received the support of the Korean Government and he came to have the confidence of the Korean people and their king. In time Doctor Allen entered the service of Korea and was for a time attached to its legation in Washington. Later he became

---

[1] Arthur J. Brown, "The Mastery of the Far East" (N.Y., 1921), p. 199.

secretary of the American Legation in Seoul, and early in the McKinley Administration he had been made Minister Resident and Consul General.[1]   In 1905 Doctor Allen had been the American diplomatic representative in Seoul for nearly eight years and he had lived in Korea for more than twenty years.   It was President Roosevelt's policy in making diplomatic appointments after his inauguration in 1905 to replace all diplomatic representatives who had been at their posts for more than eight years.   To President Cyrus Northrop of the University of Minnesota, who had interceded for a certain minister in Europe who had already had a long tenure of office, the President wrote, February 8, 1905:

> In my judgment eight years is the very limit that one of our Ministers should reside at any foreign court.

Under the circumstances it would appear to have been very difficult to exclude Doctor Allen from the application of this very sensible rule.

We have already described how President Roosevelt had made up his mind on the Korean question early in January, 1905.   We have also noted how the Japanese Government had negotiated two agreements during the war in which Korea had consented to the establishment of a virtual Japanese protectorate.[2]   After the summer of 1904 Korea's foreign relations, by Korea's consent, were under Japanese direction.   Soon after the Portsmouth Conference Japan pressed upon the Emperor to sign a protocol which would officially and legally complete the establishment of the Japanese protectorate.   On Novem-

---

[1]"Am. in East. Asia," pp. 478, 483, 505, 557, 569, 616.
[2]See pp. 109-10.

ber 17th the Emperor was forced to sign this agreement and thus virtually surrendered his kingdom. Nearly a month earlier Mr. Homer B. Hulbert, an American citizen who had been employed as a teacher by the Korean Government since 1886, was dispatched to Washington with a message from the Emperor to President Roosevelt asking for the good offices of the American Government in the settlement of the difficulty arising out of the demand of Japan that the Emperor relinquish his imperial rights.[1]

Mr. Hulbert, trailed by Japanese detectives, reached Washington late in November. He had an interview with Secretary Root but was unable personally to deliver the Emperor's letter to President Roosevelt. The letter was, however, placed before the President and the latter replied as follows:[2]

I have carefully read through the letter of the Korean Emperor handed to you by Mr. Hulbert, an American long resident in Korea, to whose hand this letter had been entrusted. I understand from you that the Korean representatives here, so far as you know, are unacquainted with the existence of such a letter and that Mr. Hulbert understands that it is the wish of the Emperor that the existence of the letter should be kept secret and nothing said to any one about it, and particularly not to the Japanese. Of course, these facts render it impossible for us to treat the letter as an official communication, for there is no way in which we could officially act without violating what Mr. Hulbert says is the Emperor's wish. Moreover, since the

---

[1] An abstract of the records of the Department of State covering this period in Korean-American relations was presented to the Senate and printed February, 1916, as Senate Document 342 64th Cong., 1st Sess. For Mr. Hulbert's own account of his mission, see his book, "The Passing of Korea," pp. 220, 223.

[2] Roosevelt to Root, November 25, 1905.

letter was written we have been officially notified that the Korean Government has made the very arrangement with Japan which in the letter the Emperor says he does not desire to make. All things considered I do not see that any practical action on the letter is open to us.

On November 24, 1905, Secretary Root directed Minister Morgan to close the United States Legation at Seoul.

A second communication with reference to Korea was received at the Department of State from Min Yeung-Tchan, a special envoy without credentials, on December 11, 1905. This communication contained the information, which was only too true, that the protocol of November 17th had been signed under duress. Mr. Root replied that he was unable to take official cognizance of this information because Korea had already placed herself, by the agreements of February 23, and August 22, 1904, "so completely under the protection of the Government of Japan as to render completely impossible the application" of the good offices clause in the treaty of 1882.

It would indeed be difficult to pick a flaw either in Mr. Root's or President Roosevelt's reasoning from the facts before them. The Emperor of Korea, in his last effort to play one Power against another, had been entangled in his own crooked ways and there was no help for him. As President Roosevelt himself wrote many years later, Japan treated her engagements with Korea like a scrap of paper,[1] but one is unable after most careful search of the evidence to see how or where the American Government could properly intervene. Korea was betrayed not by President Roosevelt but by her own Emperor and for the most sordid

---

[1] *Outlook*, September 23, 1914, p. 174.

of motives.   With even less character and ability he had essayed the rôle of a Tsar in the 20th Century.

From Herbert Croly's biography of Willard Straight we learn (Chap. VI) that the Emperor of Korea and the Foreign Office had been advised some months earlier, both by Senator Newlands, who was a guest in Seoul, and by U. S. Minister E. V. Morgan to make a dignified protest such as could be recognized in international law, but Korean diplomacy could never rise from the level of intrigue.[1]

---

[1]For a review of Korean-American relations down to 1900 see "Am. in East. Asia," pp. 502 ff.

CHAPTER XII

More Criticisms—China

AMERICAN business interests were divided into two schools of thought with reference to the Japanese victory in the Far East.

The American Asiatic Association, composed mainly of business men interested in Far Eastern trade, strongly supported Japan. Its secretary, John Foord, maintained that "the true peril of Asia, and of the world, is the Muscovite, and not the yellow peril."[1] At the annual dinner of the Association in January, 1905, Prince Fushimi was the guest of honour and the Hon. Stewart L. Woodford spoke to the toast: "The United States and Japan—Guardian of the Portal and the Defender of the Open Door."[2] In its August number the *Journal* of the Association strongly supported the Japanese demand for indemnity, and its enthusiastic editor expressed the belief that Japan was on the point of winning another great victory in Manchuria. When the terms of peace were published the editor wrote:

By the friends of Japan the terms of peace have been received with a feeling of disappointment strongly tempered with pride . . . it would be hard to find in all history a finer example of national greatness of soul and elevation of senti-

---

[1] *Journal* of the American Asiatic Association, April, 1904, p. 78.
[2] *Ibid.*, January, 1905, p. 355.

ment than are involved in the resolution to spare the pride of a vanquished adversary by humbling oneself.[1]

The *Journal* continued its support of Japan consistently after the conclusion of the peace and it was not until September, 1906, that a definite charge that Japan was discriminating against American trade in Manchuria and seeking a monopoly was even admitted into the columns of the *Journal*, and then only as a part of a defence of Japan.[2] The attitude of the American Asiatic Association may be taken as typical of that portion of American business men who accepted the hint given by Baron Kaneko in the *International Quarterly* two years before, that American trade in the Far East could not afford to disregard the Japanese influence in China.[3] The reasoning would appear to have been that American trade would receive a greater net benefit from working with Japan than from opposing her. In so far as President Roosevelt gave any attention to this phase of the subject—and he may not have thought much about it—this was his opinion.

THE JAPANESE VICTORY AND AMERICAN TRADE

On the other hand, there was another section of American business men who held a very different opinion. In a series of attacks on the American Asiatic Association in the New York *Commercial*, Nov. 26, 28, and 29, 1904, Mr. Foord was characterized as a "discredited adjunct, so to speak, of the Japanese consulate." No disruption of the association followed, but spokesmen of importance came

---

[1] *Journal* of the American Asiatic Association, September, 1905, p. 225.

[2] *Ibid.*, September, 1906, p. 228.

[3] See p. 35.

forward on the outside to point out that Japan and the United States were natural rivals in the Pacific and the Far East and that American trade might expect to profit most either by direct approach to China or by working through Russia rather than through Japan. John Hays Hammond advocated a more or less pro-Russian view.[1] He predicted that Japan would keep Korea and would seek to dominate Manchuria. Presumably, with the vast mineral resources of north China and eastern Siberia in view, argued Mr. Hammond, American trade would be likely to find larger opportunities through supplying Russia than through supplying Japan. He regretted that the war had ever been permitted to begin and took the ground that England, Japan, and the United States should have taken "concerted action" to curb Russia in Manchuria. He wrote:

That this course would have been incompatible with American traditions I admit, but the history of the next few years is likely to demonstrate that it would merely have been anticipatory of a policy which will become imperative should we, and the other nations chiefly concerned, not be able otherwise to protect our interests in the exploitation of the commerce and industry of the coveted markets of the myriad-peopled Orient.

This advocacy of a triple alliance with Japan and England is not so difficult to reconcile with Mr. Hammond's apprehensions about Japan as at first appears. By thus joining with Japan in the support of her legitimate interests, which were American interests, too, instead of per-

---

[1]See address of Hammond at the April, 1905, meeting of the American Academy of Political and Social Science, *Annals*, Vol. XXVI, No. 1, pp. 85-88; also an article in *World's Work*, June, 1905, pp. 6277 ff.: "The Menace of Japan's Success."

mitting Japan to fight the battle of the United States against Russia in Manchuria, Japan would have been placed under obligation to the United States, and under obligation to England greater than was created in the Anglo-Japanese Alliance. This obligation could have been used to prevent Japan from adopting a policy of monopoly in the Far East which would be inimical to American interests. Mr. Hammond feared, just as did President Roosevelt, although more strongly, that the Japanese success would create an extremely difficult political and commercial situation in China. As for the triple alliance, President Roosevelt, likewise, had he been able to secure the support of Congress, would have favoured it.[1] It would have been the height of political wisdom.

Rumours of Japanese monopolistic ambitions in Manchuria were current early in 1905.

"The Japanese are playing a big game before the world," said Stanley Washburn, in substance, to Ambassador Meyer in Rome, on his return from the front as a war correspondent,[2] "and for the moment are playing it straight and for all it is worth. They at heart do not care for any whites, not even for the English and Americans, who are useful to them now, and they are working them for all they can. They laugh in their sleeves about the Open Door in Manchuria, for when the time comes they can beat us in manufacturing, due to cheap labour, and therefore get the trade. They are most untruthful and deceitful as well as tricky in business transactions and think nothing of breaking a contract if not profitable." Mr. Washburn may have been smarting under the restraints which were

[1]See p. 116.

[2]January 20, 1905, Meyer to Roosevelt, Howe's "Meyer," p. 112.

placed upon the war correspondents, and his opinion is worthy of record merely as reflecting the beginnings of an American public sentiment toward Japan which greatly increased in volume during the next decade.

Similar charges, supported by some little evidence, were made by J. Gordon Smith, another press correspondent, in an article in *World's Work*, June, 1905.[1] The Japanese traders had already begun to rush into Manchuria behind the Japanese armies, although all other foreign merchants were excluded by the Japanese Government. They were already laying the foundations for a very extensive Japanese trade. Smith asserted that not only were they thus taking an unfair advantage, since other foreigners were excluded from the opportunity, but they were engaging in extensive imitation of foreign trade-marks and doing irreparable damage to the trade already established. He mentioned, for example, the display of a certain well-known brand of American tooth powder which purported to have been made in Chicago. To the label, however, had been added the tell-tale line:

"These Teeth-powdrs IS beSt fr Leeving Teeth-ache."

Of more importance as an indication of the probable course of events in Manchuria was the experience of E. H. Harriman in his efforts to secure a joint interest in the South Manchuria Railway which Russia was forced to relinquish at Portsmouth.[2]

Mr. Harriman, who was closely associated with Kuhn, Loeb & Company, who had aided the Japanese Govern-

---

[1] Pp. 6267 ff.

[2] The facts with reference to this episode are drawn from George Kennan, "E. H. Harriman, A Biography" (2 vols., Boston and N. Y., 1922), Vol. II, Chap I. This chapter was also published separately under the title "E. H. Harriman's Far Eastern Plans" (Garden City and N. Y., 1917).

ment in floating its war loans in the United States, conceived the idea of a round-the-world system of transportation by'way of his transcontinental railway lines, the Pacific Mail Steamship Company, the Manchurian railway, trackage rights over the trans-Siberian system to the Baltic, and thence by steamship across the Atlantic.   Mr. Kennan leads us to infer that preliminary discussions with Japanese representatives in New York and Tokio encouraged Mr. Harriman to believe that Japan might be willing to make some arrangement with him about the Manchurian line.   He appears to have had reason to suppose that trackage rights across Siberia could be secured from Russia.   Mr. Harriman reached Yokohama on August 31, 1905.   On October 12th he secured the signature of Count Katsura, Prime Minister, to a preliminary understanding that the Japanese Government would permit Mr. Harriman to form a syndicate and acquire a half interest in the South Manchuria Railway and its appurtenances.   Joint mining rights were also provided for.   A Japanese corporation was to be formed, subject to Japanese laws and to be operated under Japanese control. The Government was to reserve rights to preëmptive use of the line in case of war either with Russia or with China. The agreement was a perfect exemplification of the proposals which had been repeatedly made by Japanese financiers since 1898 that American capital should join with Japanese skill and familiarity with the Far East in the exploitation of the Chinese markets.   It was the sort of a plan that Baron Kaneko had predicted two years before.[1]

The same day Mr. Harriman sailed from Yokohama for the United States.   Three days later Baron Komura, who

---

[1]See p. 325.

had negotiated the treaty at Portsmouth, returned to Japan. He immediately opposed the agreement. He did not approve of thus turning over to a foreigner a share of Japan's richest prize obtained from the war. He offered as his excuse that the sixth article of the treaty stipulated that the Russian railway rights were transferred to Japan subject to an agreement with China. Mr. Kennan volunteers the explanation that when Count Katsura signed the understanding with Mr. Harriman he did not know of this phrase in Article VI of the treaty. The explanation is absurd. Baron Komura did not have at Portsmouth powers to sign a treaty without the express approval of the Japanese Government. While Harriman was on the Pacific, Baron Komura carried the day, and upon the former's arrival in San Francisco he was greeted with a telegram from Tokio stating that the Japanese Government wished to reconsider the agreement. Nothing came of the arrangement afterward, although in the spring of 1906 Mr. Jacob H. Schiff of Kuhn, Loeb & Company went to Japan and sought to revive the project.

Japan had again disclosed its purpose in Manchuria. By such events the school of American commercial thought which was directing its policies toward coöperation with Japan in the exploitation of the Far East was somewhat weakened, and those who held the opposite view found facts to support their contention that the Americans were face to face with a conflict with Japan. In the course of the next fifteen years this growing conflict of interests brought the two nations on several occasions to the verge of war.

The primary purpose of the present study is to exhibit a record of facts hitherto little known and much misunderstood. We have confined ourselves to a minute examination of American policy in the Far East for only the two or three years which preceded the signing of the Treaty of Portsmouth. There is not accessible to the student a sufficiently authentic and complete record of the events subsequent to January 1, 1906, to warrant the attempt to continue the study, on the present scale, into the later period. On the other hand, it is impossible to reach even an approximate estimate of the soundness of President Roosevelt's policy without facing the question whether, by helping Japan into her recognized position as a great Power, he did not raise up the most formidable rival and opponent which the United States is ever likely to be forced to contend with. In substance the question is this: Did not President Roosevelt make an unnecessary sacrifice of American commercial interests in Manchuria and in China generally? We shall seek to answer this question in the concluding chapter. Meanwhile, it becomes necessary to summarize very briefly the events of the next few years in China.

Japan had given her assent to Secretary Hay's Open Door proposal in 1899. She had professed to be strongly in favour of maintaining the integrity of China. Preliminary to President Roosevelt's efforts to bring Russia and Japan together he had requested and received from Japan the promise that she would adhere "to the position of maintaining the Open Door in Manchuria and of restoring that province to China."[1] On November 30, 1908, by an exchange of notes between Secretary Root and Ambassador Takahira the two governments reached a more formal and explicit agreement in which the two Powers declared that:

---

[1]Chap. VIII, pp. 178 and 179-80.

they are also determined to preserve the common interest of all Powers in China by supporting by all pacific means at their disposal the independence and integrity of China and the principle of equal opportunity for commerce and industry of all nations in that Empire.

It would therefore appear that President Roosevelt took precautions, so far as agreements are concerned, to safeguard American interests in China. It is regrettable, however, in the light of subsequent events, that these agreements had not been made much more detailed and specific.[1]

In the judgment of President Taft and Secretary Knox, Japan, supported by Russia, England, and France, departed very much from the spirit and even from the letter of these agreements.[2] To meet this situation, which was having the effect of embarrassing and even excluding American business interests from Manchuria, Secretary Knox put forward in December, 1909, a plan for the neutralization of the Manchurian railways. He proposed that the railway investments of Russia and Japan be purchased by an international syndicate and henceforth that these railways, as well as any others which might be built, should be under international control.[3] The plan was indignantly rejected by Russia and Japan, acting together, and was not supported by England and France.

It is plain that we have here a very different kind of diplomatic practice from that of President Roosevelt in

---

[1] "For. Rel." (1908), pp. 510-11. For the documents relating to this period, see Thomas F. Millard, "Our Far Eastern Question" (N.Y., 1916), Appendix; also, by the same author, "America and the Far Eastern Question" (N.Y., 1909).

[2] For a careful and judicial survey of the facts upon which this judgment was based, see Stanley K. Hornbeck, "Contemporary Politics in the Far East" (N.Y., 1916), Chap. XV: "South Manchuria: Ten Years of Japanese Administration"; for a statement of the European background see Millard's "Our Far Eastern Question," Chap. I: "A Shift of Policies."

[3] "For. Rel." (1910), p. 236; Millard, "Our Far Eastern Question," App. A.

1905. When the President had addressed his identical notes to Russia and Japan on June 8, 1905, he was fortified by the assurance of Germany, France, and England that his good offices would be acceptable, and by the definite statements of Japan and Russia that they would give affirmative answers to his invitation. Secretary Knox appears to have had the assurance of no government to support his proposition. It had been a fundamental principle with President Roosevelt to keep step with all the foreign offices; Secretary Knox had returned to the traditional American policy of independent action.

It is, of course, extremely dangerous to attempt a generalization without all the facts before us. It would appear, however, that we have here another illustration of a deplorable weakness in the European diplomatic service of the American Government. Secretary Knox appears to have been quite ignorant of what had been going on in Europe in the few years preceding his neutralization proposal. And yet, as in so many other instances, it is in Europe that we must begin our study of the Far Eastern question. As we have already seen it had long been a favourite proposal in Europe to satisfy Russia and Japan by a division of north China between the two Powers. The Kaiser had suggested it, it had been put forward in Paris, and it was not without its supporters in England. Just before the outbreak of hostilities, "Calchas" wrote in the *Fortnightly Review* (February 1, 1904):

If British and French opinion can clearly unite in the conviction that Korea ought to become Japanese and Manchuria to remain Russian, the solution that a trial of strength could scarcely fail to enforce might be reached even at the eleventh hour, without a recourse to arms.

In January, 1904, Japan would not agree to such a division for she did not propose to relinquish her interests in south Manchuria. Immediately after the war, however, the proposition was renewed, with this difference: that while Japan retained Korea there was to be a division of Manchuria between the two recent belligerents. The British Foreign Office, carrying out its plan to reach an agreement with Russia and thus complete the isolation of Germany, seized eagerly upon the idea as one of the measures to complete the encirclement of Germany. This plan was in the process of consummation when Secretary Knox put forward his neutralization plan. Thus again Europe and Great Britain were offering up China as a sacrifice to the cause of peace in Europe.

Obviously the place where Secretary Knox should have begun, if he wished to protect the integrity of China, was in Europe. The key to President Roosevelt's success in the Far East in 1905 is to be found in the fact that he had preceded it with what amounted to a declaration that he could be counted upon to aid in preserving the peace of Europe and that he would come to the aid of Japan in case a third Power joined Russia. President Roosevelt, as we have several times repeated, had made the American Government an unsigned member of the Anglo-Japanese Alliance. The key to Secretary Knox's failure is to be found in the fact that his proposal, which would have weakened British and French plans for the encirclement of Germany, had been preceded by no assurances as to what the United States would offer in its place as a measure for the preservation of peace in Europe. In other words, under Secretary Knox, the American Government had relapsed into not only its traditional policy of isolation but also into its traditional policy in the Orient of trying to get something for nothing.

On the other hand, President Roosevelt had shown a singular carelessness about the measures by which Japan proposed to safeguard her interests in China. By his "discreet" and "courteous" notification to France and Germany at the outbreak of the war, President Roosevelt had virtually assumed the precise obligation which England had assumed in the first Anglo-Japanese Alliance. He had stated that in case a third Power went to the aid of Russia he would go to the aid of Japan. This declaration was doubtless a protection to China. The assurance in the "agreed memorandum" of July 29, 1905, was, however, of a different character. By it the American Government was committed again to act with Japan and England in the Far East. It was made on the eve of the renewal of the Anglo-Japanese Alliance which was dated August 12th. It probably led both Japan and England to believe that the American Government would become an unsigned member of the second Alliance. Depending on this assurance, Japan counted upon the support of the United States for the Japanese policy in Manchuria in 1906–10.[1] This support Secretary Knox in the Taft Administration was unwilling to give. The Knox neutralization plan was put forward for the express purpose of blocking Japanese ag-

---

[1]Herbert Croly, in his recently published biography of Willard Straight (N.Y., 1924, Chaps. VI-X), has supplied the basis for the most damaging criticism of Roosevelt's policy. "This [Root-Takahira Agreement], like the Korean withdrawal, was a terrible diplomatic blunder to be laid to the door of T. R.," wrote Straight in his diary (p. 276). True, provided one grants that Straight's comprehensive political and economic programme for China was not impractical and premature. But subsequent events, such as the withdrawal from the Six-Power Loan and the Lansing-Ishii Agreement, prove that succeeding administrations at Washington would not sustain such a programme. Nor would the American people have sustained it. Such being the case, Straight's programme could only result in a futile pin-prick policy which would incline Japan more and more toward a Russian alliance directed against the United States.

gressions in Manchuria. When the Knox proposal was made it must have looked to the Japanese Government like a maladroit repudiation of a policy of supporting Japan to which the American Government was committed by the second section of the agreed memorandum of July 29, 1905. Of course, President Roosevelt had not intended to commit his government to approve the Japanese policy in Manchuria, which was a plain violation of the Open Door principle, but, on the other hand, his action did commit his government virtually to an approval of the second Anglo-Japanese Alliance which, in turn, supported the Japanese policy in Manchuria. The memorandum had been very loosely drawn. It was wholly lacking in precise statements as to the measures which Japan intended to take for the preservation of peace in the Far East and yet it committed the American Government, in some degree at least, to their support.

We are in the midst of the most revolting aspects of European diplomacy. Notwithstanding all the assurances and promises which had been given, neither Europe nor Japan cared a gewgaw for the abstract principle of the integrity of China. The partition of China began in 1842; it was continued in 1858, 1860, 1867, 1885, and it was resumed in 1895, when Japan took the Liaotung Peninsula as well as Formosa and the Pescadores. Likewise, the doctrine of the Open Door after 1899 was an academic phrase to which Europe assented for the sake of placating America. For ten years it existed as a phrase to conjure with but not to be defined. Its definition, so far as Europe and England were concerned, depended not on the meaning of words as found in the dictionary, but on the conditions requisite for the maintaining of peace in Europe. The

ROOSEVELT AND THE RUSSO–JAPANESE WAR

American Government mistook a phrase and a promise for an event, and in a somewhat naïve and simple way Secretary Knox put forward the proposition that the theory of the Open Door be reduced to practice in Manchuria.

The impasse to which the refusal of Russia and Japan brought the American Government in 1910 resulted in an exchange of opinion between Colonel Roosevelt on the one hand and President Taft and Secretary Knox on the other. At the request of the President, Colonel Roosevelt wrote a letter on December 22, 1910, in which he framed in a very kindly and courteous way his criticism of the Knox policy. This letter was referred to the Secretary of State and drew from him an answer in the form of a memorandum. In these two documents we find a general statement of the opposing policies of the two administrations.

Our vital interest [wrote Colonel Roosevelt] is to keep the Japanese out of our country and at the same time to preserve the good will of Japan. The vital interest of the Japanese, on the other hand, is in Manchuria and Korea. It is therefore peculiarly our interest not to take any steps as regards Manchuria which will give the Japanese cause to feel, with or without reason, that we are hostile to them, or a menace—in however slight a degree—to their interests. . . . I utterly disbelieve in the policy of bluff, in national and international no less than in private affairs, or in any violation of the old frontier maxim, "Never draw unless you mean to shoot." I do not believe in our taking any position anywhere unless we can make good; and as regards Manchuria, if the Japanese choose to follow a course of conduct to which we are adverse, we cannot stop it unless we are prepared to go to war, and a successful war about Manchuria would require a fleet as good as that of England, plus an army as good as that of Germany. The Open Door policy in China was an excellent thing, and I hope it will be

320

a good thing in the future, so far as it can be maintained by general diplomatic agreement; but, as has been proved by the whole history of Manchuria, alike under Russia and under Japan, the "Open Door" policy, as a matter of fact, completely disappears as soon as a powerful nation determines to disregard it, and is willing to run the risk of war rather than forego its intention.

How vital Manchuria is to Japan, and how impossible that she should submit to much outside interference therein, may be gathered from the fact—which I learned from Lord Kitchener in England last year—that she is laying down triple lines of track from her coast bases to Mukden, as an answer to the double tracking of the Siberian Railway by the Russians. However friendly the superficial relations of Russia and Japan may at any given time become, both nations are accustomed to measure their foreign policy in sections of centuries; and Japan knows perfectly well that sometime in the future, if a good occasion offers, Russia will wish to play a return game of bowls for the prize she lost in their last contest.

To this argument Secretary Knox replied:

I greatly appreciate the frankness with which you have expressed your opinion on the Manchurian and immigration questions, and although I am aware that some Japanese statesmen have recently attempted to connect the two . . . I am unable to see any essential connection between them. . . . Why the Japanese should think that we ought to accept the observance by them of one treaty right due from them to us as an offset for the disregard by them of another treaty right due from them to us I cannot understand.

We have no desire or intention to interfere with any legitimate purpose of Japan in Manchuria. We do not care how many of her people she may send to Manchuria nor to what extent she may avail herself of her commercial opportunities there, provided in so doing she scrupulously respects the equal rights of others. Nor have we given Japan at any time just cause to think that we wished to interfere.

The opinion expressed by Lord Kitchener that Japan needs in Manchuria for any legitimate purpose any more than she now has by right, is also open to question. Commercially she is most advantageously situated and strategically she is in a position to throw troops quickly into Manchuria over her two or three lines of railways. Why the Japanese *need* Manchuria any more than does China, who owns it now, or why it is any more "vital" to them than to China is not apparent.

I admit that reference to "the Open Door" has frequently been abused, often through misunderstanding of what was meant by the expression. What we mean by "the Open Door" in Manchuria is surely nothing more than fair play for our commercial interests, which certainly are not insignificant, and for China, [integrity] territorially and administratively.

That certainly is the meaning of our policy in China as enunciated by Secretary Hay and continued and developed under your Administration. The aim of the present Administration has been merely to reduce the theory to practice. . . .

So long as we are content to confine ourselves to diplomatic generalities no one will take us very seriously and consequently no one will probably take offence. But once we attempt practically to carry out our policy to its logical end our course is bound to be more difficult; and yet I see no other way if we are to hold our own in China. . . .

Whether the American people would ever go to war or not in the defence of our interests in China I am not prepared to say. It might depend upon the nature of the provocation. But in any case it certainly is not for us to prejudice our case at the start by admitting to the world that we would *not*, under any circumstances, go to war. We can at least allow others to draw their own conclusions.

Dismissing that question, however, as academic I still believe that the wisest and best way for all concerned is for us to stand firmly on our pronounced policy and let it be known on every proper occasion that we expect fair play all round. The Japanese Government certainly is not indifferent to public opinion, and it is much better that we should continue to try to bring Japan's policy in China up to the level of ours, where we may differ, than to lower our policy to the level of hers. There are indications that we shall in the future receive more support for our policy from Great Britain than we recently have had. Braham, one of the foreign editors of the London *Times*, who was in Washington a few weeks ago on his return from a six-month visit in the Far East, reported that the sentiment among British merchants in China was practically unanimous against Great Britain's present policy of allowing Japan and Russia "a free hand" in Manchuria at the expense of British interests. Morrison, the Peking correspondent of the *Times*, now home on leave, has recently come out strongly on the same lines and there appears to be a rapidly growing sentiment among the British public in that direction. It would therefore seem an inopportune time now to let down our standard even if we had any thought of doing so; but in any event I think it would be much better for us to stand consistently by our principles even though we fail in getting them generally adopted.

Colonel Roosevelt was not convinced by Secretary Knox's argument. In his Autobiography,[1] in the course of a discussion of the Japanese immigration question, though with an evident wider application, he wrote:

Unfortunately, after I left office, a most mistaken and ill-advised policy was pursued towards Japan, combining irritation and inefficiency. . . .

---

[1] Theodore Roosevelt, "An Autobiography" (N.Y., 1913), p. 414.

Between 1905 and 1910 new factors had appeared in the Far Eastern situation. The second Anglo-Japanese Alliance was, in effect, being turned against the United States. England, already so deeply compromised in European diplomacy, had weighed her interests in north China over against her interests nearer home and had decided to sacrifice the former for the sake of the latter. No longer a restraint upon Japanese imperialism, England had become its faithful ally. Likewise Japan had, in effect, turned against the United States, had in fact entered a combination of European Powers such as President Roosevelt had envisaged in December, 1904, and had dismissed as improbable. The difference between the Knox and the Roosevelt policies in 1910 amounted to this: Knox was willing to sacrifice Japanese friendship for the sake of protecting, or for the purpose of filing a *caveat* in favour of, China and American interests in China. Roosevelt objected to a policy of bluff and felt that unless the United States was prepared to fight for the integrity of China it would be wiser to ignore the Manchurian situation or merely take advantage of it to renew the treaty with Japan and stipulate again, as the treaty of 1894 had done, the express right of the American Government to provide for the total exclusion of Japanese immigrants. Roosevelt objected to a diplomacy which brought a nation to the choice between scuttle and fight when there was no intention of fighting.

Viewed from another angle the difference was this: Colonel Roosevelt in 1910 was observing the Far Eastern problem from the viewpoint of 1905. He did not know that in the secret treaties with Russia of 1907 and 1910 Japan had virtually repudiated her promise to him to preserve the Open Door and the integrity of China as related to Manchuria. He did not realize how greatly the balance of power for which he had striven in 1905 was shifting. The neutralization plan was put forward to accomplish the exact purpose which Roosevelt had adopted in 1905, namely, the preservation of China. The essential difference between the Roosevelt and the Knox policies was merely in method. The former sought to preserve China by coöperative, the other by independent and isolated, action.

It cannot too often be emphasized that in all the history of American policy in the Far East there is not a single instance where a policy of independent and isolated diplomatic action has succeeded.[1]

CONTEMPORARY COMMENT

Baron Kaneko, "America's Economic Future in the Far East," *Forum*, April–June, 1905.

"It is most important—I should say necessary—for the Japanese company and the American corporation to form an economic alliance in their Oriental commerce, because the Americans are most anxious to extend their market in China, and they also know that they cannot do so if they disregard the importance of Japan in Chinese affairs."

O. Eltzbacher, "The Yellow Peril," *Nineteenth Century*, June, 1904.

Quoting "a prominent Japanese statesman": "We would not have China, or a part of China, for a gift, for it would only be a source of trouble and expense to us. It would cost us a lot of money for administration and bring nothing in return. We can only profit from China by trading, but trade would not increase by our occupation."

---

[1]For a critical examination, from the legal point of view, of the alleged Japanese and Russian rights in Manchuria, see W. W. Willoughby, "Foreign Rights and Interests in China."

ROOSEVELT AND THE RUSSO–JAPANESE WAR

K. Asakawa, "Korea and Manchuria under the New Treaty," *Atlantic Monthly*, November, 1905.

"The consequent régime in that territory [Manchuria] may be either a joint administration by China and Japan, as in the case of Egypt and England in the Soudan, or a supervisory rule by Japan, as that of England over Egypt, or perhaps, more likely, an entrusted administration (*Übertragene Vervaltung*) as that of England in Cyprus, or that of Austro-Hungary in Bosnia and Herzegovina."

T. Hayakawa, "Russo-Japanese Alliance," *Taiyo*, quoted in *Review of Reviews* (N. Y.), June, 1905.

"If Russia will renounce her ambition for military aggrandizement, and will extend her hand in friendly relationship to Japan, with a view of promoting her commercial interests in eastern Asia, we Japanese will gladly welcome her as our friend and ally."

Alfred Stead, "Japan and Peace," *Fortnightly Review*, June, 1905.

"Japan's paramountcy, after the recent sea-battle, carries with it as an inevitable corollary the proclamation of a new Monroe Doctrine for eastern Asia. Just as the United States has taken the American hemisphere under her wing to protect her against European aggression, so Japan will take the Asiatic Powers which are still independent and give them support to progress along their own lines."

CHAPTER XIII

Roosevelt's Contribution to the Far Eastern Policy of the United States

PRESUMABLY, in years to come, President Roosevelt's statesmanship in the Far East will be judged on the question of whether it was good policy to support Japan. This support had been somewhat qualified, for he exerted himself to preserve a balance of power. On the other hand, the support rendered to Japan had been so great that it seems very probable that if it had not been given Japan would have lost much, by the exhaustion of further warfare, by Russian victories, or, most likely, by European intervention in the settlement. Japan owed a large share of her victory at Portsmouth to President Roosevelt.

What would have been the probable result, and its effect on the Far East, if President Roosevelt had stood absolutely aside in 1904–05 and had permitted the conflict to run its natural course? Unquestionably, in some form or other, a still further weakening of the East. Would such a result have been beneficial either to the Far East or to American interests there and in the Pacific? Lord Charnwood suggests that American national interests would best be served by a weak Japan. In writing of President Roosevelt's intervention in 1905 he states:

Realpolitik would have bidden an American statesman to let the Japanese exhaust themselves.[1]

---

[1] "Theodore Roosevelt" (Boston, 1923), p. 148.

327

This opinion is shared by many. The situation in China in 1910, and later, furnishes some, though not sufficient, justification for such an opinion.

The weakening of the East was not in line with historical American policy.

The policy of the other Powers in the 19th Century had been to keep Asia under the heel of the West. The partition of Asia began so long ago that one hesitates to name a date. Steadily, persistently, the West had been advancing across Asia, and at length, in 1842, reached south China. It was not a colour conflict: it was at first purely commercial and then, in its later stages, politico-commercial. England established at Hongkong a toll-gate which, while involving only a trivial partition of the Empire, nevertheless served a similar purpose. A few years later Russia appeared on the northern coastline at Vladivostok. Then France carved out an empire in the south. The appropriation of Japan was freely discussed in 1861, but a fortunate development of European politics saved Japan for a few years. Yet Japan was saved only at the expense of yielding to the West a 5-per-cent. tariff, a tribute which had already been exacted from China. The partition of China was resumed in 1885 when France took another slice in the south. Ten years later the eastern bulwarks of the Empire were swept away. Japan took Formosa and the Pescadores, thus coming into possession of a chain of strategic islands which stand guard over all south central China. In 1895 the Chinese were definitely cleared out of Korea and forced back into Manchuria only to be driven back even behind the Great Wall at the end of the century. The Eighteen Provinces were invaded and a naval base was established at Kiaochow. Then the

328

West found a new use for eastern Asia. It had long been a treasure house; now it was selected as a victim for the altar of the Balance of Power. By this new sacrifice it was hoped to placate the gods of war and thus preserve the peace of Europe. It was proposed to complete the partition of China.

From the earliest days of American intercourse with the Far East, down through the period which now engages our attention, the great obstacle to American commercial interests was not any government in Asia but rather the European Powers. The Americans rarely favoured a gunboat policy. At old Canton, in the pre-treaty days, the American merchants were so satisfied of their ability to deal with the Chinese that they even asked the American naval officers to move their vessels to other waters. When it came to the opening of Japan in the first treaty, Commodore Perry did not even reserve for Americans extra-territorial rights. Throughout all the long years of the treaty revision controversy the American Government gave its support to Japan. No important instance can be cited where the United States had taken an action with the intention of weakening the East or keeping it down. The reason was simple. The United States was so situated, geographically, commercially, politically, that it could not share in the partition of the East, nor could it be other than injured by the closing of any door to commercial equality among the foreign traders. The American Government found it profitable to seek the good will of the East. However, the United States was not in a position to give any substantial help or protection. Only one course was left, namely, to favour the growth of states sufficiently strong to be their own doorkeepers.

ROOSEVELT AND THE RUSSO–JAPANESE WAR

The partition of China in 1900 and the establishment on the western shores of the Pacific of European capitals would have meant the extension to eastern Asia of the added blight of European jealousy and militarism. It would have destroyed the foundations of peace in the Pacific. For the American Government it would have created a political condition comparable to the extension of European imperialism in South America.

It was the intention of the European Powers to partition the Chinese Empire at the first convenient opportunity. By such a measure it was hoped to apply a poultice to international relations and draw off some of the irritation and corruption that were bringing the Old World to Armageddon. Russia was put forward as the protagonist of Europe—Russia, the home of dull, conscienceless autocracy; Russia, almost a synonym for everything that government ought not to be. The first step in the European programme was the Russian appropriation of Manchuria and other portions of north China.

In the face of this menace to American interests what had the United States to offer? Nothing. Nothing except the Open Door notes of Secretary Hay in 1899 and some very clever diplomacy in 1900. The partition of China and the closing of the door went straight on.

In 1903 Russia was firmly lodged in Manchuria. She displayed every intention to remain. It was her declared purpose to close the markets to free commercial opportunity. Americans as well as other merchants were excluded from the interior of a region where American trade was growing rapidly. Secretary Hay wrote some more notes and secured some more verbal victories, but the Russians were still there. In 1903 the situation reduced itself to this: Russia could not be dislodged without force and the American people in 1903, just as again in 1910, were not prepared to use force. The United States would not fight for the integrity of China. The American Government, notwithstanding the effrontery and the falsehoods and the broken pledges, was "not in an attitude of hostility to Russia."

Japan came forward and dislodged Russia. The effort cost the United States not a life nor even a cent. It cost Japan about $1,000,000,000; it cost her the labour of one fifth of her productive male population for more than a year and a half, and it cost her the lives of nearly one in every hundred of her male productive workers. Russia was stopped. Europe also was stopped. The partition of China was delayed and probably will never take place. This result was a commercial and political benefit to the United States.

From this point of view the American policy in 1902–05 appears to be very similar to that of 1842 when the United States allowed England to open the Five Ports without lifting a hand to help and then stepped in to share the benefits. Similar also to 1858 when the American Government righteously refused to join the Anglo-French Alliance to help in the further opening of China, and yet eagerly came forward to share in the fruits of the victory. There was, however, a vast difference between 1904–05 and 1842 or 1858.

The American Government would not join the first Anglo-Japanese Alliance to demand of Russia the fulfilment of her pledge to evacuate Manchuria. President Roosevelt was utterly unable to alter the prejudices of his people, however much he may have seen their folly.

ROOSEVELT AND THE RUSSO-JAPANESE WAR

The Constitution rarely admits of anything but hindsight in the control of foreign relations. The President did not, however, find in this situation an excuse for doing nothing. He gave to Japan every support which was constitutionally within his power. He went even further and served notice on Europe that if a third Power went to the aid of Russia he would join in the support of Japan. The action may have been unconstitutional, but it was honest—more honest than that of President Buchanan in 1858. Whatever it may have been in constitutional history, it was one of the most honourable declarations in the history of American foreign relations. So long as Japan was fighting the battle of America in Manchuria—and no one can go through the records of 1898–1904 and not feel that she was—President Roosevelt was prepared to help Japan.

This was the big contribution of President Roosevelt to Far Eastern policy. As a precedent for the future it was the largest contribution ever made, worth a thousand diplomatic notes. It was not a permanent contribution, for it did not have the support of the American people and the next Administration lapsed into the old traditional policy of expecting something for nothing, of standing back until some other Power made the effort, and then demanding a share in the fruits of victory. This, however, detracts nothing from the credit of Roosevelt for having done his honest, manly, modest best. President Roosevelt set the precedent in American history that the United States should pay for its privileges on the mainland of Asia.

On the other hand, President Roosevelt was not blind to the new danger that might arise. He believed it was better to take a chance on Japan rather than a chance on Russia and Europe. It was, however, his policy to reduce to a minimum the chances of failure arising out of the support of Japan. He believed that Russia ought to be left in eastern Asia to face Japan and moderate her action. He would leave obstacles in the way to keep Japan out of temptation. Again, as a further protection to American interests, he would place and maintain the American Navy in such a position that the United States would be in a condition of dependence upon no Power for favours. To the Anglo-Japanese Alliance he would offer no mere verbal support. Nor would he draw aloof from the struggle in Europe if the balance of power were upset. American support would be no mere verbal offering. He would give it substance. When Japan began to display that arrogance which he feared, he would send the American fleet around the world to demonstrate that the withdrawal of American approval would prove a substantial loss to any nation incurring it. In the answers to the numerous messages of congratulation which poured in upon him at the close of the session of August 29th, at Portsmouth, we find a paragraph which well expresses President Roosevelt's foreign policy:

I thank you for your letter [he wrote to William R. Thayer, September 1, 1905]. I am very grateful to have been of service in helping to bring about the peace. But, oh, my friend, do not forget that I would have been powerless to speak for peace if there had not been in the minds of other nations the belief, in the first place that I would speak with absolute sincerity and good faith, and in the second place that I did not wish peace because the nation I represented was either unable or unwilling to fight if the need arose.

ROOSEVELT AND THE RUSSO–JAPANESE WAR

We do not see how a wise statesman could have done otherwise than he did in the summer of 1905. On the other hand, we must not take Roosevelt's policy for more than it was worth. The Russo-Japanese War did not finally settle the question of the partition of China, nor did it give to Japan complete security. A weak China after 1905 was even a greater menace to Japan than a weak Korea had been since 1882. After the Treaty of Portsmouth, Japan began to count her securities. There were none. Theoretically, British and American interests in China were identical with those of Japan. The latter was in no condition to take over the administration of the Chinese Empire. This would be an impossible task for any foreign state. Japan did not want to see China divided, for the entrenchment of any Power on the mainland of Asia adjacent to Japan would prove a most serious menace. Japan needed peace and the widest possible scope for foreign trade as a means of recuperation. Japan's largest interests would be best served by the preservation of the integrity of China and the Open Door, provided her own national security could be achieved. Supporting her was the Anglo-Japanese Alliance, but the support of England was an uncertain staff to lean on. China had learned that in 1894. England, likewise theoretically, desired the preservation of the integrity of China and the Open Door, but England was preparing for a life-or-death struggle and her policy was being shaped with a view to the isolation of Germany. Japan could count on England only so far as the latter's well-being in the Far East could be made to contribute to her national defence. In the same way American interests demanded the preservation of China, but Japan could not count on more than verbal support. The policy of 1904–05 was not American policy; it was merely the policy of Roosevelt. Knowing full well that she could not count on the support of the United States either for herself or for the preservation of China, and knowing that British support would be contingent upon the necessities of imperial defence, Japan found it convenient to forget the assurances given to President Roosevelt about Manchuria and turned to find security in the paths of old-world diplomacy.

After 1905, and indeed for many years before then, the place to begin to protect China was Europe. It was utterly futile to suppose, as Secretary Knox seems to have supposed, that the question of Manchuria in 1910 could be segregated from world politics and treated as though it were an abstract question of right and wrong. When Secretary Knox wrote his memorandum in reply to Colonel Roosevelt's letter the World War was only four and one half years off. The question which was being presented to the American Government, although the fact was not recognized, was where the United States would line up at Armageddon. In 1910 the American Government was being directed, in its foreign relations, by lawyers —by constitutional lawyers. Five years earlier the situation had been quite otherwise.

The weakness of Roosevelt's policy lay in the fact that it could not be continued except at the expense of the Constitution of the United States. President Roosevelt had asserted the position which the United States had held potentially since 1898, and he claimed the leadership of world politics. He lifted the scales over Europe, and he threatened to tip them—but always in favour of peace. His interpretation of the powers of the executive was

335

repudiated by his successor. American leadership in world affairs also was surrendered. We do not see how President Roosevelt could have won his victory for the preservation of the integrity of China in 1905 if he had not first served notice on France and Germany that he was prepared to take the side of Japan if either Power came forward to assist Russia in the partition of the Empire. We do not believe that he would have been permitted to carry the Portsmouth Peace Conference to a successful conclusion if he had not already intimated that the balance of power in Europe must be preserved. On the other hand, there is scant reason to suppose that such intimations could ever have been given in 1904-05 "by and with the advice and consent" of two thirds of the Senate, or that they could have been renewed with similar approval in 1909.

In the course of our narrative for the sake of literary smoothness we have often used the terms "America," "the American Government," and "the United States" where we might with greater accuracy have continued to repeat the name Roosevelt. In truth, he was the Government. Congress had no part. Senators were rarely consulted. The President's Cabinet made few contributions. The influence of the American diplomatic service, with the single exception of Ambassador Meyer, was negligible. And yet President Roosevelt attained this position less from choice than from the fact that no one else had any contribution to make. The President, in 1905, was not in the position of having to choose between plans offered by his advisers. Nothing of any importance was proposed. It fell to his lot both to blaze the trail and to make it.

ROOSEVELT'S FAR EASTERN POLICY

One could wish that President Roosevelt had known European politics more intimately, but he knew the subject better than any other President of the United States since John Quincy Adams. As the director of the international relations of his government he was more competent than any Secretary of State since Seward and, far more than Seward, he held and merited the confidence of foreign Powers. No statesman of modern times, not even Palmerston, left so large or so significant an impress on the East. When the passage of time has set events in their true perspective, it may appear that President Roosevelt made the most important treaty in the ninety years which followed the Congress of Vienna. Indeed, we cannot refrain from asking: If the American Government had stood in 1914 where Roosevelt stood in 1904–05, would Germany ever have marched into Belgium?

While the answer to the above question carries us afield from our present study and introduces us to the ranges of speculation one cannot forbear from introducing at this point a paragraph from a letter written October 3, 1914, by Colonel Roosevelt to his old and intimate friend Sir Cecil Spring-Rice, then British Ambassador at Washington. There were parallels between the situation in 1904 at the outbreak of the Russo-Japanese War and the situation in July, 1914. In both cases a local conflict was threatening to become general. It was a problem for statesmen in July, 1914, to keep the conflict localized if possible. There had been a similar problem in 1904 and Roosevelt appears always to have believed that it was his warning to France and Germany which localized the earlier conflict to the Far East. In view of the action taken by Roosevelt, then, the following paragraph is of peculiar interest, for in it he describes the measures he would have taken in the last two days of July, 1914, either to avert or to localize what became the World War. Be it remembered that on those days England was still wavering and Germany was still supposing that England would not enter the war. What would have been the effect if the President of the United States had taken the action outlined in the following letter?

If I had been President, I should have acted on the thirtieth or thirty-first of July, as head of a signatory power of the Hague treaties, calling attention to the guaranty of Belgium's neutrality and saying that I accepted the treaties as imposing a serious obligation which I expected not only the United States but all other neutral nations to join in enforcing. Of course I would not have made such a statement unless I was willing to back it up. I believe that if I had been President the American people would have followed me. But whether I am mistaken or not as regards this, I am certain that the majority are now following Wilson. Only a limited number of people could or ought to be expected to make up their minds for themselves in a crisis like this. It would be worse than folly for me to clamor now about what ought to be done, or ought to have been done, when it would be mere clamor and nothing else.

It is the verdict of history that such unrestrained powers as Roosevelt, an individual exercised in the control of foreign relations, powers hardly less than those of the Tsar, cannot safely be entrusted to rulers. Yet, in this instance, there need be no apology for the result. Justice was not sacrificed to secure national interest or personal fame. Peace, not war, resulted.

How little there was of self-seeking in his motives must

have already appeared. A brief summary is, nevertheless, impressive. Out in the mountains of Colorado he received the first intimation that his good offices would be desired. He waited six weeks before committing himself or his government. When he came forward early in June to ask the belligerent Powers to peace negotiations he had been invited by Japan in the most formal way; he had the assurance of Germany, France, and England that his good offices would be acceptable, and he had the word of the German Emperor that Russia likewise would prefer his services to those of France. His diplomatic technique was perfect. He tried to fix the place of meeting, not at Washington, but first in Manchuria and then at The Hague, two places as far as possible removed from his direct personal influence. Not until August 18th, when it was clear that Russia and Japan at Portsmouth were unable to make peace without mediation, did he come forward as the peacemaker. And then at the conclusion of the treaty, although he was charged with selfish motives, with having yielded to the Kaiser, with having favoured both Japan and Russia, and although in Japan his picture, once so popular, was now turned to the wall, he refrained from public utterance in his own defence. Even to the end of his days he kept silent about the facts which, when known, are alone sufficient to give him his place as a world statesman, though not always a constitutional one.

BIBLIOGRAPHICAL LIST

Manuscripts

Letters or Telegrams from Roosevelt to:

Abbott, Dr. Lyman, October 16, 1905
Baldwin, Elbert F., September 20, 1905
Durand, Sir H. Mortimer, August 18, 1905
Eliot, Pres. Charles W., August 16, 1905
Griscom, Lloyd C., July 27, 1905
Harvey, George, September 6, 1905
Hay, John, May 1, 1902; January 13, 1905; January 28, 1905
Hull, Hon. J. A. T., March 16, 1905
Lodge, Henry Cabot, June 5, 1905; June 16, 1905; July 11, 1905
Kaneko, Baron Kentaro, April 23, 1904; August 22, 1905; August 23, 1905; September 11, 1905
Kennan, George, May 6, 1905; October 15, 1905
Meyer, George von L., December 24, 1904; February 6, 1905; May 24, 1905; June 5, 1905; June 8, 1905; June 16, 1905; August 21, 1905; August 23, 1905; August 25, 1905
Northrop, Pres. Cyrus, February 8, 1905
Pierce, H. H. D., Third Ass't. Sec'y. of State, August 18, 1905
Reid, Whitelaw, June 15, 1905
Rockhill, W. W., August 29, 1905
Root, Elihu, November 25, 1905
Schneder, Dr. D. B., June 19, 1905
Spring-Rice, Sir Cecil, December 27, 1904; May 13, 1905; May 26, 1905; July 24, 1905; September 1, 1905; October 3, 1914

BIBLIOGRAPHICAL LIST

Strachey, J. St. Loe, September 11, 1905
Taft, William Howard, February 9, 1905; April 20, 1905; April 27, 1905; December 22, 1910
Takahira, Kogoro, June 15, 1905
Thayer, William R., September 1, 1905
Tower, Charlemagne, February 16, 1905; July 13, 1905
Wheeler, Benjamin Ide, June 17, 1905
William II, June 5, 1905; June 16, 1905; July 11, 1905; August 27, 1905.

Letters or Telegrams to Roosevelt from:

Cassini, Count, June 6, 1905
Durand, Sir H. Mortimer, September 5, 1905
Kaneko, Baron Kentaro, April 20, 1904; February 9, 1905; July 31, 1905; August 19, 1905
Kennan, George, January 8, 1904; March 30, 1905; October 15, 1905
Meyer, George von L., January 20, 1905; February 14, 1905; February 21, 1905; June 2, 1905; June 9, 1905; June 18, 1905; July 1, 1905; July 8, 1905; August 18, 1905; August 23, 1905; August 24, 1905; August 28, 1905
O'Laughlin, J. C., June 29, 1905; August 19, 1905; August 20, 1905
Pierce, H. H. D., Third Ass't. Secretary of State, August 25, 1905
Reid, Whitelaw, June 24, 1905
Spring-Rice, Cecil, about November 5, 1904; about January 15, 1905; about July 10, 1905
Sternberg, Baron Speck von, January 5, 1905; March 6, 1905; June 11, 1905; August 18, 1905
Taft, William Howard, May 2, 1905
Takahira, Kogoro, May 31, 1905; June 3, 1905
Tower, Charlemagne, February 4, 1905; June 4, 1905; June 9, 1905; July 13, 1905

Other Letters or Telegrams in the Roosevelt Papers:

Barnes, B. F., to William Loeb, Jr., April 18, April 25, 1905

Conger, Edwin H., to Secretary of State, March 31, 1905

Griscom, Lloyd C., to Secretary of State, June 10, 1905; June 16, 1905; June 29, 1905

Lansdowne, Marquis of, to Sir H. Mortimer Durand, June 5, 1905; June 3, 1905

Loomis, F. B., to William Loeb, Jr., May 19, 1905

Meyer, George von L., to Secretary of State, June 2, 1905; June 7, 1905; June 12, 1905; June 16, 1905; July 3, 1905

Reid, Whitelaw, to Secretary of State, June 15, 1905

Wilhelm II to Charlemagne Tower, June 4, 1904

BOOKS

Asakawa, K., "The Russo-Japanese Conflict," Boston and N. Y., 1904

Bernstein, Herman, "The Willy-Nicky Correspondence," N. Y., 1918

Bishop, Joseph Bucklin, "Theodore Roosevelt and His Time," 2 vols., N. Y., 1920

Brown, Arthur J., "The Mastery of the Far East," N. Y., 1919

Charnwood, Lord, "Theodore Roosevelt," Boston, 1923

Croly, Herbert, "Willard Straight," N. Y., 1924

Dennett, Tyler, "Americans in Eastern Asia," N. Y., 1922

Dennis, A. L. P., "The Anglo-Japanese Alliance," University of California Publications, Bureau of International Relations, Vol. 1, No. 1.

———, "The Foreign Policy of Soviet Russia," N. Y., 1924

Dillon, E. J., "The Eclipse of Russia," London and Toronto, 1918

Eckardstein, von Hermann Freiherrn v., "Die Isolierung Deutschlands," Leipzig, 1921

BIBLIOGRAPHICAL LIST

Franke, Otto, "Die Grossmächte in Ostasieu von 1894 bis 1914," Braunschweig and Hamburg, 1923.

Gooch, G. P., "History of Modern Europe, 1878–1919," N. Y., 1923

Gubbins, J. H., "The Making of Modern Japan," N. Y., 1922

Hamilton, Angus, "Korea," N. Y., 1904

Hornbeck, Stanley K., "Contemporary Politics in the Far East," N. Y., 1916

Hayashi, Count, "Secret Memoirs," edited by A. M. Pooley, N. Y., 1915

Howe, M. A. DeWolfe, "George von Lengerke Meyer," N. Y., 1919

Hulbert, Homer B., "The Passing of Korea," N. Y., Chicago, etc., 1906

Kennan, George, "E. H. Harriman, A Biography," 2 vols., Boston and N. Y., 1922

——, "E. H. Harriman's Far Eastern Plans," Garden City and N. Y., 1917

Kobayashi, Ushisaburo, "War and Armament Taxes of Japan," N. Y., 1923

Korff, Serge A., "Russia's Foreign Relations During the Last Half Century," N. Y., 1922

Korostovetz, M., "Pre-War Diplomacy," London, 1920

Kuropatkin, General, "The Russian Army and the Japanese War," 2 vols., N. Y., 1909

Levine, Isaac Don, "Letters from the Kaiser to the Tsar," N. Y., 1920

McCormick Frederick, "The Tragedy of Russia in Pacific Asia," 2 vols., N. Y., 1907

McKenzie, F. A., "Korea's Fight for Freedom," N. Y., Chicago, etc., 1920

Mevil, André, "De la Paix de Francfort à la Conférence d'Algesiras," Paris, 1909

Millard, Thomas F., "Our Eastern Question," N. Y., 1916

Millard, Thomas F., "America and the Far Eastern Question," N. Y., 1909

Morse, H. B., "International Relations of the Chinese Empire," 3 vols., N. Y., 1910, 1918

Ogawa, Gotaro, "Expenditures of the Russo-Japanese War," N. Y., 1923

Pares, Bernard, "Russia and Reform," London, 1907

Pooley, A. M., "Japan's Foreign Policies," London, 1920

Reventlow, Count, "Deutschlands auswärtige Politik," Berlin, 1916

Roosevelt, Theodore, "An Autobiography," N. Y., 1913

Rosen, Baron, "Forty Years of Diplomacy," 2 vols., N. Y., 1920

Schmitt, Bernadotte E., "England and Germany," Princeton, 1916

Scott, James Brown, "The Hague Court Reports," N. Y., 1916

Stone, Melville S., "Fifty Years a Journalist," N. Y., 1922

Stuart, Graham H., "French Foreign Policy," N. Y., 1921

Tardieu, André, "France and the Alliances," N. Y., 1908

Thayer, William Roscoe, "Life and Letters of John Hay," 2 vols., Boston and N. Y., 1915

Weale, B. L. Putnam (Pseud. for Bertram Lenox Simpson), "The Truce in the East and Its Aftermath, N. Y., 1907

Witte, Count, "Memoirs," N. Y., 1921

Whigham, H. J., "Manchuria and Korea," N. Y., 1904

Willoughby, W. W., "Foreign Rights and Interests in China," Baltimore, 1920

GOVERNMENT DOCUMENTS AND COLLECTIONS OF TREATIES, ETC.

Great Britain:

China No. 1 (1898) c 8814

China No. 1 (1899) c 9131

China No. 2 (1904) cd 1936

BIBLIOGRAPHICAL LIST

Japanese Government:

Annual Return of Foreign Trade of the Empire of Japan. Department of Finance, Tokio, 1902–03

Correspondence Regarding the Negotiations Between Japan and Russia, 1904

Protocoles de la Conférence de Paix entre le Japon et la Russie, Tokio, 1906

Russia:

The Orange Book (Protocols of the Portsmouth Conference)

United States:

Senate Ex. Doc. 30, 36–1

Senate Doc. 342, 64–1

Foreign Relations, 1894, Appendix I; 1901, Appendix; 1901; 1902; 1903; 1904; 1905; 1908; 1910

Advance Sheets of Consular Reports, 1901–04

Commercial Korea in 1904, Monthly Summary of Commerce and Finance, January, 1904

Wharton, Francis, "Digest of International Law," 3 vols., Washington, 1887

Moore, John Bassett, "Digest of International Law," 8 vols., Washington, 1906

MacMurray, J. V. A., "Treaties and Agreements With and Concerning China," 2 vols., N. Y., 1921

Korea Treaties and Agreements, Washington, 1921

CONTEMPORARY MAGAZINES AND REVIEWS

"Anglo-American," "Some Revelations of the War," *North American Review*, April, 1904

Asakawa, K., "Korea and Manchuria Under the New Treaty," *Atlantic Monthly*, November, 1905

Boulger, Demetrius P., "The 'Yellow Peril' Bogey," *Nineteenth Century and After*, January, 1904

Buell, Raymond Leslie, "The Development of Anti-

Japanese Agitation in the United States," *Political Science Quarterly*, Vol. XXXVII, December, 1922

"Calchas," "First Principles in the Far East," *Fortnightly Review*, February, 1904

——, "The War and the Powers," *Fortnightly Review*, March, 1904

——, "The New German Intrigue: A Note of Warning," *Fortnightly Review*, September, 1904

Cassini, Comte, "Russia in the Far East," *North American Review*, May, 1904

Chéradame, André, "Les Causes de la Guerre," *Le Correspondent*, May 23, 1904

China Review, June 7, 1905

Dayton, Edwin Winthrop, "What Russia Fights For," *World's Work*, April, 1904

Dennett, Tyler, "American 'Good Offices' in Asia," *American Journal of International Law*, Vol. XVI, January, 1922

——, "Early American Policy in Korea," *Political Science Quarterly*, Vol. XXXVIII, March, 1923

——, "American Choices in the Far East in 1882," *American Historical Review*, Vol. XXX, No. 1, October, 1924

Dilke, Sir Charles W., "The War in the Far East," *North American Review*, April, 1904

Dillon, E. J., "Our Friends, Our Allies, and Our Rivals," *Contemporary Review*, May, 1904

——, "Official Narrative of the Peace Conference," *Harper's Weekly*, September 16, 1905

Eltzbacher, O., "The Yellow Peril," *Nineteenth Century and After*, June, 1904

——, "The Balance of Power in Europe," *Nineteenth Century and After*, May, 1905

——, "The Indemnity Due Japan," *Nineteenth Century and After*, July, 1905

Fay, Sidney B., "The Kaiser's Secret Negotiations with the

Tsar, 1904–1905," *American Historical Review*, Vol. XXIV, October, 1918

Foord, John, *Journal* of the American Asiatic Association, January, 1904–September, 1906

Gale, James S., "Korea in War Time," *Outlook*, June 25, 1904

Hammond, John Hays, *Annals of American Academy of Political and Social Science*, Vol. XXVI

——, "The Menace of Japan's Success," *World's Work*, June, 1905

Hayakawa, T., "A Russo-Japanese Alliance," *Taiyo*, quoted in *Review of Reviews*, N. Y., June, 1905

Hillier, Walter C., "Korea: Its History and Prospects," *Fortnightly Review*, June, 1904

Holcombe, Chester, "Some Results of the Eastern War," *Atlantic Monthly*, July, 1905

Hulbert, Homer B., *Korean Review*, Seoul, 1904–05

"Ivanovich," "The Russo-Japanese War and the Yellow Peril," *Contemporary Review*, August, 1904

"Junius," "The Overlord of the Pacific and the Admiral of the Atlantic," *National Review*, April, 1905

Kaneko, Baron Kentaro, "Japan and the United States: A Proposed Economic Alliance," *International Quarterly*, VII, December–March, 1903–04

——, "The Yellow Peril Is the Golden Opportunity for Japan," *North American Review*, November, 1904

——, "America's Economic Future in the Far East," *Forum*, April–June, 1905

Kennan, George, "The Sword of Peace in Japan," *Outlook*, October 14, 1905

Korff, Baron S. A.,"Russia in the Far East," *American Journal of International Law*, Vol. XVII, April, 1923

Low, Sydney, "President Roosevelt's Opportunities," *Nineteenth Century and After*, December, 1904

ROOSEVELT AND THE RUSSO-JAPANESE WAR

Low, A. Maurice, "American Affairs," *National Review*, April, 1904; March, 1905

Leroy-Beaulieu, Pierre, "Le Japon et Ses Ressources," *Revue des Deux Mondes*, March 15, 1904

de Marmande, R., "French Public Opinion and the Russo-Japanese War," *Fortnightly Review*, August, 1904

Maxey, Prof. Edwin, "Why We Favor Japan in the Present War," *Arena*, August, 1904

Millard, Thomas F., "Financial Prospects of Japan," *Scribner's Magazine*, September, 1905

Okuma, Count, "Japan's Policy in Korea," *Forum*, April, June, 1906

Paullin, C. O., "The Opening of Korea," *Political Science Quarterly*, Vol. XXV

Pinon, René, "La Guerre Russo-Japonaise et l'Opinion Européenne," *Revue des Deux Mondes*, May 1, 1904

Pownall, C. A. W., "Russia, Japan and Ourselves," *Nineteenth Century and After*, March, 1904

Reid, Thomas H., "The Menace of the East," *Contemporary Review*, May, 1905

Reinsch, Paul S., "Japan and Asiatic Leadership," *North American Review*, January, 1905

——, "An Unfortunate Peace," *Outlook*, September 16, 1905

Roosevelt, Theodore, "The World War: Its Tragedies and Its Lessons," *Outlook*, September 23, 1914

Seaman, Louis F., "The Oriental Armistice," *Outlook*, September 16, 1905

Shigeoka, K., "What Japan Should Do for Korea," *Seiyo*, translation in *Review of Reviews*, N. Y., September, 1904

Smith, J. Gordon, "Japan's Closing of the Open Door," *World's Work*, June, 1905

Stead, Alfred, "The Far Eastern Problem," *Fortnightly Review*, January, 1904

348

BIBLIOGRAPHICAL LIST

Stead, Alfred, "A Question of Good Faith and National Expediency," *Fortnightly Review*, January, 1905

——, "Japan and Peace," *Fortnightly Review*, June, 1905

Suyemetsu, Baron, "How Russia Brought on the War," *Nineteenth Century and After*, September, 1904

——, "Japan and the Commencement of the War with Russia," *Nineteenth Century and After*, August, 1904

Takahira, Kogoro, "Why Japan Resists Russia," *North American Review*, March, 1904

——, "What Japan Is Fighting For," *World's Work*, April, 1904

Times, London, September 5, 1904; August 22, 1905; September 4, 1905

Ular, Alexander, "Le panmongolisme japonais," *La Revue*, February 15, 1904

White, Arnold, "Anglo-Russian Relations", *Fortnightly Review*, December, 1904

INDEX

INDEX

INDEX

354

INDEX

INDEX

Millard, Thomas F., 299, 315
Miller, Henry B., U. S. Consul, 126–130
Missionaries, 104, 106
Mongolia, 125
Moore, John Bassett, "Digest," 28
Morgan, Edwin V., 302, 306
Morocco, 59; Roosevelt's comment on, 76, 83, 84, 86, 90
Moroccan crisis, 2, 5, 6, 21, 70; significance of, 87, 151, 182; Lansdowne, 214
Morrison, Dr. George, 124, 323
Motono, Japanese, Minister in Paris, 174, 176
Mukden, 11, 49, 68, 83, 91, 132, 140, 150, 157, 321

National Review, 20, 21, 94, 146
Navy, Roosevelt believes in strong, 89
Near East, 69, 153
Neutral zone, 101, 102
Neutrality: of China, 11, 27, 69, 80; of Korea, 98, 104; British, 168
Neutralization of Manchuria, 158; Knox plan, 315
Newchwang, 124, 125ff., 140, 152
Newlands, Senator, 306
Nicholas II, *see* Tsar
Nineteenth Century and After, 18, 21, 40, 62, 93, 147, 169
North American Review, 20, 21, 94, 148, 167
Northrop, Cyrus, Pres., Roosevelt to, 303

Okuma, Count, 19, 117, 203
O'Laughlin, J. C., 195, 206, 249, 252
Open Door, 78, 80, 130; development of policy of, 135ff., 146; Japan pledges, 158, 178, 180, 307, 310, 314; Knox defines, 322, 325, 334
Outlook, 1, 19, 278, 286, 305
Oyster Bay, 22

Pacific Ocean, 3, 50, 108, 153, 263, 330
Panama Canal, 6, 137, 164
Peace Negotiations, 2, 43; begin, 171ff.
Peking, 125; Russian designs on, 151
Philippine Islands, 4, 6, 31, 47, 48, 108, 112, 137; Japan and, 159ff.

Pierce, H. H. D., Asst. Secy. of State, 249, 251, 257
Pinon, René, 61
Plancon, M. de, 133
Plehve, 44, 119, 140
Pooley, A. M., 57
Port Arthur, 27, 54; lease of, 66, 68, 73, 83, 101, 122, 150, 156; Roosevelt on, 161, 173, 263
Portsmouth, 239, 243ff.; Peace of, 4, 5, 23; Treaty of, 121
Propaganda, Russian, 17; Japanese, 17, 102, 133, 264

Radolin, Prince, 79
Reid, Ambassador Whitelaw, 37; Roosevelt to, 211
Reinsch, Paul S., 20, 167, 278–79
Reventlow, Count, 55
Revue des Deux Mondes, 21, 61, 168
Rockhill, W. W., 119, 124
Roosevelt, President: Papers, v, 10, 11; description of, 13ff., 21, 92; and Balance of Power, 1; policy of, 4, 20; warns France and Germany, 30, to Kaneko, 35; on Kaiser, 89–91; on Korea, 110; on Russia, 119; opportunities, 147; on China, 153ff.; Manchuria, 157; policy in the Pacific, 159ff.; and navy, 163–4; to Lodge, 192ff.; Manchuria, 248; intervenes at Portsmouth, 249ff.; and critics, 278ff., 314ff.; to Taft, 320; on Open Door, 320–21
Root, Elihu, 121, 249, 285; Roosevelt to, 304–05; Takahira agreement, 314–15
Rosen, Baron, 13, 45, 138, 237; visits Oyster Bay, 252, 295; "Rosen-Nissi Agreement," 96, 99, 142
Russia, 2, 5, 26, 31, 32, 148, 328; and England, 168; Roosevelt on, 47, 89, 333; in Manchuria, 57, 148, 296; and Germany, 63ff.; Treaty, 70, 85
Russian Revolution, 90, 140; and Japan, 186; Meyer, 190, 205, 281, 288ff.; and Kaiser, 170, 209
Russo-Chinese Bank, 121, 127
Russo-Japanese War, v, 1, cost of, 297; origins of, 9, 26, 53, 53ff., 94; European background, 91

INDEX

DATE DUE